D1228664

Women of Value

Women of Value

Feminist Essays on the History of Women in Economics

Edited by (in alphabetical order)

Mary Ann Dimand

Instructor in the Department of Economics and Management, Albion College, US

Robert W. Dimand

Professor of Economics, Brock University, Canada and Visiting Fellow at Yale University, US

Evelyn L. Forget

Associate Professor of Economics, University of Manitoba, Canada

Edward Elgar
Aldershot, UK • Brookfield, US

Published by
Edward Elgar Publishing Limited
Gower House
Croft Road
Aldershot
Hants GU11 3HR
UK

Edward Elgar Publishing Company
Old Post Road
Brookfield
Vermont 05036
US

British Library Cataloguing in Publication Data
Women of Value: Feminist Essays on the
History of Women in Economics
  I. Dimand, Mary Ann
  330.082

Library of Congress Cataloguing in Publication Data
Women of value : feminist essays on the history of women in economics
  / edited by Mary Ann Dimand, Robert W. Dimand. Evelyn L. Forget.
     p. cm.
  Includes bibliographical references and index.
  1. Women economists—United States—History. 2. Economists—
  United States—History. 3. Feminism—United States—History.
  I. Dimand, Mary Ann, 1960– . II. Dimand, Robert W. (Robert
  William), 1956– . III. Forget, Evelyn L., 1956– .
  HB74.8.W66 1996
  330'.082—dc20   95–7191
                                                        CIP

ISBN 1 85278 959 X

Printed and bound in Great Britain by
Biddles Ltd, Guildford and King's Lynn

Contents

Contributors

Mary Ann Dimand is a doctoral student in economics at Yale University, New Haven, Connecticut and Lecturer in Economics at Albion College, Albion, Michigan.

Robert W. Dimand is Professor of Economics at Brock University, St Catharines, Ontario, and Visiting Fellow at Yale University.

Evelyn L. Forget is Associate Professor of Economics at the University of Manitoba, Winnipeg.

James P. Henderson is Professor of Economics at Valparaiso University, Valparaiso, Indiana.

Rita McWilliams Tullberg is author of *Women at Cambridge – a Men's University, though of a Mixed Kind* (Gollancz, 1975), editor of *Alfred Marshall in Retrospect* (Edward Elgar, 1990) and editor (with E.F. Biagini and T. Raffaelli) of the forthcoming *Alfred Marshall's Lectures to Women* (Edward Elgar, 1995).

Bette Polkinghorn is Professor of Economics at California State University, Sacramento.

Michèle Pujol is Assistant Professor of Women's Studies at University of Victoria, British Columbia.

William D. Sockwell is Associate Professor of Economics at Berry College, Mount Berry, Georgia.

Alison Comish Thorne is Professor Emerita at Utah State University, Logan.

Introduction

This collection of essays began as a modest attempt on the part of the authors to learn from one another. We wanted to enhance our particular knowledge, but also to articulate our collective ignorance, with the goal of determining what research needs to be done in order to better understand the lives and the work of the women who helped to build our discipline. This volume is neither complete nor exhaustive and all of the authors represented in this collection acknowledge with gratitude the immense work done by others who are also trying to reconstruct the contributions of women.

An historical paucity of women economists is often claimed in casual conversation. William J. Baumol (1985) wrote that 'before World War I, as today, a (distressingly) few women *were* contributing to the literature'. Yet the five volumes of the *Index of Economic Journals* (American Economic Association, 1961), covering articles from 1886 to 1959, are a marvellous cache of data on the rather extensive contributions of women to economic scholarship. This volume of essays addresses some questions which arise from the activity of women economists before 1960. Why is it often thought that women were unimportant or virtually absent from the field? What were women economists writing about,[1] and what were their contributions to the literature, to the profession and to the shaping of their society? Who listened to them, supported them or hindered them?

The essays in this collection fall into two broad classifications, but each chapter raises issues and questions which echo and amplify the concerns raised in other chapters in this volume. The first group of chapters attempts to clarify our understanding of the sociology of the discipline of economics, particularly in the first decades of the twentieth century. Robert Dimand's 'The Neglect of Women's Contributions to Economics' unearths a treasure of writing by women economists and suggests that the usual techniques of bibliographic research will do little to enhance our knowledge of this work because of systematic misattribution and lack of citation of the work of women economists. His call for a collective biography of women economists is echoed by Evelyn Forget, who examines the dissertation research topics of American women economists in the first 40 years of the twentieth century. She asks whether we can account for the apparent differences between the breadth and degree of research undertaken by women doctoral candidates, as

compared with their contributions to key economics journals, by examining
the strategies these women adopted to build careers in the context of a
sometimes hostile professional environment. Mary Ann Dimand undertakes
the prodigious task of trying to uncover the personal relationships and networks of influence within which women economists laboured before 1940.
Her work is a most welcome attempt to move beyond the 'great writer'
approach and to document the intellectual contexts that helped individual
writers to emerge.

Alison Comish Thorne's contribution, entitled 'Women Mentoring Women
in Economics in the 1930s' is a gem that deserves a category of its own. A
personal memoir, it explores the networks that Mary Ann Dimand discusses
from the perspective of a woman graduate student studying under the influence of women and men economists. This chapter yields a great deal of
insight into the sociology of the economics profession during the 1930s, but
it also celebrates the personal characteristics and significant achievements of
the author's teachers and colleagues. If further evidence of the need for a
collective biography of women economists were needed, this chapter settles
the case.

Alison Comish Thorne's contribution acts as a bridge to the second group
of essays collected in this volume, which focus on particular women or
groups of women in the history of economic thought. The original authors
honoured in these chapters are not a complete set of 'great women economists'; nor are they necessarily those authors one might expect to see in a list
of the most 'important' women economists. The selection is as idiosyncratic
as the authors and the subjects of these chapters, but they all share the
characteristic that the subjects chosen are significant women economists.
Moreover, the relationships between these chapters create a synergy that
ensures that this collection is greater than the sum of the individual contributions.

Bette Polkinghorn shares her insight into the motivations and experiences
of Jane Marcet and Harriet Martineau. These two women did more than any
other nineteenth-century writer to popularize political economy, and to ensure that the language of economics was the language in which public discourse would be conducted.

Michèle Pujol's chapter on Harriet Taylor explores that writer's work on
utilitarianism, the roles of women in society and the labour force, the education of women and the desirability of social reform. This contribution is
particularly interesting in the context of Robert Dimand's work on the neglect
of women's contributions to economics, because Harriet Taylor is virtually
known only through her relationship with Mill. Castigated for having had too
much influence on Mill, and dismissed for having had too little, her own
work has never received attention on its own merits. William Sockwell's

'Barbara Bodichon and the Women of Langham Place' picks up Taylor's interest in women's rights and the employment of women, and discusses the influence of these feminist writers during the 1850s and 1860s. Mary Ann Dimand explores similar ground in her chapter, 'The Economics of Charlotte Perkins Gilman', arguing that Gilman's economics has been undervalued. A pioneer in the use of an analytical framework encompassing exploitation and surplus value to discuss the status of women working in the home, Gilman has become a victim of the systemic neglect that Robert Dimand documents.

Rita McWilliams Tullberg's contribution on Mary Paley Marshall examines the evidence about her life that remains, and tries to answer the often-raised question: if Alfred 'Marshall's character had been other than it was, could this have been a Webb, a Bosanquet, or even a Myrdal-type partnership, with both partners contributing equally to the intellectual output of the team?' The parallels with Michèle Pujol's discussion of Harriet Taylor are clear enough.

James Henderson's chapter, 'Women's Wage Rates and Total Earnings: Two Early 'Scientific' Studies; picks up, once again, the thread of compensation for women workers. He examines two studies financed by the British Association for the Advancement of Science in the first two decades of the twentieth century dealing with the role of women in industry. Henderson examines the role that formal organizations played in helping to establish research networks among women economists in England, thereby augmenting Mary Ann Dimand's contribution on 'networks' as well as those which document the shared concern of various women economists with labour economics and women's wages. This interest appears in the chapters on Harriet Taylor, Charlotte Perkins Gilman and Barbara Bodichon, as well as Henderson's analysis, and is documented at a more abstract level in Chapters 1 and 2.

The ten chapters are not linked in any linear fashion, but rather share to various degrees a variety of themes. One issue that emerges over and over again is the formal and informal relationships that women forged in order to encourage and support one another's work. Another shared theme is the persistent interest of women economists in labour economics. But the most pressing conclusion that can be drawn from this volume is the recognition that formal analysis which relies on the standard tools and techniques of historical and bibliographic research must be augmented by biographical research which can uncover the lives and contributions of individual women economists in the context of the formal and informal relationships that they built. Alison Comish Thorne, by sharing her memories of working as an economist in the 1930s, leads us to recognize the role that oral history can play in fleshing out our knowledge of the early years of this century. A historian of economics in search of a research topic could do worse than to

interview the women who lived and worked as economists before World War
II.

We will consider this volume a success if it provides a useful reference or
raises an interesting question for others. We will be pleased if a reader is
moved to question our sources, our methods or our conclusions. But we will
be overjoyed if those who take the time to read any of the contributions in
this volume will stop for a moment to imagine the courage and the humour
that are reflected by the stories of the lives, the trials and the triumphs of the
women we write about.

NOTE

1. Because we find this question an interesting one, this volume does not contain essays on
   Joan Robinson, Rosa Luxemburg or others whose contributions are relatively well known
   to economists now.

REFERENCES

American Economic Association (1961), *Index of Economic Journals*, 5 vols,
    Homewood, IL: Richard D. Irwin.
Baumol, William J. (1985), 'On Method in U.S. Economics a Century Earlier',
    American Economic Review, **75**, 6, December, 1–12.

1. The neglect of women's contributions to economics

Robert W. Dimand[1]

1.1 INTRODUCTION

To judge from references in the literature, one might suppose that women contributed very little to economic knowledge until quite recently. Such a supposition would be mistaken. This chapter is a preliminary attempt to explore the extent to which women's contributions to economics have been overlooked and undervalued.

To posit the possibility that the work of woman economists may be neglected is to recognize that many of the usual techniques for chasing down academic prey may not help. Fortunately, the American Economic Association (AEA) *Index of Economic Journals*, while it does not list articles in all relevant journals, does list all articles in a fair assortment of journals, and yields many leads. In addition to the journals covered by the *Index*, women economists also published in such periodicals as the *Publications of the Association of Collegiate Alumnae* and, in the case of Minnie Throop England, the University of Nebraska *University Studies*. Millicent Garrett Fawcett's essays on voting theory, which would now be considered part of the economic theory of public choice, appeared in *Macmillan's Magazine* in 1870 and 1871, and were republished as pamphlets, before the founding of narrowly economic journals in English. The *Index of Economic Journals* provides more information than just its listing of articles. It was issued in the name of a committee of five eminent male economists, but the interested reader who studies the introduction to the first five volumes (covering 1886 to 1959) will encounter mention of Dorothy F. Livingston, director of the project, Truus W. Koopmans, chief of classification, Mary C. Withington, of the Yale University Library, by whom the 'prodigious task of proofreading was accomplished with meticulous care', and Louise S. Stevens, of the Irwin Editorial Staff, 'who supervised and largely performed the arduous task of transforming the thousands of entries on individual paper slips into the finished pages which follow'.

1

The career of Ruth P. Mack of the National Bureau of Economic Research indicates how a woman might produce a substantial body of work in economics without that being detectable from the *Index of Economic Journals*. According to the *Index*, before 1953 Mack published only a single article, in 1948. However, the biographical note accompanying her survey of 'The Economics of Consumption' in the AEA *Survey of Contemporary Economics* (Ellis, 1952, xv, 39–78) indicates that she published books in 1936 and 1941, was co-author of *Taxing to Prevent Inflation* in 1943 with Carl Shoup and Milton Friedman (not usually associated with fiscal policy to deal with inflation) and had a fourth book forthcoming, apart from contributions to the NBER series, *Studies in Income and Wealth*.

1.2   WOMEN IN THE COLLECTIVE MEMORY OF THE DISCIPLINE

The invisibility of women's contributions of economics to what Michèle Pujol terms the 'malestream' of the profession is striking even in such a seemingly objective, authoritative reference work as *Economists' Papers 1750–1950: A Guide to Archive and Other Manuscript Sources for the History of British and Irish Economic Thought*, compiled by R.P. Sturges (1975). Sturges lists 146 economists, including three women. Two of them, Clara Collet and Jane Marcet, are among the 43 whose names are marked with asterisks to indicate that the location of their papers is not listed in the volume. The locations of Harriet Martineau's papers are given. The papers of Marcet, a highly important popularizer of classical political economy, still exist, and were used by Bette Polkinghorn in her biography of Marcet. Clara Collet had a long and distinguished career – she was the only author to publish in both the first and the fiftieth volumes of the *Economic Journal*. The curious reader who notices in the entry for H.S. Foxwell that three letters from Foxwell to Clara Collet survive in the Collet papers will thus learn that the otherwise unidentified Collet papers whose location is given in 'Details of Private Collections Cited in the Text by Number' relate to Clara Collet. Sturges does not mention Dame Millicent Garrett Fawcett, the women's suffrage leader whose *Economic Journal* articles offered a pathbreaking analysis of low wages for women (see Pujol, 1992, 57–61, 75–6, 80–84). The entry for Henry Fawcett does note, however, that his papers are not in the Fawcett Library, thereby implying the existence of that feminist library. The entry for Sidney Webb turns out to cover Beatrice Webb as well. She might reasonably have been included in the list of economists and the title of the entry. It was Beatrice, not Sidney, who issued the Minority Report of the Poor Law Commission, generally considered their most important contribution to economics (apart from founding the London School of Economics) and the Minority Report of the War Cabinet Committee on Women in Industry (see Pujol, 1992, 84–92).

No other study of a nation's economic thought can compare in coverage to Joseph Dorfman's magisterial *The Economic Mind in American Civilization 1606–1933* (five volumes, 1946–59). The 2263 pages of text and 219 pages of notes and bibliography of this great work constitute the collective memory of the American economics profession for the period before 1933. The History of Economics Society has aptly named its dissertation award after Dorfman. Dorfman did not give much attention to the economic mind of women. Edith Abbott wrote 19 articles in the *Journal of Political Economy* (*JPE*) between 1904 and 1925, adding up to 374 journal pages, as well as *American Economic Review* (*AER*) articles and books on *Women in Industry: A Study in American Economic History* (1910/1969) and *Public Assistance* (1940). Dorfman mentions neither Abbott nor Sophonisba Preston Breckinridge, co-author of two *JPE* articles with Abbott and sole author of six other *JPE* pieces. Katharine Coman wrote books on the *Industrial History of the United States* (1917) and *The Economic Beginnings of the Far West* (1912/1969). Her monograph on contract labour in Hawaii was published by the AEA in 1903 before the launching of the *American Economic Review*, to which she contributed, as well as to the *JPE* and the *Journal of the American Statistical Association* (*JASA*). Her name does not appear in Dorfman's work, nor does that of Katharine Bement Davis, author of four *JPE* articles from 1898 to 1900, nor that of Helen L. Bliss, who published six *JPE* articles from 1895 to 1905.

John Andrews and Helen Sumner each received a PhD in economics from the University of Wisconsin in 1908. In the 19-volume Senate Report on Woman and Child Wage Earners, Andrews and W.D.P. Bliss wrote Volume X, *History of Women in Trade Unions, 1825 to the Knights of Labor* (1911), while Sumner wrote Volume IX, *History of Women in Industry in the United States* (1910; first chapter excerpted in Schneir, 1972, 255–67). The *Index of Economic Journals* does not credit Andrews with any journal publications. Andrews and Sumner were co-authors with John R. Commons of *A History of Labor in the United States* and co-editors with Commons of the ten-volume *A Documentary History of American Industrial Society* (works attributed by Dorfman to 'John R. Commons and associates', except in one footnote). Dorfman recorded in *The Economic Mind* (IV, 112) that John Andrews was a student of Commons and became secretary of the American Association for Labor Legislation, but did not mention Helen Sumner.

The published research of such women as Abbott, Bliss, Breckinridge and Coman may be compared with that of two men mentioned by Dorfman, Edgar S. Furniss and Norman S. Buck, professors of political economy at

Yale, each of whom served as provost of the university. Dorfman cites Furniss
for his dissertation, which won the Hart, Schaffner & Marx Prize, and cites
both Furniss and Buck as co-authors, with Fred R. Fairchild, of a popular
introductory textbook (based on an earlier textbook by their colleague, Irving
Fisher). The *Index of Economic Journals* credits Furniss with a two-page
'Bibliography of Professor Thomas S. Adams' and does not record any
journal publication whatsoever by Buck.

Minnie Throop England wrote four major articles on crises, totalling 65
pages, in the *JPE* and *Quarterly Journal of Economics* (*QJE*) from 1912 to
1915, as well as earlier monographs in the *University Studies* of the University of Nebraska, where she taught. In the preface to the second edition of
The Purchasing Power of Money (1913, xiii), Irving Fisher cited England and
John Maynard Keynes as the two authors whose criticisms of the book he
would take into account if he were to revise the text. Her work on promotion
as a cause of crises was cited by Wesley Mitchell (1913) as close to his own
theory. Mitchell later recognized her theory as closer to that of Joseph
Schumpeter: 'While less complete in its formal logic, Mrs. England's exposit-
ion runs in more realistic terms and cites more evidence. It should be studied
by those who feel that Schumpeter's sketch lacks substance' (1927, 22).
Schumpeter, who was a visiting professor in Mitchell's department at Columbia in 1913–14, discussed England in his *History of Economic Analysis*
(1954, 1128), but Dorfman omitted her. Her writings in the University of
Nebraska *University Studies* were as much part of professional discourse as
her journal articles, with Schumpeter and Fisher writing reviews of her 1906
and 1907 essays, respectively. Harold Somers included only one of England's
four journal articles, and none of her three relevant *University Studies* essays,
in his 'Classified Bibliography of Articles on Business Cycle Theory' (1944).
Raymond Saulnier did not include any of her work in his 'Selected Bibliography of Books and Articles on the Theory of Money and the Business Cycle'
(Saulnier, 1938, 393–416).

Without pursuing early twentieth-century American women economists
through the alphabet to the economic historian Agnes Wergeland (a *JPE*
article each year from 1900 to 1905, adding up to 138 journal pages), it is
clear that Dorfman's neglect of women gives a misleading account of the
discipline at the time. Women were publishing books and journal articles,
teaching in women's colleges (as with Balch and Coman at Wellesley) and
state universities (as in the case of England), doing graduate study in economics (Helen Campbell as a student of Richard Ely; Edith Abbott, PhD
University of Chicago, 1905; Helen Sumner, PhD University of Wisconsin,
1908) – and winning awards from the AEA (Helen Campbell, for her monograph *Women Wage-Earners*, published in 1893 with an introduction by Ely).
Women were also active in presentations at scholarly conferences, as when

Edith Abbott, Katharine Coman, Jessica Peixotto and Susan Kingsbury gave papers in a session on the 'Economic Efficiency of Women' in San Francisco at the 1908 annual meeting of the Association of Collegiate Alumnae (Antler, 1987, 131, 384). Peixotto and Kingsbury served as vice-presidents of the AEA. Women collaborated on collective works such as *Women's Work in America*, edited by Annie Meyer (1891), as in Britain they collaborated on *Woman in Industry from Seven Points of View* (Gertrude Tuckwell, 1908). Male economists joined women economists on policy issues: petitions to Congress in 1930 in support of public works to reduce unemployment were signed not only by such prominent male economists as John Bates Clark, John Maurice Clark, John R. Commons, Paul Douglas, Frank A. Fetter, Irving Fisher, Edwin Kemmerer and Frank Taussig, but also by Edith Abbott, Emily Green Balch, Sophonisba Breckinridge, Joanna C. Colcord, Hazel Kyrk, Mary K. Simkhovitch and Lillian Wald (Rothbard, 1975, 222, 333–4). British women also published in American economic journals: among the contributors to Tuckwell (1908), Clara Collet published in *QJE* and Constance Smith in the *Journal of Political Economy*.

Such activity by women in economics can be found in many countries. Six women were among the 185 founding members of the Australian Economic Association in 1887, and volumes III and IV of the *Australian Economist* (1893–6) carried articles on the economic position of women by Louisa McDonald, Florence Gordon, Rose Scott and Edith Badham (Groenewegen and McFarlane, 1990, 68, 70).

Non-economists anthologizing classic statements on the economic status of women often group Thorstein Veblen's *Theory of the Leisure Class* (1899) with *Women and Economics* (1898b) by Charlotte Perkins Gilman, 'the greatest writer that the feminists ever produced on sociology and economics, the Marx and Veblen of the movement' (Sinclair, 1965, 272). Miriam Schneir (1972) reprinted excerpts from the two books side by side, while Aileen Kraditor (1968) paired excerpts from Veblen's book with articles by Gilman, including an 1898 article, 'Economic Basis of the Woman Question'. In fact, Gilman's comparison of humans with other species, as well as her analysis of male rationales for the marginalization of women and their work as masculine possessions, parallels Veblen (1899). Gilman's name does not appear in *The Economic Mind*. Dorfman's two mentions of her in *Thorstein Veblen and His America* (1934, 194, 196) recorded that Edward Ross recommended Veblen's book to her and that she enjoyed its satire, but did not indicate who she was or that she had ever written anything, let alone a book and article the previous year that overlapped in topic with Veblen's work. David Reisman's *Thorstein Veblen: A Critical Interpretation* (1953) and Douglas Dowd's *Thorstein Veblen* (1964) make no mention of Gilman. John Diggins (1978, 158–61), however, examines the 'striking resemblance' between Veblen and

Gilman. Wherever one draws the dividing line between sociology and institutional economics, Veblen and Gilman surely belong on the same side, yet Gilman is now known almost exclusively to noneconomists. This was not always so: Gilman's *The Home* (1903/1972), advocating a market solution to the problem of housework, was the subject of a 12-page review article by Caroline Hill in the *Journal of Political Economy* in 1904.

One section of *The Economic Mind* on 'The Rise of Consumption Economics' (V, 571–8) is, however, about the work of three women. Hazel Kyrk of the Food Research Institute, Stanford, and the University of Chicago (jointly appointed in economics and home economics) won the Hart, Schaffner & Marx Prize for her 1920 Chicago PhD dissertation, published as *A Theory of Consumption* (1923). Theresa McMahon of the University of Washington published *Women and Economic Evolution* (1912), based on her 1909 Wisconsin PhD dissertation, and *Social and Economic Standards of Living* (1925). Dorfman discussed only the second of McMahon's books, beyond mentioning the existence of the first. Jessica Peixotto of the University of California, Berkeley, wrote household budget studies. In the one limited field of household spending, Dorfman recognized women's contributions. Even in that field, Dorfman did not mention the appearance of these women in scholarly journals: Kyrk on the economics of consumption in *AER*, *JASA*, the *Journal of Farm Economics* and the *Journal of Marketing*, McMahon in *AER*, Peixotto in *JPE* and *AER*.

Dorfman made only a single mention of Emily Greene Balch in *The Economic Mind* (III, 243), quoting her as stating that the 'most important contemporary work in economic theory is that based largely ... on the conception of marginal utility'. He did not remark that in 1893 she published a 180-page monograph on 'Public Assistance of the Poor in France' in the *Publications of the American Economic Association* (First Series, VIII, nos. 4–5), or that, after teaching at Wellesley College for 24 years, she was not reappointed to a full professorship of economics in 1918 because of her social reform and anti-war activism, or that she shared the Nobel Peace Prize in 1946 for that same activism (see Judith Ann Trolander on Balch in the *Dictionary of American Biography*, Supplement VII). One presumes that mention would have been made of a male economist removed from a professorship for social and political activism, or who won a Nobel Prize, let alone who won a Nobel Prize for the same reasons that the professorship was taken away.

Lewis H. Haney included 14 pages listing 'Chief Works of American Economists Active between 1850 and 1915', including works published at other times by economists whose careers overlapped that period, in the third edition of his *History of Economic Thought* (1936, 789–802). Some men were included on the basis of one or two publications. No women were among the 89 economists listed, although Abbott, Breckinridge, Coman, Davis, England and others published extensively before 1915. No women appeared in Haney's chapter on economics in the United States, nor was Gilman mentioned in his chapter on Veblen and institutionalism. *History of Labor in the United States* was attributed to John R. Commons 'with associates', without naming Helen Sumner or Elizabeth Brandeis (Haney, 1936, 791). H.R. Sewall (1901) did, however, appear, without indication of author's gender, in Haney's list of 'Leading Works on the History of Economic Thought' (Haney, 1936, 809). Marcet, Martineau, Luxemburg and Harriet Taylor Mill were absent from Haney's index, although Mary Paley Marshall appeared twice (for bare listings as co-author of Marshall and Marshall, 1879). Haney (1936, 447) did mention Harriet Taylor Mill in his text, to observe briefly that John Stuart Mill 'probably goes too far in ascribing to her all that is best in his writings, as he does frequently'.

The widespread neglect of women's contributions to economics by male writers (apart from Maynard Keynes's memorial article on Mary Paley Marshall and G.D.H. Cole's 1949 essay on 'Beatrice Webb as an Economist') may be due in part to the topics on which they wrote: the 'malestream' of the discipline did not care to read Abbott on *Women in Industry*, Breckinridge on *Women in the Twentieth Century* (1933), Campbell on *Prisoners of Poverty*, Gilman on *Women and Economics* or McMahon on *Women and Economic Evolution* for the same reasons that male economists wrote little on the economic experience of the female majority of the population. Thus, for example, Bessie Leigh Hutchins's *Women in Modern Industry* (1915/1978), her eight *Economic Journal* articles, her contributions to the *Journal of the Royal Statistical Society*, her Fabian Tracts (Alexander, 1988, 33–52, 164–78) and her Women's Industrial Council publications were peripheral, or antipathetic, to male interests. Helen Dendy Bosanquet's ten *Economic Journal* articles between 1891 and 1920 were on such topics as women's wages and women in industry, as well as on the causes of poverty. Choice of topic, however, cannot explain the neglect of Eveline Burns or Eleanor Lansing Dulles. While Burns wrote in *Economica* on the economics of family endowment, she also wrote on 'Recent Contributions to Economic Theory' in *Economica* in 1922, on statistics and economic forecasting in *JASA*, and on the economics of unemployment relief, the relation between institutional and orthodox economics, and financial aspects of the Social Security Act in *AER*. Dulles, later a diplomat with the rank of minister, wrote books on *The French Franc, 1914–1928* (1929), *The Bank for International Settlements at Work* (1932), *The Dollar, the Franc and Inflation* (1933) and *Depression and Reconstruction* (1936); a monograph on *The Evolution of Reparation Ideas* (1932); and a book-length report on *Financing the Social Security Act* (1937), and contributed to *AER* on Social Security (1938), the Bank for International

Settlements (1938), and 'War and investment opportunities: an historical analysis' (1942). In other fields, reasons are often adduced for such neglect of women's work. Joanna Russ (1983) and Dale Spender (1989) catalogue and explode a cornucopia of male excuses for ignoring or denigrating women's writing, primarily in the field of literature. (See Russ, 1983, 32, for contemporary male abuse of Harriet Martineau for producing books instead of children.)

The macroeconomics of the Stockholm School has attracted much attention. The first book by a member of the school to appear in English was Karin Kock's doctoral dissertation, *A Study of Interest Rates* (Stockholm Economic Studies no. 1, 1929), earlier than translations of Lindahl, Lundberg, Myrdal or Wicksell. Although most of her books and articles were in Swedish, Kock published in English on monetary policy and money markets in *Economica* (1927), *Economic Essays in Honour of Gustav Cassell* (1933) and *Review of Economic Studies* (1943), and in French in a symposium on monetary issues in *Revue d'Economie Politique* (1932). With Erik Lindahl and Einar Dahlgren, she wrote a massive and pioneering study, *National Income of Sweden, 1861–1930* (Stockholm Economic Studies nos 5A and 5B, 1937). Later she wrote on *International Trade Policy and the GATT, 1947–1967* (Stockholm Economic Studies, new series, no. 11, 1969). Her name is not in Bo Sandelin (ed.), *The History of Swedish Economic Thought* (1990) or in Bjorn Hansson, *The Stockholm School and the Development of Dynamic Method* (1982) and the *New Palgrave* has no entry on her. She is absent from 'Dramatis Personae at the end of 1937', the bibliography of non-Swedish writing by members of the Stockholm School, and 17 of the 19 essays in Jonung (1991). Rolf Henriksson includes four sentences on Kock in his essay in Jonung (1991) on the Political Economy Club, and Lars Jonung remarks in his introduction that 'Karin Kock, who worked with Myrdal on Sweden's monetary policy in the early 1930s, became the first woman cabinet minister in the late 1940s', but later in the book Bengt Metelius omits Kock from a list of Stockholm School members active in politics and policy. Her name also appears in lists of names in Jonung's introduction and the essays by Henriksson and Eskil Wadensjo, among those writing memoranda for the Committee on Unemployment or dining with Keynes in Stockholm in 1936.

Joseph Dorfman was unusual in the comprehensiveness of his coverage, not in his neglect of women's contributions. The most distinguished and comprehensive work on the history of American economics since *The Economic Mind* is *Breaking the Academic Mould*, edited by William Barber (1988), which examines economics at 14 American colleges and universities in the nineteenth century and, in the cases of Chicago, Wisconsin, MIT, Berkeley and Stanford, the first decade of the twentieth. The information given on women in economics is as follows. Helen Page Bates joined the faculty at Wisconsin after being a graduate student there, Mary Roberts Smith was an associate professor at Stanford, Jane Marcet's *Conversations on Political Economy* was used as a text at South Carolina College in 1825, William Graham Sumner was influenced by reading Harriet Martineau's *Illustrations of Political Economy* when he was 13 or 14, Millicent Fawcett's *Political Economy for Beginners* was vulgar, and Helen Sumner got a job at the Department of Labor after graduating from Wisconsin and co-editing the *Documentary History of American Industrial Society* with Commons (Barber, 1988, 330, 286, 49, 143, 188, 334, 339). Jessica Peixotto receives fuller coverage as a teacher in Mary Cookingham's essay (Barber, 1988, 275, 278, 288), but neither her research nor that of any other woman (apart from Sumner's editing) is mentioned. Barber (1988, 402) mentioned W.G. Sumner as referring to 'Marshall (*The Economics of Industry*)' but did not indicate Mary Paley Marshall as joint author. (Since Sumner's reference was made in 1883, it cannot have been to the later work of similar title by Alfred Marshall alone.) In large part, this reflects the choice of institutions to be covered, including schools such as Yale, which did not then admit women as undergraduates, and excluding women's colleges (Vassar, Wellesley, Bryn Mawr, Smith, Mount Holyoke, Connecticut College for Women), other liberal arts colleges, such state universities as the University of Nebraska (where Minnie Throop England taught) or the Chicago School of Civics and Philanthropy (Edith Abbott and Sophonisba Breckinridge). Still, the account of the University of Wisconsin does not mention Helen Campbell or Theresa McMahon, nor does that of the University of Chicago mention Hazel Kyrk, although a student winning an award from the AEA or the Hart, Schaffner & Marx Prize was a notable event. It would also be appropriate, in a history of academic economics, to consider why Edith Abbott joined the Chicago School of Civics and Philanthropy instead of getting a position at an established institution (although decades later becoming Dean of the University of Chicago Graduate School of Social Service Administration, after the university absorbed the school) and why Helen Campbell was unable to find an academic appointment, and so gradually moved into home economics.

1.3 DECLINE OF ACADEMIC EMPLOYMENT OF WOMEN

It should be kept in mind that women's achievements in American economics were accomplished despite considerable gender discrimination in hiring across academic fields. Such discrimination appears to have increased after World War I. Patricia Albjerg Graham (1977–8) has documented a decline in academic employment of women in the United States after 1930, as colleges increasingly imitated the practices of Ivy League and other leading research universities, including the hiring of only men: the percentage of women among full professors of history at coeducational liberal arts colleges declined from 16 per cent in 1930 to zero in 1970. Barbara Libby (1984) has shown that women were less well represented in the American economics profession in the interwar period than before 1920. Maxine Berg (1992, 308, 320) notes 'the female input into economic history [in Britain] which was so very important during these [interwar] years, yet declined sharply after the Second World War', and the postwar disappearance of women from the leadership of the Economic History Society.

The proportion of women among recipients of doctorates in economics in the United States also declined, from 8.5 per cent in 1920–29 (52 women receiving PhDs in economics) to 4.2 per cent (125 women PhDs) in 1950–59 (Chamberlain, 1988, 227).

The biologists Gertrude Elion, Barbara McClintock and Rosalyn Yalow, and the physicist Maria Goeppert Mayer, were all refused promotion and tenure in the 1950s, presumably because of insufficient merit, although each subsequently won the Nobel Prize. Mayer was allowed to work without pay in a university laboratory until 1963, when she won the Nobel Prize and was offered a paid position (Abir-Am, 1991, 337; Dagg and Thompson, 1988, 16). The only woman to hold a professorship in any discipline in interwar France was Marie Curie, who won two Nobel Prizes, in physics and chemistry.

In England, Joan Robinson was first appointed a lecturer at Cambridge, normally the lowest rung on the academic ladder, in 1938: five years after *Economics of Imperfect Competition* (1933) and after her macroeconomic essays, collected in *Essays in the Theory of Employment* (1937a), made her the ninth most cited macroeconomist in the English language for 1936–9 (see citation figures in Patrick Deutscher, 1990, 191). She was permitted to give a series of lectures (which became her *Introduction to the Theory of Employment*, 1937b) before being appointed to the faculty, despite opposition to her lecturing from Dennis Robertson, then chairman of the Faculty Board, and later objections by others to her appointment. This opposition led Keynes to protest that 'If there were no University lecturers and we were appointing all over again, would she not have a superior claim to some of those who now have a superior status? I should think myself that there could be no doubt about it' (Moggridge, 1992, 599–601). Harry Johnson (1978, 138–9), it may be noted, complained that Joan Robinson persecuted Dennis Robertson who 'had been prevented from receiving what he (and many others) considered was the final reward of a serious academic career, namely the professorship at Cambridge' – although in fact Robertson was elected to that chair at the earliest opportunity, upon the retirement of Pigou.

Joan Robinson's publications received the discipline's attention, even if they only led to her employment after considerable delay. However, Robert Skidelsky (1992, 448) introduces a discussion of Richard Kahn's contribution to Keynes's *General Theory* by asserting, without offering any evidence, that Kahn 'was almost certainly the creative force behind *The Theory of Imperfect Competition* [sic] by Joan Robinson'.

Such attempted reattribution of a woman economist's work to a man sometimes occurs while the woman is still alive and active. While Eleanor Lansing Dulles was in Paris in 1926, revising her Harvard–Radcliffe dissertation as a book, she was visited by Professors Robert Murray Haig and James Harvey Rogers of Columbia: 'Haig said, "You are here on a small grant and working alone, studying the nature of French inflation. Professor Rogers is working with our group and can do a more searching and complete job. We want you to turn over your notes to us and we'll carry on your work as part of our comprehensive project."' Dulles refused, publishing her own book: 'Keynes was to comment on my book in a letter to me saying it was an outstanding contribution to monetary theory' (Dulles, 1980, 100–102).

1.4   WOMEN'S REFERENCES TO WOMEN ECONOMISTS

To the extent that most women's contributions to economics were remembered, they were usually remembered by other women. Edith Abbott wrote on 'Harriet Martineau and the Employment of Women in 1836' (1906) and Clementina Black, a contributor to the *Economic Journal* on women's employment, and author of *Married Women's Work* (1915), wrote on Martineau for the ninth edition of the *Encyclopaedia Britannica*. Joan Robinson wrote an important introduction to Agnes Schwarzschild's translation of Rosa Luxemburg's *The Accumulation of Capital* (1951, 13), arguing that 'Luxemburg, neglected by Marxist and academic economists alike, offers a theory of the dynamic development of capitalism which is of the greatest interest'. Frank Hahn and R.C.O. Matthews (1967), however, omitted Luxemburg and Natalie Moszkowska from their survey of growth theory. Dorothy Lampen Thomson wrote *Adam Smith's Daughters* (1973) about Marcet, Martineau, Fawcett, Luxemburg, Webb and Robinson. This was a pathbreaking work which, however, left much further research to be done, as it was based only on the books of its subjects, thus missing, for example, the journal articles of Fawcett and Webb. Although she was a professor of economics at Lehman College, City University of New York, Lampen Thomson published her book through a vanity press.

The contributors to Berenice Carroll (ed.), *Liberating Women's History* (1976) cite the early economists and economic historians Edith Abbott, Helen

Campbell (for *Prisoners of Poverty: Women Wage Earners, Their Trades and Their Lives*, 1887/1970), Elizabeth Dexter, Bessie Leigh Hutchins, Emilie Josephine Hutchinson's *Women's Wages* (1968), Annie Meyer, Julia Spruill, Helen Sumner and Caroline Ware. Mary Lynn McDougall (1977) cites Clementina Black, B.L. Hutchins, Harriet Martineau's *The Factory Controversy: A Warning Against Meddling Legislation* (1855) and Ivy Pinchbeck's *Women Workers and the Industrial Revolution, 1750–1850* (1930/1969). Virago and other reprint houses interested in women's history have reissued books by Abbott, Campbell, Hutchins, Pinchbeck and others. Hannah Robie Sewall's *The Theory of Value Before Adam Smith*, published by the AEA in 1901, has been reprinted in the Kelley Reprints of Economic Classics. In their multicultural economic history of US women, Teresa Amott and Julie Matthaei (1991, 125) mention Edith Abbott, Sophonisba Breckinridge and Helen Sumner, together with the historian Mary Ritter Beard, as 'The new sociologists and social scientists who studied women', but only to report that they 'found professional jobs as a result of social homemaking', without making any mention or use of their writings. Recently, interest in women's contributions to economics has spread from women's history to women working in the history of economic thought, with Michèle Pujol's *Feminism and Anti-Feminism in Early Economic Thought* (1992) on British writers, Bette Polkinghorn's biography of Marcet (1993) and articles by Maxine Berg (1992) on the first British women economic historians, by Rita McWilliams Tullberg (1992) on Mary Paley Marshall and *Economics of Industry*, and by Margaret O'Donnell (1983) and Jannett Highfill and William Weber (1991) on Martineau. Michael Howard and John King give appropriately full, if unsympathetic, coverage in their *History of Marxian Economics* (1989, I, ch.6) to Rosa Luxemburg's claim to demonstrate the impossibility of stable accumulation in a closed capitalist system, and discuss (1992, II, chs 1, 7) Natalie Moszkowska's underconsumptionist theory of crises and critique of the falling rate of profit.

1.5 CONSEQUENCES OF NEGLECT

The neglect of women's writings on economics has led to misattribution of some contributions. Pujol (1992, 94) observes, citing articles by Kenneth Arrow and by Brian Chiplin and Peter Sloane as examples, that 'The economics profession has wrongly attributed to Edgeworth the development of the overcrowding theory of women's pay ... actually developed by John Stuart Mill (1965), Barbara Bodichon (1857) and Millicent Garrett Fawcett (1892, 1918).'

Roger Backhouse noted in his *History of Modern Economic Analysis* (1985, 36) that 'Ricardo's *Principles* was the subject of immediate discussion.

Ricardian ideas were presented in more accessible form in Mrs. Marcet's immensely successful *Conversations on Political Economy* (1817) and in James Mill's *Elements of Political Economy* (1821).' The curious reader who turns to page 418 to pursue the note appended to the Marcet reference will learn there that 'The first edition was in 1816, prior to Ricardo's *Principles*.' Backhouse made no further comment on the question of priority which would have been flagged by using the date of original publication, rather than of the second edition, in the text.

Rather than simply repeating Ricardo, Jane Marcet 'differed from her friends Malthus and Ricardo in her treatment of value theory. ... Rejecting the idea that the amount of labour contained in a good caused it to have value, Jane preferred the French economist J.B. Say's emphasis on "utility". ... Hers was not the "dismal science" of Malthus and Ricardo. She was more optimistic about the future than either of these writers for two reasons: first, she saw no limit to growth of output, income and wealth, as did Ricardo, and second, she was not convinced, as was Malthus, that the working class would erode all increases in the standard of living by having more children' (Polkinghorn, 1993, 52–4).

Marcet's work was well received by the economists of her day. 'Torrens wrote: "we know one female, at least, fully competent to instruct the members of our present cabinet in Political Economy". J.R. McCulloch toasted Jane at a meeting of the Political Economy Club of Edinburgh, saying she had "first shewn that women could rival men in the abstract sciences". ... David Ricardo recommended the book to his daughter who, he noted, studied it with great profit and appeared to understand it well. It was J.B. Say who wrote first to ask permission to "translate sizeable passages from her excellent book" for the students in his political economy class.' Malthus, however, tempered general praise with an objection that 'I think you have given too much sanction to Mr. Say's opinion reflecting utility' (Polkinghorn, 1993, 54–5).

The relative income hypothesis is well known as the first of the theories advanced to explain why cross-section data showed the marginal propensity to consume to be less than the average propensity (so that the average propensity would decline as income rose), while long-term time series data yielded equal marginal and average propensities. Macroeconomics textbooks which discuss this theory attribute it without exception to James Duesenberry's 1948 paper and 1949 book. His 1948 paper is reprinted in volumes of macroeconomics readings edited by Williams and Huffnagle, by Lindauer, by Mueller and by Shapiro, while Keiser reprinted the conclusion to Duesenberry's 1949 book. By contrast, the prior publication of the relative income hypothesis by Dorothy S. Brady and Rose Director Friedman in a 1947 National Bureau of Economic Research volume of *Studies in Income and Wealth* is noted in the fifth sentence of the second paragraph of the Notes and References to Chapter IX of Staffan Linder (1970, 171), in a footnote in Ruth Mack's survey of 'Economics of Consumption' (Ellis, 1952, 54n) and, most fully, in Robert Ferber's survey of 'Research on Household Behaviour' (1966, 115–17). In the same volume of *Surveys of Contemporary Economics* as Mack's paper, Moses Abramovitz and Paul Baran each attributed the relative income hypothesis to Duesenberry alone (Ellis, 1952, 150, 360). Alvin Hansen (1951, 168n) cited the Brady and Friedman paper (and an independent 1949 statement by Franco Modigliani) after Duesenberry in a footnote, but included a date only in the Duesenberry citation.

Marion Crawford Samuelson's fundamental paper on the so-called Australian case for protection to raise the return on nationally scarce factors of production (1939) is the subject of Paul Samuelson (1981) and has been cited by him elsewhere (for instance, in Stolper and Samuelson, 1941, and in the inaugural issue of the *Journal of International Trade & Economic Development*, 1992, 101), but has otherwise been ignored in the literature of trade theory. Lloyd Metzler footnoted her article in *Surveys of Contemporary Economics* in 1948, but she remains unmentioned in the surveys of trade theory by Jagdish Bhagwati, John Chipman, W. Max Corden and Gottfried Haberler in the 1960s, although Haberler must have known the paper, which was originally written for his seminar. Paul Samuelson's treatment of his late wife's contribution to trade theory is in striking and heartening contrast to Alfred Marshall's appropriation and later suppression of Mary Paley Marshall's *Economics of Industry*.

Neglect of women's contributions can also lead to distortion of historical context. The Canadian equivalent of the AEA's Richard Ely Lecture is the Harold Innis Lecture, named after the Canadian economic historian, institutionalist economist and expounder of the staple theory of economic growth. The voluminous Canadian book and journal literature on Harold Innis fails to mention that his wife, Mary Quayle Innis, wrote *Economic History of Canada* and 'The Early Industrial Development of Ontario', was Dean of Women at University College in the same University of Toronto where Harold Innis was Dean of Graduate Studies, and was a pioneer in Canadian women's history. Donald Creighton's biography of his mentor praises Mary Quayle Innis for her homemaking without hinting at her publications or her academic affiliation. It is difficult to imagine a biography of Mary Quayle Innis that would fail to mention that her husband was also an economic historian of Canada.

Ignoring the economic writings of women does not lead only to misattribution of discoveries or distortion of context. It can also mean that knowledge yielded by their research remains unknown to the discipline. Neglect in the leading textbooks on American economic history of the research of Abbott, Breckinridge, Campbell, Dexter, Spruill and Sumner on the economic experience of American women is associated with neglect of that experience itself.

Following the references to 'women' in the index of Jonathan Hughes (1990) leads to a discussion, based on Claudia Goldin's research, of the rising number of women in tertiary employment (the service sector) in the twentieth century (538, 540, 542, 577, and figure on 539) and a passing mention of sexism in a section on racism in the labour market (603). There is also an unindexed recognition on page 138 that the textile workers in Francis Lowell's Waltham, Massachusetts, mills in the early nineteenth century were women, and Caroline Ware's *The Early New England Cotton Manufacture* (1931) appears in the references for that chapter. Hughes did not include the growing right of married women to own property in his innovative chapter on property rights and economic growth.

James Willis and Martin Primack (1989, 428) devote two paragraphs to the rising service employment of women in recent decades, citing the 1987 edition of Hughes's textbook and a Goldin article, and include an unindexed sentence (132) noting that women and minors worked in textiles in New England in the early nineteenth century. Robert Puth (1988) provides slightly fuller coverage: women found it all but impossible to obtain advanced education before the Civil War (246), 'greater freedom for women' was one of several implausible causes of the Great Depression put forward by contemporaries (457), five million women joined the labour force during World War II (523) and female labour force participation is discussed (371, 566–7). Apart from references indexed under 'Women', Puth has another category, 'Mill girls' (186, 239–40). Susan Previant Lee and Peter Passell (1979, 85) mention Lowell's employment of young single women. The index to Jeremy Atack and Peter Passell (1994), the new edition of Lee and Passell, lists seven references to women – and 16 to tobacco. While all four books note that the 'mill girls' must have been better off in the factories than on New England farms, since they made that choice, none discusses wage rates, working conditions, disciplinary firing and blacklisting, the 12 or more female-led textile strikes between 1824 and 1837, or the writings of the workers, now conveniently edited by Philip Foner (1977).

All four of these books cite Anna J. Schwartz as co-author, with Milton Friedman, of *A Monetary History of the United States*, and Alice H. Jones on wealth distribution in colonial America. None cites Julie Matthaei's *An Economic History of Women in America* (1982), or Brownlee and Brownlee's *Women in the American Economy: A Documentary History, 1675 to 1929* (1976). None cites such earlier work as Dexter's books on women of affairs in the colonial and early national periods, or the writings of Abbott, Breckinridge, Campbell, Gilman, Spruill or Sumner (except that Atack and Passell include one Abbott article in a chapter bibliography). Hughes (1990,

551–2) did, however, cite recent work by Jane Humphries, Alice Kessler-Harris and Elyce Rotella on women's employment, as well as Goldin, and was unique in citing Harriet Martineau. Ratner *et al.* (1993) provide fuller coverage of women's economic experience than the other texts, citing books by Goldin, Kessler-Harris, Matthaei and Rotella, but not any works available at the time of their first edition in 1979, apart from a quotation from Sumner (1910), taken second-hand from Goldin. Some of these references, including that to Matthaei, were brought to their attention by an external reviewer for the revised edition (personal communication from reviewer). Berg (1992, 310) notes that David Cannadine (1984) cites no women other than Beatrice Webb and Barbara Hammond in his survey of literature on the English industrial revolution, omitting Alice Clark, Dorothy George, Dorothy Marshall, Ivy Pinchbeck and others.

Among writers of textbooks on the history of economic thought, E.K. Hunt gives particular attention in his revised edition (1992) to what he indexes as 'Women, exploitation of'. Under this heading he discusses the views of William Thompson (196–8), rates Thompson's understanding of the subject above that of John Stuart Mill (197), quotes Veblen (404–5) and considers William Reich on repression of sexuality (624–5) – all men. He does not mention Harriet Taylor Mill in connection with John Stuart Mill, or Charlotte Perkins Gilman in reference to Veblen. Hunt cites *Appeal of One Half the Human Race* as written by William Thompson alone, despite Thompson's declaration that part of the book was written by Anna Wheeler and that the remainder was their 'joint property' (Thompson, 1825/1983, xxi–xxiii). Hunt does, however, treat Rosa Luxemburg's economics at length (440–50, 456–9). None of Robert Ekelund and Robert Hébert (1990), Ingrid Rima (1991) or Harry Landreth (1976) mentions Luxemburg, or that Mill or Veblen or any-one else ever discussed the economic status of women. Ekelund and Hébert (1990, 450) include Martineau in a list of popularizers of classical political economy, and the bibliography of their chapter on Marshall includes articles by Michèle Pujol and Rita McWilliams Tullberg. Ekelund and Hébert (1990, 375, 414) and Rima (1991, 311) record that Alfred Marshall wrote a book with Mary Paley Marshall, and Ekelund and Hébert name the book and cite Keynes's article on her. All four texts discuss Joan Robinson.

1.6   CONCLUSION AND EXHORTATION

The economic profession has largely forgotten the substantial contributions made by women to the literature of economics before the post-1930 decline in women's representation in the profession. The extent of this neglect is strikingly illustrated by William J. Baumol's 'Digression: On Earlier Writings by Women', based on findings by his research assistant, Nicola Pearson, in an article on the centenary of the AEA. Baumol (1985, 11) made the 'observation ... that before World War I, as today, a (distressingly) few women *were* contributing to the literature' and provided a list of three articles (one in two parts) by Edith Abbott, and one each by Clementina Black, Clara Collet and, after World War I, Dorothea Kittredge. This is a meagre result for what was clearly a sincere effort to draw attention to women's writings. Even for the four women of whom Baumol knew it is inadequate: Clara Collet published 14 articles in scholarly economics and statistics journals, as well as books, one of which was reviewed in one of Mary Paley Marshall's rare contributions to the *Economic Journal*. Edith Abbott published 17 other economic journal articles and several books, while Baumol entirely missed Helen Bliss, Helen Bosanquet, Sophonisba Breckinridge, Eveline Burns, Helen Campbell, Katharine Coman, Katharine Davis, Minnie Throop England, Amy Hewes (one article in *JASA*, four in *JPE*, three in *AER*, one in *QJE* starting in 1919, mostly on the Soviet economy), Bessie Leigh Hutchins, Hazel Kyrk, Theresa McMahon, Hannah Sewall and Helen Sumner, without counting those, such as Katharine Snodgrass or Mary van Kleeck, who wrote only two or three articles, or those who, like Margrieta van der Veen (two *Economic Journal* articles in 1898) or Hansi Pollak (four articles in the *South African Journal of Economics*, from 1933), published a few journal articles in English but appear to have worked primarily in other languages.

Women were more numerous and active in economics than Baumol indicates. Peter Groenewegen and Susan King (1994) list 112 women (6.78 per cent of the 1655 contributors) who published 222 articles (5.3 per cent of the total) in five core economics journals (*AER*, *Economica*, *Economic Journal*, *JPE*, *QJE*) between 1900 and 1939. This useful and important preliminary list will be even longer in its final form, since such economists as Gladys Blakey, Marian Bowley and Elisabeth van Dorp are absent from the preliminary list. Gladys Blakey was co-author, with Roy Gillespie Blakey, of a series of ten *AER* articles on federal tax legislation of the preceding year: a 31-page article in 1919, and others in 1932 and each year from 1934 to 1941, inclusive.

Contrary to Baumol's claim, and to the implication of his list, their concerns ranged far beyond labour economics or women's issues: Elisabeth van Dorp's *Economic Journal* articles in 1919 and 1920 were on deviations in international exchanges, Lila Knudsen wrote on 'Serial or coherent correlation in price series' (*Journal of Farm Economics* 1938), while Ethel Dietrich's four *AER* and *JPE* papers between 1928 and 1935 dealt with import quotas, model trade agreements and export credit insurance. Eleanor Lansing Dulles and Karin Kock wrote on monetary and international economics. Women economists were, however, almost the only economists to concern themselves with the economic experience of the female majority and with such questions as explaining the disparity between men's and women's wages.

The history of economic thought must, if it is to portray the discipline's past, take account of the role played by women and consider why the participation of women in the economics profession declined. Even construed more narrowly as a retrospective on contributions to theory, a history of economic analysis should examine and attribute Dorothy Brady and Rose Friedman on the relative income hypothesis, Ruth Cohen's discovery of reswitching of techniques, Rosa Luxemburg on formal models of capitalist growth and breakdown, Mary Paley Marshall's share in Marshallian economics, and all the theorists of women's economic status and wage discrimination since Harriet Taylor Mill and Barbara Leigh Smith Bodichon. Economic historians of both Britain and North America would find in the writings of women economists a treasure trove of learning on the economic history of the neglected majority of the population.

There are economists who argue that the discipline's current body of knowledge incorporates everything of value from the past. This is in fact a testable empirical proposition: one can check whether, at each moment in the past, the economics profession remembered every previous contribution now considered important. For every sample period, this hypothesis can be rejected (consider, for example, what any economist between 1900 and 1960 could have learned about efficient markets, random walks, Brownian motion and rational expectations from Louis Bachelier's thesis). Vera Smith's critique of central banking (1936/1990), based on her dissertation with Hayek, was nearly half a century ahead of the revival of the theme in books by Kevin Dowd, David Glasner, George Selgin and Lawrence White, which led to the reissue of her first book. Beyond the issue of just recognition of worthy contributors to the discipline in the past, economists can still learn much, not least about the economic experience of more than half of humanity, from the writings of earlier generations of women economists.

Women's contributions are not, of course, all that is misplaced from the heritage of economics. The essays on the history of Swedish economics in Sandelin (1990) miss Robert Eagly's articles on the Swedish bullionist debate as well as missing Karin Kock. Joseph Dorfman (1946–59) made no mention of E.A.J. Johnson's *American Economic Thought in the 17th Century* (1932) and the ten-page bibliography of White (1958) lists neither Johnson nor Dorfman. The neglect of women's contributions is particularly glaring and widespread, however.

The indispensable next step in rediscovering the women economists of the past and their writings is to survey who they were and what they wrote in a *Biographical Dictionary of Women Economists*, an exercise in prosopography (collective biography or multiple career-line analysis) a technique of historical research pioneered by Beard, Merton, Namier and Syme (see Lawrence Stone, 1972). When this project is completed, it will help to diminish the neglect of women's contributions to economics and illuminate the past of the discipline.

NOTE

1. Presented at a joint History of Economics Society and American Economic Association session in Anaheim, California, 5 January 1993, and at a Kress Society seminar at Harvard, September 1993. I am grateful to Mary Ann Dimand for helpful comments and suggestions. This paper was written while I was Barbara Hogate Ferrin Term Professor of Economics at Connecticut College, New London, CT.

REFERENCES

Abbott, Edith (1906), 'Harriet Martineau and the Employment of Women in 1836', *Journal of Political Economy*, **14**, 614–26.

Abbott, Edith (1910/1969), *Women in Industry: A Study in American Economic History*, New York: D. Appleton; reprinted New York: Arno Press.

Abbott, Edith (1940), *Public Assistance*, Chicago: University of Chicago Press.

Abir-Am, Pnina (1991), 'Nobelesse oblige: Biographical Writings on Nobelists', *Isis*, **82**, 326–43.

Alexander, Sally (1988), *Women's Fabian Tracts*, London: Routledge.

American Economic Association (1961), *Index of Economic Journals*, 5 vols, Homewood, IL: Richard D. Irwin.

Amott, Teresa and Julie Matthaei (1991), *Race, Gender, and Work*, Montreal and New York: Black Rose Books.

Andrews, John and W.D.P. Bliss (1911), *History of Women in Trade Unions, 1825 to the Knights of Labor*, Washington, DC: Senate Report on Condition of Woman and Child Wage-Earners in the United States, Vol. X (Doc. no. 645, 61st Congress, 2nd session).

Antler, Joyce (1987), *Lucy Sprague Mitchell*, New Haven, CT: Yale University Press.

Atack, Jeremy and Peter Passell (1994), *A New Economic View of American History*, 2nd edn, New York: W.W. Norton.

Backhouse, Roger (1985), *A History of Modern Economic Analysis*, Oxford: Basil Blackwell.

Barber, William J. (ed.) (1988), *Breaking the Academic Mould*, Middletown, CT: Wesleyan University Press.

Baumol, William J. (1985), 'On Method in U.S. Economics a Century Earlier', *American Economic Review*, **75**, (6), December, 1–12.

Berg, Maxine (1992), 'The First Women Economic Historians', *Economic History Review*, **45**, 308–29.

Black, Clementina (1883), 'Harriet Martineau', *Encyclopaedia Britannica* (9th edn).

Black, Clementina (1915), *Married Women's Work*, London.

Bodichon, Barbara Leigh Smith (1857), *Women and Work*, London: Bosworth & Harrison, reprinted in Candida Ann Lacey, ed., *Barbara Leigh Smith Bodichon and the Langham Place Group*, London: Routledge, 1987.

Brady, Dorothy and Rose Friedman (1947), 'Savings and the Income Distribution', in *Studies in Income and Wealth*, **10**, 247–65, New York: National Bureau of Economic Research.

Breckinridge, Sophonisba P. (1933), *Women in the Twentieth Century: A Study of Their Political, Social and Economic Activities*, New York and London: McGraw-Hill.

Brownlee, W. Eliot and Mary M. Brownlee (1976), *Women in the American Economy: A Documentary History, 1675 to 1925*, New Haven, CT: Yale.

Burns, Eveline (1922), 'Recent Contributions to Economic Theory', *Economica*, **2**, 272–8.

Campbell, Helen (1887/1970), *Prisoners of Poverty: Women Wage Workers, Their Trades and Their Lives*, Boston, MA: Roberts Brothers; reprinted Westport, CT: Greenwood Press.

Campbell, Helen (1893), *Women Wage-Earners: Their Past, Their Present and Their Future*, with an introduction by Richard T. Ely, Boston: Roberts Brothers.

Cannadine, David (1984), 'The Past and Present in the English Industrial Revolution, 1880–1980', *Past and Present*, **103**, 149–58.

Carroll, Berenice (ed.) (1976), *Liberating Women's History: Theoretical and Critical Essays*, Urbana, IL: University of Illinois Press.

Chamberlain, Mariam K. (ed.) (1988), *Women in Academe*, New York: Russell Sage Foundation.

Cole, G.D.H. (1949), 'Beatrice Webb as an Economist', in M. Cole (ed.), *The Webbs and Their Work*, London: Frederick Muller, Ltd.

Coman, Katharine (1912/1969), *Economic Beginnings of the Far West*, New York: Macmillan; reprinted New York: A.M. Kelley.

Coman, Katharine (1917), *Industrial History of the United States*, New York: Macmillan.

Creighton, Donald (1957), *Harold Adams Innis: Portrait of a Scholar*, Toronto: University of Toronto Press.

Dagg, Anne Innis and Patricia Thompson (1988), *MisEducation: Women and Canadian Universities*, Toronto: OISE Press.

Deutscher, Patrick (1990), *R.G. Hawtrey and the Development of Macroeconomics*, Ann Arbor, MI: University of Michigan Press.

Dexter, Elizabeth A. (1931), *Colonial Women of Affairs: Women in Business and Affairs in America before 1776*, 2nd edn, Boston, MA: Houghton Mifflin (1st edn, 1924).

Dexter, Elizabeth A. (1950), *Career Women in America: 1776–1840*, Francestown, NJ: M. Jones.

Diggins, P. John (1978), *The Bard of Savagery: Thorstein Veblen and Modern Social Theory*, New York: The Seabury Press.

Dorfman, Joseph (1934), *Thorstein Veblen and His America*, New York: Viking Press.

Dorfman, Joseph (1946–59), *The Economic Mind in American Civilization, 1606–1933*, 5 vols, New York: Viking Press.

Dowd, Douglas (1964), *Thorstein Veblen*, New York: Washington Square Press.

Duesenberry, James (1948), 'Income-Consumption Relations and Their Implications', in *Essays in Honor of Alvin Hansen*, New York: W.W. Norton.

Duesenberry, James (1949), *Income, Saving and the Theory of Consumer Behavior*, Cambridge, MA: Harvard University Press.

Dulles, Eleanor Lansing (1929), *The French Franc, 1914–1928*, New York.

Dulles, Eleanor Lansing (1980), *Chances of a Lifetime: A Memoir*, Englewood Cliffs, NJ: Prentice-Hall.

Ekelund, Robert and Robert Hébert (1990), *A History of Economic Theory and Method*, 3rd edn, New York: McGraw-Hill.

Ellis, Howard (ed.) (1952), *A Survey of Contemporary Economics*, Vol. II, Homewood, IL: Irwin for American Economic Association.

Fawcett, Millicent Garrett (1870a), *Political Economy for Beginners*, London: Macmillan.

Fawcett, Millicent Garrett (1870b), 'Proportional Representation', *Macmillan's Magazine*, **22**.

Fawcett, Millicent Garrett (1871), 'A Short Explanation of Mr. Hare's Scheme of Representation', *Macmillan's Magazine*, **23**.

Ferber, Robert (1966), 'Research on Household Behaviour', in *Surveys of Economic Theory*, III, New York: St Martin's for American Economic Association and Royal Economic Society.

Fisher, Irving (1913), *The Purchasing Power of Money*, 2nd edn, New York: Macmillan.

Foner, Philip (ed.) (1977), *The Factory Girls: A Collection of Writings on Life and Struggles in the New England Factories of the 1840s by the Factory Girls Themselves, and the Story in Their Own Words of the First Trade Unions of Women Workers in the United States*, Urbana, IL: University of Illinois Press.

Friedman, Milton and Anna J. Schwartz (1963), *A Monetary History of the United States, 1867–1960*, Princeton, NJ: Princeton University Press for the National Bureau of Economic Research.

Gilman, Charlotte Perkins (1898a), 'Economic Basis of the Woman Question', *Woman's Journal*, 1 October, partially reprinted in Kraditor (1968), 175–8.

Gilman, Charlotte Perkins (1898b), *Women and Economics: A Study of the Economic Relation Between Men and Women*, Boston: Small, Maynard; reprinted with introduction by Carl N. Degler, New York: Harper Torchbooks, 1966.

Gilman, Charlotte Perkins (1903/1972), *The Home: Its Work and Influence*, New York: McClure, Phillips; reprinted Urbana, IL: University of Illinois Press.

Goldin, Claudia (1990), *Understanding the Gender Gap: An Economic History of American Women*, New York: Oxford University Press.

Graham, Patricia Albjerg (1977–8), 'Expansion and Exclusion: A History of Women in American Higher Education', *Signs*, **III**, 759–73.

Groenewegen, Peter D. and Susan King (1994), 'Women as Producers of Economic Articles: A Statistical Assessment of the Nature and the Extent of Female Participation in Five British and North American Journals 1900–39', University of Sydney Working Papers in Economics no. 201.

Groenewegen, Peter D. and Bruce McFarlane (1990), *A History of Australian Economic Thought*, London and New York: Routledge.

Hahn, Frank, and R.C.O. Matthews (1967), 'The Theory of Economic Growth: A Survey', in *Surveys of Economic Theory: Growth and Development*, Vol. II, New York: St Martin's Press.

Haney, Lewis H. (1936), *History of Economic Thought*, 3rd edn, New York: Macmillan.

Hansen, Alvin H. (1951), *Business Cycles and National Income*, New York: W.W. Norton.

Hansson, Bjorn A. (1982), *The Stockholm School and the Development of Dynamic Method*, London: Croom Helm.

Highfill, Jannett and William V. Weber (1991), 'Harriet Martineau: An Economic

View of Victorian Arts and Letters', *Journal of Culture Economics*, **15** (1), June, 85–92.

Howard, Michael and John King (1989–92), *History of Marxian Economics*, Princeton, NJ: Princeton University Press.

Hughes, Jonathan R.T. (1990), *American Economic History*, 3rd edn, Glensview, IL: Scott Foresman-Little Brown.

Hunt, E.K. (1992), *History of Economic Thought: A Critical Perspective*, 2nd edn, New York: Harper Collins.

Hutchins, Bessie Leigh (1915/1978), *Women in Modern Industry*, London: G. Bell and Sons, reprinted West Yorkshire: E.P. Publishing Ltd.

Hutchinson, Emilie Josephine (1968), *Women's Wages*, New York: AMS Press.

Innis, Mary Quayle (1937), 'The Industrial Development of Ontario: 1783–1820', *Ontario Historical Society Papers and Records*, **32**, 105–13; reprinted in J.K. Johnson (1975), *Historical Essays on Upper Canada*, Toronto: McClelland and Stewart.

Innis, Mary Quayle (1954), *Economic History of Canada*, 3rd edn, Toronto: Ryerson (1st edn, 1935).

Johnson, E.A.J. (1932), *American Economic Thought in the 17th Century*, London: P.S. King and Son.

Johnson, Harry (1978), 'Cambridge in the 1950s', *Encounter*, **42**, 28–39; reprinted in E.S. Johnson and H. Johnson (1978), *The Shadow of Keynes*, Chicago: University of Chicago Press.

Jonung, Lars (ed.) (1991), *The Stockholm School of Economics Revisited*, Cambridge: Cambridge University Press.

Keynes, J.M. (1944), 'Mary Paley Marshall (1850–1944)', *Economic Journal*, **54**, 268–84.

Kock, Karin (1929), *A Study of Interest Rates*, London: P.S. King.

Kock, Karin (1969), *International Trade Policy and the GATT, 1947–1967*, Stockholm: Almqvist & Wiksell.

Kraditor, Aileen (ed.) (1968), *Up from the Pedestal: Landmark Writings in the American Woman's Struggle for Equality*, Chicago: Quadrangle Books.

Kyrk, Hazel (1923), *A Theory of Consumption*, Boston and New York: Houghton Mifflin.

Landreth, Harry (1976), *History of Economic Theory: Scope, Method and Content*, Boston: Houghton Mifflin.

Lee, Susan Previant and Peter Passell (1979), *A New Economic View of American History*, New York: W.W. Norton.

Libby, Barbara (1984), 'Women in Economics Before 1940', *Essays in Economic and Business History*, **3**, 273–90.

Linder, Staffan (1970), *The Harried Leisure Class*, New York and London: Columbia University Press.

Luxemburg, Rosa (1951), *The Accumulation of Capital*, Agnes Schwarzchild, trans, London: Routledge & Kegan Paul.

Marcet, Jane (1816), *Conversations on Political Economy*, London.

Marshall, Alfred and Mary Paley Marshall (1879), *Economics of Industry*, London: Macmillan; reprinted, with introduction by D.P. O'Brien, London: Routledge and Thoemes Press, 1994.

Martineau, Harriet (1855), *The Factory Controversy: A Warning Against Meddling Legislation*, Manchester: Ireland and Company.

Matthaei, Julie (1982), *An Economic History of Women in America*, New York: Schocken.

McDougall, Mary Lynn (1977), 'Working-Class Women During the Industrial Revolution', in R. Bridenthal and C. Koonz (eds) (1978), *Becoming Visible: Women in European History*, Boston: Houghton Mifflin.

McMahon, Theresa (1912), *Women and Economic Evolution*, Madison, WI: University of Wisconsin Bulletin no. 496.

McMahon, Theresa (1925), *Social and Economic Standards of Living*, Boston: D.C. Heath.

McWilliams Tullberg, Rita (1992), 'Alfred Marshall's Attitude Toward the *Economics of Industry*', *Journal of the History of Economic Thought*, **14**, (2), 257–70.

Meyer, Annie (ed.) (1891), *Women's Work in America*, New York: Holt.

Mitchell, Wesley Clair (1913), *Business Cycles*, Berkeley and Los Angeles: University of California Press.

Mitchell, Wesley Clair (1927), *Business Cycles: The Problem and Its Setting*, New York: National Bureau of Economic Research.

Moggridge, Donald (1992), *Maynard Keynes: An Economist's Biography*, London: Routledge.

O'Donnell, Margaret (1983), 'Harriet Martineau: A Popular Early Economics Educator', *Journal of Economic Education*, **14** (4), Fall, 59–64.

Pinchbeck, Ivy (1930/1969), *Women Workers and the Industrial Revolution, 1750–1850*, London: Routledge; reprinted London: Virago.

Polkinghorn, Bette (1993), *Jane Marcet*, London: Forestwood Publications.

Pujol, Michèle A. (1992), *Feminism and Anti-Feminism in Early Economic Thought*, Aldershot: Edward Elgar.

Puth, Robert (1988), *American Economic History*, 2nd edn, Chicago: The Dryden Press.

Ratner, Sidney, James Soltow and Richard Sylla (1993), *The Evolution of the American Economy*, 2nd edn, New York: Macmillan.

Reisman, David (1953), *Thorstein Veblen: A Critical Interpretation*, New York: Scribners.

Rima, Ingrid (1991), *Development of Economic Analysis*, 5th edn, Homewood, IL: Irwin.

Robinson, Joan (1933), *Economics of Imperfect Competition*, London: Macmillan.

Robinson, Joan (1937a), *Essays in the Theory of Employment*, London: Macmillan.

Robinson, Joan (1937b), *Introduction to the Theory of Employment*, London: Macmillan.

Rothbard, Murray (1975), *America's Great Depression*, 3rd edn, Kansas City: Sheed & Ward.

Russ, Joanna (1983), *How to Suppress Women's Writing*, Austin, TX: University of Austin Press.

Samuelson, Marion Crawford (1939), 'The Australian Case for Protection Re-examined', *Quarterly Journal of Economics*, **54**, 143–9.

Samuelson, Paul (1981), 'Summing Up on the Australian Case for Protection', *Quarterly Journal of Economics*, **96**, 147–60.

Sandelin, Bo (ed.) (1990), *The History of Swedish Economic Thought*, London: Routledge.

Saulnier, Raymond (1938), *Contemporary Monetary Theory*, New York: Columbia University Press.

Schneir, Miriam ed. (1972), *Feminism: The Essential Historical Writings*, New York: Random House.

Schumpeter, Joseph (1954), *History of Economic Analysis*, New York: Oxford University Press.

Sewall, Hannah (1901), *The Theory of Value Before Adam Smith*, New York: Macmillan for American Economic Association; reprinted New York: A.M. Kelley, 1968.

Sinclair, Andrew (1965), *The Emancipation of the American Woman*, New York: Harper Colophon.

Skidelsky, Robert (1992), *John Maynard Keynes, The Economist as Saviour, 1920–1937*, London: Macmillan.

Smith, Vera (1936/1990), *The Rationale of Central Banking: And the Free Banking Alternative*, London: P.S. King and Son; reprinted Liberty Fund.

Somers, Harold (1944), 'Classified Bibliography of Articles on Business Cycle Theory', in *Readings in Business Cycle Theory*, Philadelphia: Blakiston for American Economic Association.

Spender, Dale (1989), *The Writing or the Sex?, or, Why You Don't Have to Read Women's Writing to Know It's No Good*, New York: Pergamon Press.

Spruill, Julia C. (1938), *Women's Life and Work in the Southern Colonies*, Chapel, NC: University of North Carolina Press; reprinted New York: W.W. Norton, 1968.

Stolper, Wolfgang F. and Paul Samuelson (1941), 'Protection and Real Wages', *Review of Economic Studies*, **9**, 58–73.

Stone, Lawrence (1972), 'Prosopography', in Felix Gilbert and Stephen R. Graubard (eds), *Historical Studies Today*, New York: W.W. Norton.

Sturges, R.P. (1975), *Economists' Papers 1750–1950: A Guide to Archive and Other Manuscript Sources for the History of British and Irish Economic Thought*, Durham, NC: Duke University Press.

Sumner, Helen L. (1910), *History of Women in Industry in the United States*, Washington, DC: Senate Report on Condition of Woman and Child Wage-Earners in the United States, Vol. IX (Doc. no. 645, 61st Congress, 2nd session).

Thompson, William (1825/1983), *Appeal of One Half the Human Race, Women, Against the Pretensions of the Other Half, Men, To Retain Them in Political, and Thence in Civil and Domestic Slavery*; reprinted London: Virago.

Thomson, Dorothy Lampen (1973), *Adam Smith's Daughters*, Jericho, New York: Exposition-University Press.

Tuckwell, Gertrude (ed.) (1908), *Woman in Industry*, London: Duckworth & Co.

Veblen, Thorstein (1899), *Theory of the Leisure Class*, New York: Macmillan.

Ware, Caroline (1931), *The Early New England Cotton Manufacture*, Boston: Houghton Mifflin; reprinted New York: Russell and Russell, 1966.

White, Virgle Glenn (1958), *Founders of American Economic Thought and Policy*, New York: Bookman Associates.

Willis, James and Martin Primack (1989), *An Economic History of the United States*, 2nd edn, Englewood Cliffs, NJ: Prentice-Hall.

2. American women economists, 1900–1940: doctoral dissertations and research specialization

Evelyn L. Forget[1]

2.1 INTRODUCTION

In a 1985 essay on the early history of the *AER*, William Baumol credits his research assistant Nicola Pearson with the observation that 'before World War I, as today, a (distressingly) few women *were* contributing to the literature. However, even more than today, their topics were predominantly specialized in "women's issues", of considerable interest in themselves, but unrelated to the subjects that were attracting the bulk of the profession' (1985, 11). But Peter Groenewegen and Susan King, in the process of compiling a data base covering the nature and extent of women's participation in *AER*, *Economica*, *Economic Journal*, *JPE* and *QJE* between 1900 and 1939, were led to ask, '"How so Many?" rather than "Why so Few?", given the enormous barriers that existed to women doing academic research in economics over this period' (1994, 23). Groenewegen and King demonstrate that 'Labour Economics; Social Policy (especially noticeable when Health, Education and Welfare are combined with Regional Planning, Development and Housing); Comparative Economic Systems and Industry Studies were the various branches of the subject to which women were contributing significantly above the average of their overall contribution to the journal literature' (1994, 19) and note that articles in these areas grew increasingly rare in the journals studied as the twentieth century progressed. Strober and Reagan (1976, 307) report that the tendency of women to specialize in areas of economics associated with 'helping people' (such as labour economics, development and social policy) persisted well into the 1970s.

This chapter has two purposes. First, it examines the thesis topics pursued at American universities before 1940, as reported in the *AER*,[2] and draws some general conclusions about the sexual division of labour at the doctoral dissertation stage. The data suggest that the topics chosen by women, although less diverse than those chosen by men, were concentrated in the same general areas throughout the period studied. And in fact, by 1935 the distribution of topics chosen by men and women were very similar. That is, the thesis topics chosen by women were not unrelated to the subjects that were attracting the bulk of the profession during the period. Moreover, while the pattern is similar, thesis topics chosen by women demonstrate a slightly broader range of specialization than journal articles contributed by women.

The second purpose of this chapter is to speculate about the nature of the constraints faced by women in the economics profession during the early decades of the twentieth century and how women dealt with them. Four strategies – superperformance, subordination, separatism and innovation – have been identified as creative attempts by women professionals in other fields to live reasonable lives despite the obstacles their own socialization and the larger society placed in their paths (Glazer and Slater, 1987, ch.6). The data available to us suggest that these same strategies may have been pursued by women economists, with some implications for the differences observed between the breadth of dissertation research as compared with journal publication.

2.2 THE SEXUAL DIVISION OF LABOUR AND DISSERTATION TOPICS

The PhD was a qualification sought by those who wanted to teach and do research in colleges and universities, although some graduates found work in business, government, social agencies and banks. While it is certainly the case that not all college teachers obtained higher degrees, particularly at the smaller regional colleges that employed many women, it is clear that higher degrees became increasingly important throughout the period for those who planned academic careers. If we examine all fields of study in which PhDs were awarded, by 1920 some 10 per cent were earned by women. By 1930, that figure had reached its peak at approximately 15 per cent, and persisted at that level until 1940, before beginning a 30-year decline. Only in the past 20 years has the figure recovered (Glazer and Slater, 1987, 25; Solomon, 1985, chs 8, 11; Carter, 1981, 684, 687). In economics, by contrast, PhD dissertations by women, as a percentage of the total number of dissertations in economics, seemed to reach their peak in 1920 and then show a general decline until 1940 (see Table 2.1).

The expansion of women's colleges in the first four decades of this century was at least partly responsible for creating both the demand for and the supply of women doctoral candidates. They offered the most certain employment for newly minted PhDs, and even those colleges which did not have doctoral programmes and could not directly produce women economists

Table 2.1   *PhD dissertations by women as a percentage of the total number of PhD dissertations in economics, 1912–40*

Year	Women (%)	Year	Women (%)	Year	Women (%)
1912	6.15	1922	14.55	1932	10.54
1913	6.77	1923	12.50	1933	9.94
1914	10.81	1924	12.77	1934	10.21
1915	10.95	1925	12.02	1935	10.06
1916	11.16	1926	11.68	1936	9.15
1917	12.08	1927	13.24	1937	12.09
1918	16.89	1928	13.64	1938	9.70
1919	16.89	1929	13.18	1939	9.52
1920	19.29	1930	10.94	1940	6.94
1921	15.45	1931	10.73		

Note: In most cases, the first name was adequate to identify the author as female. In ambiguous cases, we attempted to identify the author through other biographical sources. In those few cases where no such identification was possible, the entry was counted as part of the total but not female. Therefore the estimate of women PhD candidates in economics may be biased downwards.

Source: 'Dissertations in Progress', as listed in the *American Economic Review*.

were nevertheless responsible for encouraging their own undergraduates to pursue graduate work. Many of the women writing dissertations in economics between 1912 and 1932 received first degrees from the seven sisters, Barnard, Bryn Mawr, Mt. Holyoke, Radcliffe, Smith, Vassar and Wellesley. Moreover, Bryn Mawr had a thriving PhD programme. And, of course, Radcliffe generated its own PhDs at least in part to save Harvard the ignominy of admitting women to its hallowed halls in the early years.

Nevertheless, women economists studied, by and large, at the same schools as their male colleagues. Between 1912 and 1932, 57 women chose to write economics dissertations at Columbia University. The University of Chicago was the next most popular venue, with 26 women. Bryn Mawr and the University of Pennsylvania both produced 15 women graduates, the University of Wisconsin 14 and Radcliffe ten. Nebraska, Cornell, Stanford, Indiana, Illinois, California, Johns Hopkins, Minnesota and Michigan each produced between one and four women PhDs.

If American women were studying economics at the same institutions as their male counterparts, they were not necessarily choosing dissertation topics in the same areas, particularly in the early part of the century. In order to determine how the pattern of specialization differed between men and women and changed over time, we examined 'Doctoral Dissertations in Political Economy in Progress in American Universities and Colleges', listed in the *American Economic Review* in three separate years: 1915, 1925 and 1935. The classification scheme is that used by the AEA during the period.

The data in Table 2.2 should be read as follows: of the total number of women writing doctoral dissertations in economics in 1915 at American universities and colleges, 4.3 per cent were writing on theory and its history, while 5.3 per cent of the men writing theses chose a topic in this area. In some fields, the total number of theses in progress during any year was so small that the 'percentages' tended to fluctuate wildly, but the fields that attracted the most interest tended to be more stable. We looked at three distinct years in order to minimize the problem of double-counting theses reported more than once, sometimes with slightly different titles.

Some very broad conclusions can be drawn. In 1915, women seemed to focus on two areas: Economic History and Geography; and Labour and Labour Organizations. Social Problems and Reforms, and Population and Migration were also areas of significant concern, while other topics received little or no attention. Men also favoured Economic History and Labour, but they were much less concentrated in those two fields than were women. Public Finance was an area of significant concern for men. The range of dissertation topics chosen by men fell into 16 different fields, as compared to only eight for women.

By 1925, women had expanded their range to include 13 fields. A smaller proportion of women wrote in the area of Economic History and Geography, while topics such as Theory and its History, Public Finance, Manufacturing Industries and Social Problems and Reforms gained in popularity. The main area of interest remained Labour and Labour Organizations. Men, by contrast, increased their attention to Agriculture, Mining, Forestry and Fishing; Accounting and Business Methods; Money, Prices, Credit and Banking; and Social Problems and Reforms. Dissertation topics covered a range of 17 fields.

By 1935, the distribution by field of topics chosen by men and women were very similar. There was a slight tendency for female writers to focus disproportionately on Economic History and Social Problems and Reforms, while men chose Accounting and Public Finance. The most popular area for both women and men (unsurprisingly, in 1935) was Money, Prices, Credit and Banking. But what the data show most clearly is how the distribution of dissertation topics chosen by women and men tended to become more similar over time.

These results are particularly interesting in the light of Strober and Reagan's (1976) finding that Labour Economics and Social Policy remained the most popular areas of research among women PhD candidates in the 1970s. In the

Table 2.2 Dissertations in progress by field (by women as a percentage of total dissertations in progress by women authors, and by men as a percentage of total dissertations by men)

	1915		1925		1935	
	Women	Men	Women	Men	Women	Men
Theory and its History	4.3	5.3	6.8	4.1	5.6	6.4
Economic History and Geography	30.4	12.3	11.9	6.6	14.8	6.6
Agric., Mining, Forestry and Fishing	0	6.4	1.7	11.5	11.8	11.2
Manufacturing Industries	0	7.5	5.1	3.2	3.7	4.1
Transportation and Communication	0	7.5	3.4	4.5	5.6	5.0
Trade, Commerce and Commercial Org.	0	4.3	1.7	4.8	5.6	5.8
Accounting and Business Methods	0	4.3	3.4	11.1	7.4	15.1
Capital and Capitalistic Org.	4.3	3.7	0	3.2	0	2.2
Labour and Labour Org.	30.4	13.9	28.8	13.8	9.3	7.7
Money, Prices, Credit and Banking	4.3	4.3	5.1	8.8	18.5	16.8
Public Finance, Tariffs and Trade	4.3	12.9	6.8	9.5	3.7	10.1
Population and Migration	8.7	4.3	0	2.9	0	0.6
Social Problems and Reforms	13.0	7.0	18.6	10.2	7.4	2.5
Insurance and Pensions	0	4.3	5.1	1.6	3.7	3.5
Socialism and Cooperative Enterprises	0	1.1	0	0.7	0	0.4
Statistics and its Methods	0	1.1	1.7	2.9	1.9	3.1
Pauperism and Charities	0	0	0	0.7	1.9	0.4

Note: Columns do not add to 100 per cent, owing to rounding.

first four decades of this century, it seems that women and men were choosing dissertation topics from similar fields of study. Women continued to focus on these same fields until very late into the twentieth century, while men (and, given the gender balance, therefore the discipline) turned their attention to other areas.[3]

It is, of course, possible that women were specializing in particular areas within these broad classifications at the dissertation stage of their careers, but a (necessarily) subjective inspection of thesis titles suggests otherwise. If we define 'women's issues' as all topics that deal specifically with women, such as 'Women in the Labour Market' and all topics in areas of traditional concern for women (such as household budget studies), then we find that the percentage of women writing on 'women's issues' was very low – less than 20 per cent over the entire period. Even given the very subjective definition of 'women's issues' and the difficulty of determining the content of a dissertation from its title, it appears that the proportion of women specializing in women's issues was not large. (Suppose our estimate is incorrect and that we have caught only half the women writing in this area. Even at the peak of specialization in 1924, we would still have only slightly more than a third of women writing in these areas.) Moreover, there is no reason to believe that thesis titles are either more or less revealing in 1940 than they were earlier in the century, and therefore the trend apparent from the data in Table 2.3 should reflect the declining specialization of women in areas of traditional concern over the period.

This suggests that women hardly 'focused' on 'women's issues' in their choice of dissertation topic. And yet our very casual survey of the journal literature allows us cautiously to support Pearson's claim that women contributing to the journal literature were more likely to focus on these areas than were women writing dissertations. It is certainly true, as Robert Dimand shows in his contribution to this volume, that women were writing books and journal articles on a much wider set of topics than simply labour economics and women's issues, but women writing in the key mainstream journals in economics were focusing on these topics to a greater extent than one would expect from the choice of dissertation topic. Nevertheless, at least as far as dissertation research was concerned, the topics that attracted the attention of women were very similar to those that attracted the attention of men before 1940.[4]

As limited as our knowledge is, some general conclusions can be drawn about the sexual division of labour among PhD candidates in American universities and colleges in the first four decades of this century. First of all, women constituted a higher proportion of PhD candidates than they did authors of articles in the leading journals (Groenewegen and King, 1994, 6). If women PhD candidates were increasing as a proportion of the whole over

Table 2.3 *Percentage of female candidates writing dissertations on 'women's issues', 1912–40*

Year	%	Year	%	Year	%
1912	7	1922	10	1932	3
1913	0	1923	14	1933	4
1914	10	1924	19	1934	4
1915	4	1925	12	1935	2
1916	15	1926	6	1936	2
1917	13	1927	4	1937	0
1918	12	1928	9	1938	2
1919	8	1929	6	1939	6
1920	12	1930	5	1940	0
1921	8	1931	2		

Notes: Dissertations focusing on 'women's issues' were flagged by title using a very subjective classificatory scheme which defined all topics dealing specifically with women and all topics dealing with areas of traditional concern to women (such as household budget studies). The 'data' should be treated with a good deal of caution. If the same thesis appeared more than once, it was counted only the first time it appeared.

the entire period, we might expect their representation in the journals to appear with a lag. But, in fact, that does not seem to have happened. Second, while there was a very slight tendency towards a sexual division of labour early in the century, with women disproportionately favouring Economic History and Labour, by 1935 men and women were virtually indistinguishable insofar as area of specialization was concerned. Throughout the period, women chose topics in fewer fields than did men, but the areas women chose were the fashionable areas of research. There is no significant evidence that women were specializing exclusively in 'women's topics' within these broad fields of study. And, perhaps more interesting, Strober and Reagan (1976) suggest that these areas of study remained popular with women while the attention of men, who formed the bulk of the profession, shifted.

These data on PhD dissertation topics before 1940 are particularly interesting in the light of Libby's research (1984, 1987, 1990), Groenewegen and King's data (1994) and Pearson's observation about the representation of women in the journal literature before 1940. Why should women appear to concentrate on a smaller range of topics in the journal literature than they did in their selection of dissertation topics? Why should fewer women than men who earn PhDs subsequently appear in the major journals? Why should women continue to focus on areas of research fashionable in the early years of the century, while men turned their attention (and the orientation of their journals) in other directions? Why should the proportion of PhD candidates who are women reach their peak earlier in economics than in other disciplines, and decline for decades? The answers to these questions require much more information about the nature of the constraints that women faced in a rapidly professionalizing discipline, and the strategies they chose to deal with them.

2.3   THE CONTEXT OF PROFESSIONALIZATION

The process by which the modern professions emerged has attracted a great deal of attention of late (Solomon, 1985; Glazer and Slater, 1987; Scott, 1988). During the late nineteenth century, a period of rapid social and intellectual change, professionals were attracted to the possibility of developing new bodies of knowledge with profound implications for the betterment of society. Motivated in large part by a desire to monitor standards of performance, many groups moved towards controlling entry into the new professions and upgrading and lengthening the educational requirements for practitioners. The ideology developed alongside this process emphasized merit, performance standards and service to the community. A 'vulgar' preoccupation with salaries and profits was dismissed as unseemly, even though a cynic (or an economist) might focus on the rents to be earned in a profession with limited access. In any case, economists were something of a breed apart. Richard Ely tells us a great deal about monetary concerns, while reminiscing about the early years of the AEA:

> The apparent absence of careers at that time … was undoubtedly an obstacle in the development of economics in the United States. (…) It was along toward the middle of the nineties when Dr. H.C. Taylor received an admonition from Secretary of Agriculture Wilson …: 'Taylor, you are a young man. Some day you will want to get married and have a family. Agricultural economics will never support you. Take up some practical subject like plant pathology and I will give you a job!' (Ely, 1936, 142–3)

But it was 'science' rather than careers that drove professionalization.

Glazer and Slater claim that 'the rise of modern science and the decline of religion marked a major intellectual shift' and that 'science was seen as the key to a series of modern possibilities – controlling the environment, harnessing new forms of energy, solving human problems, and accelerating social progress' (1987, 235). Scott relates that women were admitted to the American Historical Association, founded in 1884, if 'they had some university training and self-consciously practised the scientific method considered so crucial to the new professional history' (1988, 180). Economics was no different. Richard Ely's chatty tale of the founding of the AEA in 1885 assures us that

> the founding of the American Economic Association was greeted with an enthusiasm which cannot now easily be understood. Why? On the one hand, those who were scientifically inclined saw opening up before them a vista and a vision. Economics was not a dead thing of the past, but a live thing of the present, inviting young men to put the best they had into this field. On the other hand, humanitarians felt that no longer were their efforts for improvements balked and frustrated by the so-called laws of economics. (1936, 146)

Ely's anecdote is more revealing than he might have realized; although women were admitted to the AEA from its foundation, he recalls quite clearly that its invitation was issued to 'young men'. The rise of the professions heralded the establishment of a meritocracy which was, nevertheless, a bastion of middle-class virtue. The women who vied for success in this milieu shared the socialization of their brothers, and were almost exclusively of the same race and class as their male competitors. Now this was partly the result of institutional constraints. Just because the colleges had begun to admit women, this does not mean that they were prepared to freely admit blacks or Jews (Solomon, 1985, ch.9), and the paucity of fellowship support for women doctoral students constrained the aspirations of many who could not count on parental support (Solomon, 1985, 146). Reynolds claimed that in 1923, as was the case earlier, the median family income of women attending private, non-sectarian women's colleges ($5140) was significantly higher than that of women in state universities ($3349) or non-state coeducational institutions ($3091) (Reynolds, 1927, 23–5).

But if women bought into the ideology of the aspiring professional classes, they nonetheless faced qualitatively different constraints than their male counterparts when it was time to leave college and take up a career. Limiting the discussion specifically to academic employment, it is clear that full-time, well paying professorial appointments were considerably less open to women than to men, *except* at the traditional women's colleges which were, for the most part, keen to add women to their faculty during the early decades of this century. Susan Carter (1981) has calculated that women comprised over 70 per cent of the faculty at women's four-year colleges between 1900 and 1940, whereas they represented less than 20 per cent of the faculty at the private coeducational institutions and an even smaller proportion at the land grant institutions. Teachers's colleges and normal schools also offered faculty appointments to women in significant numbers. These numbers undoubtedly seem large from a present-day perspective, where many institutions struggle with a female/male faculty ration of less than 20 per cent, but the raw numbers are misleading. Coeducational and male institutions rarely appointed women to faculty rank; appointments virtually always carried an adjunct or inferior status.

Moreover, throughout the period of our investigation, the social awkwardness of trying to combine marriage, children and a career was paramount. The women's colleges had created an atmosphere where intellectual pursuits were encouraged and it became possible for women to embark actively upon an academic career, but they imposed a significant constraint. It was widely understood that marriage and career were not compatible. President Mary Woolley of Mount Holyoke, for example, informed her board of trustees in 1923 that 'weddings have wrought havoc in the ranks of the faculty and staff', with many 'resigning or refusing reappointments at the close of the last academic year for that reason' (quoted by Glazer and Slater, 1987, 58). The 'marriage question' continued to attract a good deal of attention throughout the 1930s.

How, then, did women respond to the differential social and economic constraints in the way of their complete participation in the professions? They did as well as they could in the circumstances, changing the constraints when conceivable and creating alternatives when the barriers persisted. Glazer and Slater identify four strategies that, they claim, were used by women in various professions to deal with the constraints they faced (1987, ch.6). Looking at the roles that women played in the economics profession early in the twentieth century from the perspectives of these different strategies can help us to understand a little bit more about the career choices they made. It also provides a partial explanation for the apparent changes in the nature and extent of the research women undertook as professional economists from that they did as doctoral candidates.

Superperformance has always been a strategy available to the few. Some women in all areas were the pathbreaking pioneers, outperforming their male colleagues on most measures of professional success and commitment. These are the women now attracting the attention of new generations of historians who are always a little astounded by the accomplishments of their 'forgotten' ancestors. The 'Joan Robinson phenomenon', to borrow Groenewegen and King's label, can be understood as superperformance. There are few ways to account for it, except by noting individual drive and genius and circumstance. The only way to understand it is by intense biographical research into the lives of these outliers. But most women, like most men, are not possessed of superhuman energy or incomparable intellect, and these women typically adopted one or a combination of other responses.

A second strategy is that of subordination. This is the path chosen by (or imposed upon) women who taught for years at major institutions but always in the capacity of an adjunct or an assistant, or who were otherwise marginalized. Clearly, this could contribute to the apparent underrepresentation of women contributors in the key journals as compared with their representation as doctoral candidates, if these positions carried with them very heavy teaching loads and other duties. This strategy, however, is one that requires closer examination because it does not necessarily represent exploitation. The women's colleges, for example, were quite adept at creating jobs for their graduates and keeping them around for years as assistants or associates or librarians and so on. At least sometimes, these created positions carried with them the freedom to engage in independent intellectual work in a supportive social environment. This may indeed have been a path freely chosen and much preferable to the perceived alternatives. The nature of the careers of academic women, and the role that these careers played in determining the nature and extent of women's participation in the profession, need further investigation, and the only apparent way to learn more is, again, through detailed biographical work.

Separatism is another such strategy, and represents an attempt on the part of women to carve out a career for themselves in the context of differential constraints. For academic women could most easily be identified in the expansion and development of the women's colleges in the first four decades of this century. If women were not getting jobs in large numbers at the coeducational institutions, and if those who were hired were effectively prevented from full participation in the governance of the institution by the nature of their appointments and ranks, the women's colleges provided an alternative area of employment. Here men were marginalized, more or less overtly, depending on the institution and the nature of its president (Glazer and Slater, 1987, ch.2; Solomon, 1985, chs 6,7,9). But there are other types of separatism: creating niches in journal publication by focusing on areas ignored by the larger profession, or taking positions in home economics departments despite one's specific area of training, or contributing to the 'betterment of society' through urban missionary work with the settlement houses or the charities. In fact, we know that women economists were disproportionately housed in 'home economics' departments (Solomon, 1985, 86–7). Groenewegen and King (1994) argue that the creation of specialist journals in female-intensive areas of research accounts for much of the decline in the proportion of women contributors to five leading English-language journals. The *Social Service Review* was created specifically to publish the research of the Chicago women economists. It is not too great a leap to suggest that the narrowing of research interests among women publishing in the leading journals, as compared with the research interests evident in the choice of dissertation topic, reflects this same phenomenon. Perhaps women chose to write articles in particular areas because they had a comparative advantage in doing the research. Perhaps, cut loose from the restrictions of graduate school, they followed their 'natural' inclinations. More likely, separatism was adopted as a strategy and women published in these areas because there was less male competition. That is, they had a comparative advantage in publishing their results. The extent to which editorial policy explicitly encouraged this strategy remains an open question.

The fourth strategy Glazer and Slater identify is that of innovation. We often find ourselves in the position of trying to understand how women reacted to the constraints imposed upon them, and how their decisions in the context of these constraints influenced their performance vis-à-vis the discipline's traditional standards of success. A slightly different perspective encourages us to ask whether women ever challenged the constraints directly and whether they had a measurable impact on the nature of the discipline itself. The expansion of home economics departments, the creation of specialist journals and the expansion of settlement house work have all been identified as forms of separatism above, but they could just as easily be seen as innovative attempts on the part of women to modify the constraints themselves. The distinction between separatism and innovation is subtle and turns upon individual motivations not easily uncovered. The results are the same: there are new journals and faculties and areas of research. But we will know more about the nature of our discipline and about the creative spirits of the women who contributed to it if we can understand how they perceived their professional decisions. It need hardly be said that the only way we can hope to understand more is through detailed biographical work.

2.4   A FINAL WORD

If we examine the experience of women in the economics profession in isolation from the experiences of their sisters in other professions, we tend to look for explanations for the statistical patterns we find in degrees awarded and articles published in the changing nature of the discipline, which we somehow imagine to be distinct from the people who contribute to it. That is, we note the early presence of women in the profession and see the decline in the proportion of women contributing to the journals as the century progressed as evidence that the increasing statistical and mathematical focus of the discipline after Keynes and Samuelson drove women out. We look at the titles of the articles published by women in the journals and note a disproportionate focus on 'special interests'. It seems inevitable to wonder whether women have always been marginal participants in the profession, not really interested in contributing to the mainstream concerns of the discipline.

But when we look at the statistical data available on PhD dissertations in progress at American universities, and compare the results to the participation of women in the professional journals, a slightly different picture begins to emerge. Women focused on topics that are unfashionable by late twentieth-century standards, but so did men. Dissertation topics chosen by men and women were very similar. The proportion of PhDs granted to women began to decline long before the mathematization of the discipline. We know that, as this century aged, the discipline became narrower in scope and more rigorous in method. As that process developed, women became increasingly marginalized. What is not at all clear is whether the two processes were related and, if they were, in what direction the causation flowed. But the most striking feature of the data on PhD dissertations in progress is the breadth of women's research agenda indicated in their dissertations, relative to that apparent from the articles by women published in leading journals.

When we look at economics in the larger context of professionalization, and examine the careers of those 'ordinary' women who were not super-performers, different questions again emerge. What constraints helped shape the career decisions of those women who earned PhDs at American universities between 1900 and 1940? How did they react to those constraints, and what effects did their decisions have on their own careers, on the discipline of economics itself and on the opportunities available to those women and men who came after them? Our data on PhD dissertations, in the context of what we know about the roles of women in economics in the early part of the century, suggest that women economists engaged in creative attempts to build careers for themselves in the face of considerable constraints. Detailed biographical work will help us learn more about those constraints and about the impact of the strategies individual women adopted to deal with them.

NOTES

1. I would like to thank Sandra Daycock for careful and thoughtful research assistance, and for many very helpful comments and criticisms of an earlier draft of this chapter.
2. The data reported are dissertations in progress at American universities and colleges. I do not have data on the proportion of theses reported as 'in progress' by either men or women which did not result in a degree. Nonetheless, 'dissertations in progress' are a better guide to the research undertaken by graduate students than are completed degrees.
3. Changing intellectual fashions emerged early enough, as is apparent from A.C. Pigou's inaugural lecture where he (undoubtedly) recalled Marshall, his predecessor at Cambridge:

    I shall be glad if a man comes to Economics because he has been interested by Professor Edgeworth's Mathematical Psychics or Dr. Fisher's Appreciation and Interest: just as I shall be glad if he comes to it because he is looking forward to business and wishes to learn something of the broader aspects of his future career; but I shall be far more glad if he comes because he has walked through the slums of London and is stirred to make some effort to help his fellow men. Wonder, Carlyle said, is the beginning of philosophy: social enthusiasm, one might add, is the beginning of economic science. (Hutchison, 1975, 284)

That Social Problems and Labour were considered suitable areas of study for male economists is clear enough.

4. There is, of course, the possibility that 'thesis topics' were not chosen by students, but
    selected by thesis supervisors and imposed upon students. In that case, one might argue
    that one would expect women and men to write on the same topics. But it is at least as
    likely that supervisors would ensure a sexual division of labour at the doctoral dissertation
    stage, imposing topics for which they supposed students had a comparative advantage.

REFERENCES

Baumol, William J. (1985), 'On Method in U.S. Economics a Century Earlier',
    American Economic Review, **75**, (6), December, 1–12.
Carter, Susan (1981), 'Academic Women Revisited: An Empirical Study of Changing
    Patterns in Women's Employment as College and University Faculty, 1890–1963',
    Journal of Social History, **14**, summer, 615–97.
Ehrenberg, Ronald G. (1992), 'The Flow of New Doctorates', *Journal of Economic
    Literature*, **30**, June, 830–75.
Ely, Richard E. (1936), 'The Founding and Early History of The American Economic
    Association', *American Economic Association, Papers and Proceedings*, **26**, (1),
    March, 141–50.
Glazer, Penina Migdal and Miriam Slater (1987), *Unequal Colleagues: The Entrance
    of Women Into the Professions, 1890–1940*, New Brunswick, NJ: Rutgers.
Groenewegen, Peter D. and Susan King (1994), 'Women as Producers of Economic
    Articles: A Statistical Assessment of the Nature and the Extent of Female Partici-
    pation in Five British and North American Journals 1900–39', University of Syd-
    ney Working Papers in Economics no. 201.
Hoffman, Elizabeth (1992), 'Report of the Committee on the Status of Women in the
    Economics Profession', *American Economic Association, Papers and Proceed-
    ings*, **82**, (2), May, 610–14.
Hutchison, T.W. (1975), *A Review of Economic Doctrines 1870–1929*, Westport, CT:
    Greenwood Press.
Libby, Barbara (1984), 'Women in Economics Before 1940', *Essays in Economic
    and Business History*, **3**, 273–90.
Libby, Barbara (1987), 'Statistical Analysis of Women in the Economics Profession',
    Essays in Economic and Business History, **5**, 179–89.
Libby, Barbara (1990), 'Women in the Economics Profession 1900–1940: Factors in
    Declining Visibility', *Essays in Economics and Business History*, **8**, 121–30.
Reynolds, O. Edgar (1927), *The Social and Economic Status of College Students*,
    New York: Teachers College, Columbia University.
Scott, Joan Wallach (1988), *Gender and the Politics of History*, New York: Columbia
    University Press.
Solomon, Barbara Miller (1985), *In the Company of Educated Women: A History of
    Women and Higher Education in America*, New Haven, CT: Yale University Press.
Strober, Myra (1975), 'Women Economists: Career Aspirations, Education and Train-
    ing', *American Economic Review*, **65**, (2), 92–9.
Strober, Myra and Barbara B. Reagan (1976), 'Sex Differences in Economists, Fields
    of Specialisation', *Signs*, **3**, (2), 303–17.

3. Networks of women economists before 1940

Mary Ann Dimand[1]

3.1 INTRODUCTION

This chapter constitutes a preliminary attempt to trace the connections between and personal influences upon women economists up to 1940 in the United States and England. For the purpose of this paper, I define women economists as women who wrote what was considered economics when they were writing (so that political economists are included) or what is considered economics now. This definition de-emphasizes non-publishing academic appointees. Throughout the period investigated, relatively few women economists had academic appointments, and public acceptance of women as economists was not notable. Despite this, quite a few women wrote works of economics. Writing is hard work – these women must have known they had an audience. I make an initial attempt to examine whom they were writing for, and who gave them encouragement to write. A thorough inquiry would require the reading of reams of women's (and men's) personal papers: I have not done this, but have relied on published sources. The principal consequence of this lapse is weakness in tracing the connections between individuals.[2] I discuss only the numerous connections I have happened to come across. I am sure that there are many more.

Few colleges and universities were prominent catalysts in women economists's lives, and either the organization of a college or student experience at one was likelier to figure in a woman's life than faculty appointment. Faculty appointments for women were rare outside the London School of Economics in England, and even the remarkable Joan Robinson notably was not appointed lecturer at Cambridge until 1938. As more women's colleges were founded in the United States, there were (initially) a larger number of faculty appointments for women, yet faculty appointments for women were still relatively rare. Newcomer (1959, 190–91) noted that, in 1956, women scholars[3] were 5 per cent of all American scholars in the social and behavioural sciences, although women took 14 per cent of all doctoral degrees between

39

1900 and 1950. Economics has long employed fewer women than the other
social sciences, so presumably fewer than 5 per cent of American economics
scholars were women. Evelyn Forget's chapter in this volume gives further
data on American economics dissertations by women (Table 2.1).

Moreover, those women who were academically employed did not necessarily find the experience particularly fruitful. At the University of California
at Berkeley, the first women faculty members (in 1903) were Lucy Sprague
and Jessica Peixotto. Sprague felt that her academic background was inadequate for her job, making the condescension of male academics appropriate,
but that 'Jessica Peixotto was their equal in training and intelligence, and
they acted the same way toward her appointment because she was a woman'
(Antler, 1987b, 110).[4]

Newcomer's chart (1959, 203) showing the percentages of men and women
University of Chicago PhDs by date of degree receipt who were at the ranks
of professor, associate or assistant professor, or instructor indicates disparity
between men and women in academe. In

> a study by the Institute of Women's Professional Relations concerning all women
> who had received the Doctor of Philosophy Degree in the years 1877–1924, while
> nearly 75% of respondents observed that they would advise others to take the
> degree, it is significant that in their letters, women Ph.D.s in every field com-
> plained of discrimination in appointments, promotions and salary. ... Several
> women mentioned that they felt that even with their higher degrees they had
> inadequate career options. (Antler, 1987a, 382)

Antler gives two responses by women economists which are worth quoting:

> From a professor of Economics, Ph.D. 1915–24: 'The field for women with Ph.D.
> in economics is decidedly limited. Women may be given minor positions,
> instructorships, etc., in first class colleges and universities, but would rarely be
> considered for one of major rank. A good college embarrassed for funds may
> rather unwillingly take a woman.'
> From a Ph.D. in Economics, obtained 1915–24, unemployed: 'There are no
> openings for a woman in economics. Ordinarily I am a fairly sane woman of thirty,
> but on this matter of advanced degrees I own that I am considerably disillusioned ...
> The prejudice is marked. I had both an A.M., and M.S. plus two years' experience
> when I taught at the university. I received $500 less per year than boys with only the
> A.B. and no experience. As a result of the worry and strain, I have been an invalid
> for a year. I am convinced that it is wrong to encourage women to do graduate work
> unless it is for personal satisfaction. (Antler 1987a, 387–8)

Even women with academic qualifications in economics typically looked
to relationships which were more than merely professional to supply a public
for their work and credence in them as thinkers. Women who worked on
economic problems without such qualifications of course did so as well.

Apart from individual interactions, I discuss the roles of academic organizations, charity organizations and social work, labour groups, political organizations (including suffrage groups) and journals as nexuses for women economists.

3.2   INDIVIDUALS

The earliest woman economist I know of, Jane Marcet, published the enormously popular *Conversations on Political Economy* in 1816 and other books in 1833 and 1851. Polkinghorn's biography of Marcet (1993) and chapter in this volume discuss her life and accomplishments. As a very wealthy woman, Marcet perhaps needed relatively little support to write. Thomson (1973, 11–13) indicated that Marcet was influenced by the work of Mary Wollstonecraft, and she and her husband were on friendly terms with Ricardo and James Mill (Polkinghorn, 1993, 40, 43–4, 48–9). Harriet Martineau was influenced by Marcet's *Conversations* to write her own *Illustrations of Political Economy* and became part of the Marcet social circle. Bette Polkinghorn (1986, 1993) writes of Malthus's, Say's and Torrens's largely favourable reactions to the *Conversations*, both in reviews and in correspondence with Marcet.

The Owenite Anna Wheeler is known for *Appeal of One Half the Human Race* (1825), a work of political economy written in response to James Mill by her friend William Thompson. Thompson, however, stated in an introductory letter to her which begins the work that the book is a product of his and Anna Wheeler's inextricably intertwined thought, although she wrote only a few pages. He cited her publications (written under a feigned name which he unfortunately did not give), so there is no reason to think she could *not* have written the book (Thompson, 1825, 'Introductory Letter to Mrs. Wheeler'). Bentham, Charles Fourier and Robert Owen were her friends as well as Thompson, and she was influenced by Mary Wollstonecraft. Disraeli 'described her as "something between Jeremy Bentham and Meg Merrilies, very clever, but awfully revolutionary"' (Spender, 1983, 396). John Stuart Mill 'was very well acquainted' with Thompson, whom he found 'a very estimable man' (Mill, 1924, 87), so he perhaps knew Anna Wheeler as well.[5]

Harriet Martineau, like Marcet an explicator of political economy and part of her circle, was also connected to Harriet Taylor, John Stuart Mill and William Johnson Fox, the Unitarian minister and publisher. According to Rose (1983, 103), Martineau was at a dinner party at Taylor's house when Mill first met his future co-author and wife. Banks (1986, 135) places Martineau with Harriet Taylor and Barbara Bodichon within Fox's sphere of influence. Martineau, along with John Stuart Mill 'and the rest' of 'the eminent of both sexes' visited Barbara Leigh Smith's (later Bodichon) father, at whose house Barbara acted hostess (Hamilton, 1936, 44; Spender, 1983, 405, states rather that it was Barbara's house Martineau visited).

John Stuart Mill may be the best-known male feminist, and his autobiographical claims as to Harriet Taylor's de facto co-authorship of his work have long been discussed and disputed. (Having found Taylor's 'Enfranchisement of Women' a work of economics superior to Mill's 'Subjection of Women', I believe Mill.) Mill was an influence on Olive Schreiner (Banks, 1986, 134), the author of works (*The Story of an African Farm*, 1883; and *Woman and Labour*, 1911) which, though more sociology than economics, influenced women economists. Mill was an associate of both Henry Fawcett, Marshall's predecessor as professor of political economy at Cambridge, and his wife and sometime co-author, Millicent Garrett Fawcett, who were his fellow members in Thomas Hare's Proportional Representation Society, and both Fawcetts were devotees of the early works of Mill. No doubt Mill's and Taylor's influence were even wider.

Mill credited his stepdaughter, Helen Taylor, with inheriting 'much of [her mother's] wisdom, and ... all her nobleness of character' (Mill, 1924, 184) and declared his reliance on her help after her mother's death. Mill's belief that Helen's name would become notable was not justified. Helen Taylor is a curious figure in nineteenth-century reform and economic circles: she appears in many quarters but, apart from editing Mill's posthumous chapters on socialism, is seldom said to have done anything in particular. Along with Barbara Bodichon, Emily Davies (a founder of Girton College, Cambridge) and Elizabeth Garrett Anderson (sister of Millicent Garrett Fawcett and first British woman physician), she was a member of the Kensington Society, which promoted education for women (Spender, 1983, 417) and was a catalyst of the Women's Suffrage Committee. She was a close enough associate of Eleanor Marx for Marx to tap her for 40 marks to aid families of persecuted German socialists (Kapp, 1972, 212–13). She attended the second meeting for the formation of the Fabian Society, but then seems to vanish from it (MacKenzie and MacKenzie, 1977, 25).

Barbara Leigh Smith Bodichon, nucleus of the 'Langham Place group', wrote a number of pamphlets on women's status under the law and the economic status of women as workers, giving the 'first coherent feminist treatment of women's work' (Pujol, 1992, 15–16). Bessie Rayner Parkes, Bodichon's intimate friend and another member of the group, also wrote economic pamphlets on women as workers. (Some of their works are reprinted in Lacey, 1987.) Although most of the group would seem, by their pamphlets, to have been social scientists, promoters of public welfare and women's education, rather than economists, they furnished a milieu for Bodichon to work in. The group 'focused specifically at women's rights to wider employment opportunities, so long as they enlarged the scope for the practice of women's domestic and nurturing qualities' (Lown, 1990, 218). I suspect, however, that she was more a support to the group than it was to her. Bodichon was active as a painter, as a publisher of the *English Woman's Journal*, as a promoter of women's education, and in the suffrage movement. She knew many of the intellectual women of her time, being a close friend of George Eliot (Marian Evans)[6] as well as of Octavia Hill (Strachey, 1928, 130), members of the Langham Place group and of the Kensington Society. Bodichon met John Stuart Mill in her teens and was associated with him in his early fight for women's suffrage, but she may have been more of an influence on him than he on her. Number 19 Langham Place become an intellectual gathering place for women in London, and it was there that Elizabeth Garrett was first fired with the thought of becoming a physician (Hamilton, 1936, 45).[7]

Henry Fawcett was the author and co-author, with his wife Millicent Garrett Fawcett, of many essays and books on political economy which explicated Mill's economics and Hare's voting scheme. Millicent, who married at 18, was exposed early to the idea that education and careers should be opened to women, but it was probably Henry who stimulated her interest in political economy. Millicent was an early and tenacious partisan of women's suffrage, along with other women economists, but it is not clear that she had much influence on them. (Eleanor Marx damned her as a 'fine-lady suffragist' (Kapp, 1976, 559).) Perhaps her greatest influence was through her role in the equal-pay-for-equal-work debates in the *Economic Journal* with Sidney Webb and Eleanor Rathbone. This debate is thoroughly and elegantly discussed by Michèle Pujol (1992).

Charles Booth, compiler/author of *Life and Labour of the People in London*, employed a number of women as investigators and writers. These included his cousin by marriage Beatrice Potter[8] (later Webb) (MacKenzie and MacKenzie, 1977, 120, 130, 133–4) and Clara Collet. Collet wrote on the economics of women's work in the *QJE*, *Journal of the Royal Statistical Society* and, most frequently, in the *Economic Journal*, where she was the only person to publish in both first and fiftieth volumes, as well as many between. Edith Abbott, an economist who was to found the social service movement in the United States, also met Booth (Uglow, 1989), and Jane Addams, an influence on many American women economists, exhibited familiarity with his work (Addams, 1910, 163).

Eleanor Marx, whom Addams met briefly (Addams, 1910, 264), is marginal as an economist: her claim lies in having edited ten previously unpublished works of her father, rather as Helen Taylor edited writings by Mill. Eleanor Marx is not marginal as a nexus for women economists, however. While she thought the Fabians 'wrongheaded', though 'above the suspicion of harbouring spies', she had many friends among them and frequently shared a platform with them (Kapp, 1976, 68). Clementina Black, who published in the *Economic Journal* on women's work, was a family friend who read to the dying Mrs Marx (Kapp, 1972, 219, 226). Elizabeth Garrett Anderson was Eleanor Marx's doctor, although Marx thought so ill of Millicent Garrett Fawcett as a suffragist. Olive Schreiner was her friend (Spender, 1983, 646; Kapp, 1972, 235), as was Clara Collet, whose father, Collet Dobson Collet, published essays by Karl Marx (Kapp, 1976, 269) and she was associated with Helen Taylor, as noted above.

Olive Schreiner's work was widely read and moved a number of women economists strongly. Mabel Atkinson (author of 'The economic foundations of the women's movement', reprinted by Alexander, 1988) and Bessie Leigh Hutchins (who wrote on women's work in the *Economic Journal* and the *Journal of the Royal Statistical Society*) introduced Schreiner's work to the Fabian Women's Group (Berg, 1992, 312). Charlotte Perkins Gilman greatly admired Schreiner's work and berated her friend Martha Lane for her lack of appreciation (Hill, 1980, 176–7, 221, 286).

Beatrice and Sidney Webb, with whom Eleanor Marx was acquainted, formed a nexus for women economists through the Fabian Society. Sidney, as well as Booth and Hill, inclined Beatrice towards economics. There can be no doubt of the staunchness of his belief in her: during their courtship, 'Sidney astonished her by telling her that he had read all six hundred pages of Alfred Marshall's *Principles of Economics* on the previous evening. Though it was a great book, he remarked, it still left someone the chance of remaking economics. "Who is to do it? Either you must help me to do it; or I must help you"' (MacKenzie and MacKenzie, 1977, 138). His suggestion that women could improve their wages by eating beef and drinking beer instead of consuming tea and toast (Webb, 1891) does not, however, suggest much helpfulness towards women in general. Beatrice began her career by refusing to study women's labour despite Charles Booth's and Marshall's urging (MacKenzie and MacKenzie, 1977, 133) and signed a manifesto against political enfranchisement of women in *Nineteenth Century* (MacKenzie and MacKenzie, 1977, 13; Strachey, 1928, 285) although she changed her mind in 1906. Pujol (1992) discusses Beatrice Webb's contributions to the equal-pay-for-equal-work debates, which at least eclipse Sidney's. Edith Abbott met the Webbs (Uglow, 1989), as did Charlotte Perkins Gilman (Hill, 1980, 289), but it is not clear that this influenced them, though Abbott kept up with the Webbs's work. The Webbs were probably most supportive of women as founders of the London School of Economics, where Beatrice taught Bessie Leigh Hutchins.

In the United States, two male academics seem to have supported women economists to some extent. Wesley Clair Mitchell was close friends with Sadie Gregory, who was trained as an economist, although she quit after one year's teaching at Wellesley, and with Jessica Peixotto (Antler, 1987b, 122). That he may have discussed economics with them is suggested by his support of his wife's activities as an educator (Antler, 1987b). Richard Ely, on the other hand, explicitly 'acknowledged and encouraged the entry of women into economics' in his published work (Nelson, 1993, 141). Charlotte Perkins Gilman, author of *Women and Economics* (1898) and of many articles, told her future husband that she had read some of Ely's economics and been influenced by it (Lane, 1990, 203). Ely lectured on economics at Hull House, where a number of women economists lived, worked or passed through (Hill, 1980, 274). Helen Campbell, a close friend of Gilman, studied under Ely. 'Having received Ely's blessing, but not a Ph.D., ... [she was] invited to teach at the University of Wisconsin, again with Ely's backing. ... Well-respected publications notwithstanding,[9] she was never offered the permanent Wisconsin academic post she apparently hoped for and to some extent expected' (Hill, 1980, 239, 245–6). Deprived of an academic position in economics, Campbell eventually turned to publication on home economics. Edward Ross, another Ely student invited to teach at Wisconsin, attained a tenured position even though one of the courses he taught was on marriage and the family (Newcomer, 1959, 99).

Jane Addams's Hull House served as a focus for American women interested in economic or social concerns. Sophonisba Breckinridge, who taught economics in the Department of Household Administration at the University of Chicago, was an associate of Addams's from 1908 to 1920 (Bernard, 1964, 245, 247; Muncy, 1991). Edith Abbott, who, like and with Breckinridge, published extensively in the *JPE* for 20 years, lived at Hull House from 1908 to 1920, but had relatively little to do with its activities (Bernard, 1964, 247; Muncy, 1991). Her sister Grace Abbott, however, was an active associate of Addams. Beatrice Webb visited Hull House in 1898 (Muncy, 1991, 10). Charlotte Perkins Gilman was so impressed by Hull House that she initially thought to become a social worker, roping Helen Campbell into heading a settlement in a part of Chicago called 'Little Hell' (Hill, 1980, 272–82). Gilman loathed it so much that she quit quite soon. Emily Balch, one-time head of Wellesley's Department of Economics, was an Addams associate (Sicherman and Green, 1980, 42) and later active with Addams in the Women's Peace Movement (Uglow, 1989) for which, like Addams, she eventually won the Nobel Peace Prize.

Although I have not delved for individual influences among early women economists, what little information I have unearthed indicates the complexity of the relationships and communications among them, and with other public figures. Other personal relations, as well as institutional ones, were developed through the founding of, attendance at, or teaching at educational institutions.

3.3   ACADEMIC ORGANIZATIONS

Bedford College (founded in 1849, a year after Queen's College) was the second institution of higher education open to women in Great Britain, and may have figured more profoundly than I have learned among women economists. Harriet Martineau was a secretary of the school on its founding (Uglow, 1989) and it differed from Queen's in having a mixed rather than wholly male board (Strachey, 1928, 62). Barbara Bodichon was one of the first students there (Spender, 1983, 406; Strachey, 1928, 124). Spender (1983, 407) suggests, however, that 'it offered only a glimpse of the possibilities of women's research rather than practical training in how to do it'.

The National Association for Promotion of Social Science, founded in 1857, encouraged women's participation and thus a concern for women's education from the outset. Its offices were at 19 Langham Place, and it had strong connections with the *English Woman's Journal* and the Langham Place group (McWilliams Tullberg, 1975, 27; Lewenhak, 1977, 60–61; Spender, 1983, 414–15). Barbara Bodichon attended at least one of its meetings (Lacey, 1987, 8) and Bessie Rayner Parkes presented papers at its meetings.

Barbara Bodichon was one of the founders of Girton College, Cambridge in 1869 (Stephen, 1933, 4; Strachey, 1928, 145). She was not named to the first Committee because Emily Davies feared that the unpopularity of women's suffrage, in which Bodichon was involved, would prejudice many against a women's college at (or, at that stage, connected with) Cambridge (Stephen, 1933, 17). Bodichon was, however, a member of Girton College from 1869 to 1891 and contributed handsomely to its foundation. John Stuart Mill and Helen Taylor also contributed (Strachey, 1928, 160). Mary Paley was one of the first class of Girton students and later lectured there (McWilliams Tullberg, 1975, 60–62, 67). Later Mrs Alfred Marshall, Mary Paley was the initial author (and eventual co-author with Alfred) of *Economics of Industry*, and her work and personality were celebrated in obituary by John Maynard Keynes (*Economic Journal*, 1944, 54, 268–84). Eileen Power, doyenne of English economic history, took a history first at Girton in 1911 and was Director of Studies in History from 1913 to 1921. Barbara Wootton (later Baroness Wootton) served as Director of Studies in Economics in 1920 and Joan Robinson took her first degree at Girton in 1925 (Uglow, 1989).

Newnham College, Cambridge was founded not long after Girton. Its origin has been traced to meetings at the home of the Fawcetts in 1869, which inaugurated very well attended lectures for women at Cambridge (Gardner, 1921, 12; Hamilton, 1936, 89; McWilliams Tullberg, 1975, 56). Millicent Garrett Fawcett was on the first executive of the Association for Promoting the Higher Education of Women in Cambridge (Gardner, 1921,

13) and later protested the withholding of Cambridge degrees from women (McWilliams Tullberg, 1975, 91–2). Mary Paley Marshall was the chief founder of a society for Cambridge ladies to read papers, but this led primarily to Newnham College settlement work (Gardner, 1921, 73–4). Helen Bosanquet (author of ten *Economic Journal* articles) took her first degree in moral science at Newnham (Hamilton, 1936, 129).

As indicated above, it was probably in founding the London School of Economics that the Webbs had their greatest influence on women economics scholars. Maxine Berg has published on the women economic historians of LSE, but cautions that 'the place of women in the institution should be kept in perspective: there were still relatively small proportions of women studying economics-related subjects' – specifically, 100 between 1900 and 1932 (Berg, 1992, 318). Nonetheless, Berg cites Vera Anstey, Eleanora Carus-Wilson, Alice Clark (although she abandoned economics after her dissertation, *Working Life of Women in the Seventeenth Century*, to return to the family business), Margaret Cole, Barbara Hammond, Bessie Leigh Hutchins (taught by Beatrice Webb), Lilian Knowles and Eileen Power, who did her doctorate at LSE between 1911 and 1913 and taught there from 1921 (Uglow, 1989). Knowles became Dean of the Faculty of Economics of the University of London and, like Carus-Wilson and Power, held a professorship in economic history at LSE. Edith Abbott went to LSE on a Carnegie Fellowship (Uglow, 1989).

In the United States, the University of Chicago seems remarkable as a source of women economists' PhDs and, to a lesser extent, of jobs for them. It is not clear what caused this. It might, as Hill (1980, 246) suggests, be due to the wide-open policies of John Dewey as chair of the Department of Philosophy, Psychology and Education. It might be due to Paul Douglas's (later) position in economics, since Douglas published with at least two women, or to what became the Graduate School of Social Service Administration under Sophonisba Breckinridge and Edith Abbott. In any case, Emily Balch did postgraduate work there (Sicherman and Green, 1980, 42). Sadie Gregory, Wesley Clair Mitchell's friend, did her PhD at Chicago (Antler, 1987b, 93) and Emilie Louise Wells, who was later an inspirational teacher at Vassar, did graduate work there (Mills *et al.*, 1934). Edith Abbott earned a PhD there in 1905 (Uglow, 1989), later returning to aid Breckinridge and eventually head the Graduate School of Social Service Administration, where they gradually hired a predominantly female faculty (Bernard, 1964, 246–7). Hazel Kyrk received her PhB in 1910 and PhD in 1920 from the University of Chicago. She later served on the faculties of economics and home economics from 1925 to 1952, attaining the rank of full professor in 1941. It might surprise Gary Becker to learn that it was Kyrk who 'broadened the economics curriculum to include consumer topics and established Chicago as the premier university for the study of family and consumer economics' (Sicherman and Green, 1980, 405).

The American women's college most supportive of female economists would seem to have been Vassar (founded 1865), which Bernard (1964, 126) shows to have employed a relatively high percentage of women in the social science and history faculty, which were one until quite late. Although Maria Mitchell, who taught astronomy at Vassar, realized on Matthew Vassar's death that the position of women was being undermined as new appointments went to men, and travelled to campaign against this (Spender, 1983, 382), women's position in social science was apparently not eroded at all. This must be attributed to the influence of Herbert Elmer Mills who advised Vassar students to 'fight passionately' for suffrage against Vassar president Henry Noble MacCracken's advice (Mills *et al.*, 1934, xiii of MacCracken's introduction). It may have been due to his influence that Vassar graduates in the Women's Trade Union League brought women labour speakers to talk at college, and 'dozens of students from Vassar, Bryn Mawr, Barnard, and Wellesley served as volunteer pickets' in a garment strike (Foner, 1979, 331–2). Katharine Bement Davis (who published four papers in *JPE*) took a baccalaureate at Vassar in 1892 (Rogers, 1940, 125–6) and Julia Lathrop of Hull House was also a graduate (Mills *et al.*, 1934, ix; Rogers, 1940, 126). Emilie Louise Wells took a Vassar baccalaureate in 1894, and returned to rise from assistant to instructor to assistant professor to associate professor before dying in 1910. Mills *et al.* (1934) gave her an encomium. Mabel Newcomer, who published extensively in public finance, was a professor and her sometime co-author Ruth Gillette Hutchinson rose at least to associate professor at Vassar.

Wellesley (founded 1875) was the next most notable American women's college. Graham Wallas, H.G. Wells and William Clarke (also a Fabian) visited and spoke there (Converse, 1939, 144). Edith Abbott and Wesley Mitchell's friend Sadie Gregory each taught there for a year (Antler, 1987b, 93). Emily Balch, the first economist to gain a Nobel Prize (for Peace) was in the first class graduating from Bryn Mawr (Uglow, 1989) and taught at Wellesley for 18 years, becoming department head before she failed to be rehired because of her pacifism (Converse, 1939, 95).[10] Katharine Coman, who did extensive work in American economic history (including two volumes reprinted by Augustus Kelley in Reprints of Economic Classics), also taught at Wellesley, succeeding Balch as head of the department of economics (Converse, 1939, 68).

Edith Abbott and Sophonisba Breckinridge's flight into social work indicates one of the incentives acting on women who might normally have been academic economists. In the United States, where women made social work an academic subject, the separation between social work or charity and academe was not as marked as it was in Great Britain.

3.4 CHARITY AND SOCIAL WORK

Robyn Muncy has argued that American women created a domain for themselves in social work because

> women in male-dominated professions like law, ministry, the social sciences, the physical sciences, and many medical specialties encountered blatant discrimination in education, hiring, promotion, and salaries. Moreover, the entrance of some intrepid women into these professions did not represent an opening wedge for younger women. Often, the struggle to maintain their own positions was so exacting and uncertain for pioneers or the profession so structured that these women could not serve as mentors to younger women or in any way help ease them into professional life.
>
> Women's experience in female-dominated professions revealed different patterns. Entrants to these fields did not have to tough out discrimination just to obtain a job, and they could count on female mentors. Nevertheless, women in professions such as nursing, teaching, or librarianship found their entire professions dependent on and circumscribed by separate male groups – for instance, doctors or school administrators. As a result, these female professions simply could not develop the autonomy necessary to full professional privilege.
>
> Somewhere in between these two groups lay the experience of women in new female professions created during the Progressive era. Here I include especially social work, public health nursing, and home economics, in addition to a large proportion of doctors in female specialties. (Muncy, 1991, xiii–xiv)

Thus Jane Addams set herself up at the head of Hull House, and Edith Abbott, who disliked teaching at a women's college, helped to develop the Chicago School of Civics and Philanthropy and then the University of Chicago Graduate School of Social Service Administration, which she eventually headed. College settlements provided at least interim employment for many women graduates. Katharine Coman was active in the Wellesley College Settlements Association (Converse, 1939, 95) and Emily Balch had worked in a Boston settlement (Sicherman and Green, 1980, 42) before rejecting social work as a career. Of 12 chapters on postgraduate work in Mills *et al.* (1934), four are on social work of one type or another.

In England, many woman economists were connected with the Fabians, or had views of the equal-pay-for-equal-work debates analogous to those of Millicent Garrett Fawcett, rather than those of Eleanor Rathbone (whom Pujol, 1992, describes as an early welfare or maternal feminist). Emily Townshend, on the Fabian National Executive from 1915 to 1916, wrote 'The case against the Charity Organization Society' (Fabian Tract 158, 1911; Kareh, 1987). Amber Reeves claimed that her parents' socialism was primarily about 'being fair to the poor' (Alexander, 1988, 2), but Fabian publications indicate more interest in the reform of the wage system. (Beatrice Potter worked intermittently for the Charity Organization Society from 1883 to

1888 (Thomson, 1973, 79) but this was while she was still dallying with Tories, before marriage to Sidney Webb or her connection with the Fabians.) Rathbone was a member of the Liverpool Central Relief Society and honorary secretary of the Women's Settlement Association (Jeffreys, 1985, 151), positions consistent with her views on government payments to mothers. Helen Bosanquet headed the Charity Organization Society in which Octavia Hill worked (MacKenzie and MacKenzie, 1977, 319). Yet Rathbone and Bosanquet were outliers among British women economists, while Abbott, Breckinridge, Campbell and others were not in the United States.

By comparison, English women economists were much more prominent in labour movements than the Americans. This may be partly due to the suspicion Margaret Dreier Robins, president of the National Women's Trade Union League (founded in 1903 as the American branch of the international WTUL) had of Grace Abbott and Sophonisba Breckinridge, precisely because of their welfare tendencies (Payne, 1988, 2).

3.5   LABOUR GROUPS

Despite Robins's suspicion, the WTUL supported Abbott's and Breckinridge's campaign for a federal agency to collect data on working women (Sealander, 1983, 15). Emily Balch co-founded and presided over the Boston chapter of the National WTUL in 1902 (Kenneally, 1978, 44). Hazel Kyrk was on the board of the Chicago WTUL (Sicherman and Green, 1980, 406). Charlotte Perkins Gilman contributed to WTUL's *Life and Labor* (Kenneally, 1978, 88), published an article in the WTUL *Union Labor Advocate* on housework as economic production (Foner, 1979, 315–16) and appeared in a WTUL-sponsored debate with Anna Howard Shaw (Kenneally, 1978, 123). A song by Gilman was sung at yearly meetings of the WTUL (Foner, 1979, 470).

In England, Harriet Martineau was on the Committee of the WTUL when it was the Women's Protective and Provident League (Lewenhak, 1977, 70) some time between its founding in 1874 and her death in 1876, which seems rather startling. Clementina Black became secretary of the League, remaining active after the name change and through the remainder of her life (Foner, 1979, 296; Kapp, 1976, 380; Lewenhak, 1977, 77).

The Consumers League, founded by Clementina Black (Uglow, 1989) as an organization supporting 'fair treatment' of workers, also served as a nexus for women economists of England and the United States. Florence Kelley (a member of the Hull House circle) learned of the concept of a minimum wage from Beatrice Webb and persuaded the League to support it (Foner, 1979, 479). As a member, Emily Balch pressed for a minimum wage policy after abandoning protective legislation as a goal (Kenneally, 1978, 35–6). Katharine Coman also worked in the Consumers League (Converse, 1939, 95).

Clementina Black supported the London Match Girls Strike, and was active in the National Anti-Sweating League, serving as its vice-president, and in the Trade Union Congress, where she initiated an equal pay resolution in 1888 (Uglow, 1989). She was leader and 'chief inspector' of the Women's Industrial Council (Mappen, 1985, 19). Barbara Wootton was active in the Trade Union Congress from 1922 (Uglow, 1989) and Bessie Leigh Hutchins was an early member of the Women's Industrial Council (Mappen, 1985, 18), of whose Liverpool branch Eleanor Rathbone was unpaid secretary (Jeffreys, 1985, 151).

Earlier, Barbara Bodichon had founded the Women's Employment Bureau, which opposed the restriction of women's labour and publicized the crowding theory of women's wages (Pujol, 1992, 410). Eleanor Marx organized English gasworkers in 1888 (Lewenhak, 1977, 89; Foner, 1979, 297). Millicent Garrett Fawcett, however, would seem to lie quite outside the labour movement. She was a shareholder in the Bryant & May match factory and opposed restrictions on the use of yellow phosphorus (Lewenhak, 1977, 74). Working with yellow phosphorus poisoned many of Bryant & May's largely female workforce: phosphorus, as well as pay, was an issue fomenting the London Match Girls Strike which Clementina Black supported, and in which Annie Besant (then a Fabian) was a central figure (MacKenzie and MacKenzie, 1977, 91–2).

Other political concerns, as well as membership in frequently woman-oriented labour groups, united women economists, especially in England. Many women had Fabian connections, and more worked for suffrage. The first political movement uniting women economists, however, was as early attempt at getting a Married Women's Property Bill legislated.

3.6   POLITICAL GROUPS

Barbara Bodichon was a veteran petitioner. She took her 'Brief Summary in Plain Language of the Most Important Laws concerning Women' (reprinted by Lacey, 1987) before the Law Amendment Society, which drafted a report proposing a Married Women's Property Bill. Bodichon (then Smith) drafted and circulated a petition, gaining the support of Harriet Martineau, among 26 000 other men and women (Spender, 1983, 408; Strachey, 1928, 71–3, 76, 89). Although the bill failed before Parliament on its presentation in 1857, Smith Bodichon's political life had begun.

It was Bodichon, 'chief originator of the movement for the emancipation of women' (Stephen, 1933, 172–3), who proposed the Women's Suffrage

Committee in 1865 (Strachey, 1928, 103) and organized the petition which John Stuart Mill, supported by Henry Fawcett, bore brilliantly but unsuccessfully to Parliament (Spender, 1983, 417–18; Strachey, 1928, 104–5).[11] Millicent Garrett Fawcett, who wrote the chapter on Great Britain for Anthony and Stanton's *History of Woman Suffrage* in 1922 (Spender, 1983, 267), was a member of Bodichon's suffrage society (Strachey, 1928, 111). As suffrage societies burgeoned and competed considerably later, the National Union of Women Suffrage Societies was formed, with Fawcett as its president, in 1897 (Strachey, 1928; Pujol, 1992). She was succeeded by her opponent in the equal pay debates, Eleanor Rathbone (Pujol, 1992, 76). The women of the Fabian Society, many of them economists, were also heavily involved with the suffrage movement. This will be discussed below.

American women economists tended to be less active in the suffrage movement. This may have been partly because more of them had academic positions which they feared losing if they were 'strident'. Some of them may have agreed with Charlotte Perkins Gilman, who argued (unpopularly) that, while suffrage was necessary for women to achieve a role in society commensurate with their inputs, it was far from sufficient. Nonetheless, Gilman helped plan and attended annual meetings of the California Women's Congress (Hill, 1980, 248–53), where she met Jane Addams in 1897 (Uglow, 1989) and Sophonisba Breckinridge was vice-president of the American Women's Suffrage Association in 1911 (Bernard, 1964, 247).

While the Fabian Society was founded by women as well as men in 1884, its status as a group which would encourage women to work in economics is problematic. Pugh reports that 'In the mid-1890s the society attempted to produce a tract stating the claims of all women to share the civil and political rights then enjoyed by men but abandoned the project in despair' (Pugh, 1984, 106). Whose despair about what is not clear, but Beatrice Webb had been involved in the attempt at a time when she was anti-feminist. In the wake of agitation by H.G. Wells, a Special Committee was formed which made a report that, if ratified, would have drastically changed the form of the Society.

> Certain Fabian women, led by Maude Pember Reeves, threatened to vote for the Special Committee Report unless a clause advocating equal citizenship for men and women was inserted in the aims of the Basis. The Executive gave way without a struggle but in a manner implying that the women were a little silly to insist because in the Society equality had always been taken for granted: a complete misinterpretation of the women's demand for active advocacy of equality. (Pugh, 1984, 88)

In response, Maud Pember Reeves, a member of the Fabian National Executive during 1907–19 (Kareh, 1987), formed the Fabian Women's Group to work on the problems she had hoped the Society would tackle, including pressing for women's suffrage (Pugh, 1984, 106). The Women's Group published pamphlets on women as workers, including two in which physicians examined popular claims about women's unfitness as workers,[12] and works on the economic condition of women in prison and budgetary studies.

Charlotte Wilson, 'an ardent anarchist, [elected] to the Executive' and an important member of the group (Terrins and Whitehead, 1984, 15), persuaded others to read and analyse Marx's *Capital* (Pugh, 1984, 7). She was on the National Executive from 1911 to 1915 (Kareh, 1987). Mabel Atkinson, whose work 'was taken up ... in several ... works of [LSE economic] historians during the interwar years' (Berg, 1992, 312), was on the Local Government Committee, the Suffrage Section and suggested the Fabian Summer School (Pugh, 1984, 96, 112, 177). Alice Clark and Bessie Leigh Hutchins were members of the group (Berg, 1992, 312) and group publications were quoted by Millicent Garrett Fawcett (Pujol, 1992, 76).

The Society as a whole was hospitable to women thinkers, despite its unwillingness to push for their rights. Clementina Black lectured on women's labour to the Society in 1888 (Kapp, 1976, 268) and Clara Collet was a member. Bessie Leigh Hutchins was on the National Executive from 1907 to 1912, Beatrice Webb from 1912 to 1933, Barbara Wootton from 1941 to 1943, and they, as well as Barbara Hammond, published extensively in Fabian outlets (Kareh, 1987).[13] While Margaret Cole's administrative influence on the society occurred largely after 1940, she taught in the Women's Educational Association from 1925 to 1949, and co-founded the New Fabian Research Bureau in 1935 with her husband (Uglow, 1989). After Charlotte Perkins Gilman met a number of Fabians on a trip to England, she was invited to become a contributing editor of *American Fabian* (Hill, 1980, 292–3, 333).[14] Later Gilman was to publicize such Fabian events as Emmeline Pethick-Lawrence's American lecture tour in her own paper (*The Forerunner*, 1915).

Kareh's interesting bibliography (1987) indicates that women's Fabian publications in the late 1910s and 1920s are increasingly on social welfare topics: public education, public feeding of infants, and so on. There are few publications of any sort by women in the 1930s and 1950s, and not many in the 1940s. This pattern was common to journals as well.

3.7 MAGAZINES AND JOURNALS

Examination of the *Index of Economic Journals* discloses immediately that the *Economic Journal*, *JPE* and *Journal of the Royal Statistical Society* published many articles by women economists from the 1890s to the 1920s, although this and the women who published there have been largely forgotten. At that point the representation of women in these and other journals declined sharply, for no clear reason. But earlier, during this period and later, other less officially economics-related journals served as means of communication for women economists.

William Johnson Fox, mentioned above as an individual sponsor of women intellectuals, also edited *The Monthly Repository* from 1833 to 1836. He transformed the Unitarian journal from one principally concerned with theology and missionaries to one which served 'as an important source of feminist ideas' (Banks, 1986, 135). Fox published many works on political economy and women's rights by Harriet Martineau, Harriet Taylor and John Stuart Mill. Moreover, he wrote and published a number of essays in which he defended Martineau and Taylor from their critics, most of whom seem to have criticized them chiefly as women. Fox was eventually ousted from editorship by the Unitarian Church. A letter written by him in his defence indicates that many of the objections against him were due to his feminism.

The English Woman's Journal (1858–64), edited by Bessie Rayner Parkes (and for a time by Emily Davies), operated primarily from 19 Langham Place and was printed by Emily Faithfull at the Victoria Press from 1860 on. Its two aims were to direct women into employment in new service sectors such as insurance and to report on the National Association for Promotion of Social Science, with particular emphasis on its openness to women and concern with women's employment issues.[15] The *Journal* published many papers read before the Association's meetings by women. It was the only periodical for women as workers, and published articles on Mill's economic theory of women's labour, legislation relating to women's work and new professions opening to women, such as printing, insurance and medicine (with essays by Elizabeth Garrett Anderson). Fiction in its pages often exhorted women to work in new fields and explicitly embodied economic theory. Its tone was much milder than that of Fox's *Repository*, but that failed to save it from the acrimony of the *Saturday Review*, which repeatedly published articles denouncing Parkes's and Bodichon's statements that the crowding of women into professions such as governess could influence governesses' wages. After it had ceased publication because of continual financial losses, Jessie Boucherett revived it under the title *The Englishwoman's Review* (1866–1910) (Herstein, 1988).

The *Woman's Journal* (1870–1931(?)) was the official organ of the American Woman Suffrage Association: Gilman frequently published in it (Hill, 1980, 333–4; Lane, 1990, 104) and it offered Helen Campbell's *Prisoners of Poverty* as a premium for getting subscriptions (Foner, 1979, 238). The *Woman's Journal* also offered reviews of women's economic publications and information on their activities, including gossip about Philippa Fawcett's treatment by Cambridge dons.

Gilman wrote and edited *The Forerunner* (1909–17) entirely by herself. This meant that she included only her own economic articles and didactic fiction, and it is somewhat difficult to know how much the magazine influenced woman economists. However, she frequently recommended the *Woman's Journal*, the *Englishwomen's Review* and *The Englishwoman*, and cited articles on women's work and suffrage from them.

The Englishwoman (founded 1909 and continuing at least to 1919) was a suffrage and women's labour journal with strong Strachey[16] and Fabian connections, which also published Millicent Garrett Fawcett and Clementina Black, and defended Gilman's *Women and Economics* (1898) ten years after its initial publication. Fabian contributors included Beatrice Webb, Marion Phillips, Bessie Leigh Hutchins, Emily Townshend and George Bernard Shaw. The journal focused on the economics of women's work and legislation concerning it (including Poor Laws) and the progress of legislation towards women's suffrage.

The *Social Service Review* was founded by Edith Abbott and Sophia Breckinridge (Uglow, 1989) and with its first issue in 1927, they promptly stopped publishing in *JPE*. Papers in the first few issues indicate some of the connections between women economists and their nexuses: Edith Abbott, 'The Webbs on the English Poor Law', III(2); Clara Collett, 'Some Recollections of Charles Booth', I(3); 'Source materials: Mrs. Sidney Webb before the Royal Commission on Unemployment Insurance', VII(2); Ray Strachey, 'The Centenary of Josephine Butler: An Interview with Dame Millicent Garrett Fawcett' II(1).

These journals and magazines, probably with others, helped to nourish the web of connections between American and British women economists, and to stimulate entrance into the area by new women.

3.8   CONCLUSION

The period before 1940 has generally been thought nearly devoid of women economists, despite the pathbreaking work of Michèle Pujol (1992). Because we know that the academic and governmental employment of women economists was limited in this period, we tend to think they did not exist. There were, however, a surprising number of women in the United States and England publishing interesting work on economics. We tend, then, to wonder what might have stimulated them to this effort. This chapter, an early and partial attempt at learning whom the early women economists were speaking to, has established that individual and institutional relations between these women and sympathetic men were pervasive and complex. Further study, while much needed, can only confirm that women economists were in touch with each other and with an audience long before present economists believe them to have existed.

NOTES

1. I have benefited from conversation and correspondence with Robert W. Dimand, Evelyn Forget, James P. Henderson, Shirley Kessel, Bette Polkinghorn, Malcolm Rutherford, Lawrence Shute, John B. Davis and Alison Comish Thorne. The original paper was presented at a joint History of Economics Society and International Association for Feminist Economics session at the Allied Social Science Associations, Boston, January 1994.
2. That a woman was related to a male economist unfortunately does not indicate that he encouraged her. McWilliams Tullberg calls Alfred Marshall 'an early deserter from the women's side' and gives a history of his thought on women's role so macabre as to be funny (1975, 88, 236). McWilliams Tullberg (1992) discusses Marshall's suppression of Mary Paley Marshall's and his *Economics of Industry*. In 1902, however, long after he decided 'that woman was a subordinate being' (McWilliams Tullberg, 1975, 236), he wrote to Helen Bosanquet quite civilly about her work, addressing her as an economist (Bosanquet, 1903, 'Preface to Second Edition')! I am wary about reaching conclusions based solely on relationship, or even on co-authorship.
3. 'Scholars', for Newcomer, were those listed in the *Dictionary of American Scholars* or *American Men of Science*. I believe her definition stemmed from the sorts of data problems she encountered, which persist.
4. While Peixotto, appointed instructor in sociology in 1904, achieved full professorship in 1918 and retired only in 1938, her pioneering contributions to the studies of poverty and the economics of the household have been forgotten by the mainstream of the economics discipline.
5. Mill's praise of Harriet Taylor and her daughter Helen in his autobiography has long been noted. It is also remarkable, however, how few of his women friends he mentions there. Barbara Leigh Smith Bodichon, Harriet Martineau and Millicent Garrett Fawcett go unmentioned (though Henry Fawcett is also not mentioned).
6. Whom she may have met at Bedford College, where they were both students (Strachey, 1928, 124).
7. Miss Murray, a lady-in-waiting to Queen Victoria, often called Garrett Anderson in to tell of her progress. 'My dear,' she said, 'I think you are doing quite right; and I really believe, if I were a woman myself I would do the same.' 'If you were a woman yourself?' said Miss Garrett surprised. 'I mean if I were in that station of life,' was Miss Murray's explanation (Strachey 1928, 60–61).
8. Potter also worked for Octavia Hill (MacKenzie and MacKenzie, 1977, 128).
9. 'Respect' included an AEA award for her monograph 'Women and Wages', which was published with a foreword by Ely.
10. Converse seemed to feel, rather oddly, that full amends were made when Balch was asked to speak at Wellesley decades later and agreed to do so.
11. Mill would disagree with these statements: he attributed his activity and the Women's Suffrage Committee to Helen Taylor and praised her writing of letters on the matter sent *above his signature* (Mill, 1924, 214–15).
12. 'A summary of six papers and discussions upon the disabilities of mothers as workers', for private circulation only, 1909; and 'Summary of eight papers and discussions upon the disabilities of mothers as workers', 1910 (Kareh, 1987).
13. Joan Robinson also published Fabian tracts in 1943, 1944 and 1958 (Kareh, 1987).

14. The *American Fabian* ballyhooed its acquisition of Gilman. Helen Campbell became a contributing editor at the same time.
15. Given this, it is amusing to note that *The English Woman's Journal* seems to have been the first place of publication of that syrupy Victorian favourite, 'The Lost Chord', by Adelaide Proctor, a frequent contributor.
16. J.M. Strachey was a member of the editorial committee, and both Marjorie Strachey and Alys Russell were published by the journal.

REFERENCES

Addams, Jane (1910), *Twenty Years at Hull House*; reprinted New York: Macmillan, 1960.

Alexander, Sally (ed.) (1988), *Women's Fabian Tracts*, London and New York: Routledge.

Antler, Joyce (1987a), *The Educated Woman and Professionalization: The Struggle for a New Feminine Identity, 1890–1920*, New York and London: Garland.

Antler, Joyce (1987b), *Lucy Sprague Mitchell: The Making of a Modern Woman*, New Haven, CT: Yale University Press.

Banks, Olive (1986), *Becoming Feminist: The Social Origins of 'First Wave' Feminism*, Athens, GA: University of Georgia.

Berg, Maxine (1992), 'The first women economic historians', *Economic History Review*, **45**, (2), 308–29.

Bernard, Jessie (1964), *Academic Women*, University Park, Pennsylvania: Pennsylvania State University; reprinted New York: New American Library, 1966.

Bosanquet, Helen (1903), *The Strength of the People: A Study in Social Economics*, 2nd edn, London: Macmillan.

Converse, Florence (1939), *Wellesley College: A Chronicle of the Years 1875–1938*, Wellesley, MA: Hathaway House Bookshop.

Foner, Philip (1979), *Women and the American Labor Movement From Colonial Times to the Eve of World War I*, New York: The Free Press.

Gardner, Alice (1921), *A Short History of Newnham College Cambridge*, Cambridge: Bowes and Bowes.

Gilman, Charlotte Perkins, (1909–17), *The Forerunner*, a periodical of works by Gilman, published in seven volumes, New York: Charlton Co.

Hamilton, Mary Agnes (1936), *Newnham: An Informal Biography*, London: Faber & Faber.

Herstein, Sheila R. (1988), 'English Woman's Journal, Englishwoman's Review', in Sally Mitchell *et al.* (eds), *Victorian Britain: An Encyclopedia*, New York and London: Garland Publishing, 267–8.

Hill, Mary A. (1980), *Charlotte Perkins Gilman: The Making of a Radical Feminist, 1860–1896*, Philadelphia: Temple University Press.

Jeffreys, Sheila (1985), *The Spinster and Her Enemies*, London: Pandora Press.

Kapp, Yvonne (1972–6), *Eleanor Marx*, 2 vols, London: Lawrence & Wishart.

Kareh, Rashid (1987), *One Hundred Years of Fabian Publishing: Full Cumulative Indexes under Authors and Titles, 1883–1987*, London: The Fabian Society.

Kenneally, James J. (1978), *Women and American Trade Unions*, Monographs in Women's Studies, St Albans, Vermont: Eden Press.

Lacey, Candida Ann ed. (1987), *Barbara Leigh Smith Bodichon and the Langham Place Group*, New York and London: Routledge & Kegan Paul.

Lane, Ann J. (1990), *To Herland and Beyond: The Life and Work of Charlotte Perkins Gilman*, New York: Pantheon.

Lewenhak, Sheila (1977), *Women and Trade Unions*, London and Tonbridge: Ernest Benn.

Lown, Judy (1990), *Women and Industrialization: Gender and Work in 19th Century England*, Cambridge: Polity Press.

MacKenzie, Norman and Jeanne MacKenzie (1977), *The Fabians*, New York: Simon & Schuster.

Mappen, Ellen (1985), *Helping Women at Work: The Women's Industrial Council, 1889–1914*, London: Hutchinson.

McWilliams Tullberg, Rita (1975), *Women at Cambridge: A Men's University – Though of a Mixed Type*, London: Victor Gollancz.

McWilliams Tullberg, Rita (1992), 'Alfred Marshall's Attitude Toward the *Economics of Industry*', *Journal of the History of Economic Thought*, **14**, (2), 257–70.

Mill, John Stuart (1924), *Autobiography of John Stuart Mill*, New York: Columbia University Press.

Mills, Herbert Elmer and his former students (1934), *College Women and the Social Sciences*, New York: John Day.

Muncy, Robyn (1991), *Creating a Feminist Dominion in American Reform, 1890–1935*, New York: Oxford University Press.

Nelson, Julie A. (1993), 'Value-Free or Valueless? Notes on the Pursuit of Detachment in Economics', *History of Political Economy*, **25**, (1), 121–45.

Newcomer, Mabel (1959), *A Century of Higher Education for American Women*, New York: Harper and Brothers.

Payne, Elizabeth Anne (1988), *Reform, Labor, and Feminism*, Urbana and Chicago: University of Illinois Press.

Polkinghorn, Bette (1986), 'An Unpublished Letter from Malthus to Jane Marcet, January 22, 1833', *American Economic Review*, **76**, (4), 845–7.

Polkinghorn, Bette (1993), *Jane Marcet: An Uncommon Woman*, Aldermaston, Berkshire: Forestwood Publications.

Pugh, Patricia (1984), *Educate, Agitate, Organize: 100 Years of Fabian Socialism, 1884–1984*, London: Methuen.

Pujol, Michèle A. (1992), *Feminism and Anti-Feminism in Early Economic Thought*, Aldershot: Edward Elgar.

Rogers, Agnes (1940), *Vassar Women: An Informal Study*, Poughkeepsie, New York: Vassar College.

Rose, Phyllis (1983), *Parallel Lives: Five Victorian Marriages*, New York: Alfred A. Knopf.

Sealander, Judith (1983), *As Minority Becomes Majority: Federal Reaction to the Phenomenon of Women in the Work Force 1920–1963*, Westport, CT: Greenwood Press.

Sicherman, Barbara and Carol Hurd Green, with Ilene Kantrov and Harriette Walker (1980), *Notable American Women: The Modern Period: A Biographical Dictionary*, Cambridge, MA and London: Belknap Press of Harvard University Press.

Spender, Dale (1983), *Women of Ideas (And What Men Have Done to Them)*, London: Ark Paperbacks.

Stephen, Barbara (1933), *Girton College, 1869–1932*, Cambridge: Cambridge University Press.

Strachey, Ray (1928), *The Cause: A Short History of the Women's Movement in Great Britain*, London: G. Bell and Sons; reprinted London: Virago, 1978.

Terrins, Deirdre and Philip Whitehead (1984), *100 Years of Fabian Socialism, 1884–1984*, London: The Fabian Society.

Thompson, William (1825), *Appeal of One Half the Human Race, Women, Against the Pretensions of the Other Half, Men, To Retain Them in Political, and Thence in Civil and Domestic Slavery*; reprinted London: Virago, 1983.

Thomson, Dorothy Lampen (1973), *Adam Smith's Daughters*, Jericho, New York: Exposition-University Press.

Townsend, Emily (1911/1988), 'The Case Against the Charity Organization Society', Fabian Pamphlet No. 158; reprinted in S. Alexander (ed.), *Women's Fabian Tracts*, London and New York: Routledge.

Uglow, Jennifer (comp. and ed.) and Frances Hinton (assistant ed. on 1st edn for science, mathematics and medicine) (1989), *The Macmillan Dictionary of Women's Biography*, 2nd edn, London: Macmillan.

Webb, Sidney (1891), 'The alleged differences in the wages paid to men and to women for similar work', *Economic Journal*, **1**, 635–62.

4. Women mentoring women in economics in the 1930s

Alison Comish Thorne[1]

4.1 INTRODUCTION

Women economists were relatively rare in coeducational institutions in the 1930s but I was fortunate to have been mentored by three: Elizabeth E. Hoyt and Margaret G. Reid of Iowa State College and Hazel Kyrk of the University of Chicago. They were the only women on the economics faculty of those institutions.

The issue of women finding fields, mentors, recognition and employment was difficult in the 1930s. A relationship with home economics, which was a women's field, could prove helpful for example in providing teaching opportunities for women economists. I found that Hoyt, Reid and Kyrk sustained connections to home economics, while maintaining their identity as professional economists in good standing with their male colleagues in economics departments.

As for mentoring, this can be a complicated matter. I shall examine the mentoring by these three women not only in terms of transmission of knowledge, but also as a relationship enmeshed in dynamics of power and care.[2]

My graduate schooling began 60 years ago when I went from my parents' home in Oregon to Iowa State College to study consumption economics under Elizabeth Hoyt and Margaret Reid. They were economists in the economics and sociology department headed by Theodore W. Schultz,[3] who would later make his name at the University of Chicago and become the first agricultural economist to receive the Nobel Prize.

The Great Depression gripped the country in 1934 and I felt fortunate to receive a departmental scholarship of $25 a month. My father, Newel H. Comish, himself an economist, first at Oregon State and later at the University of Oregon, supplemented my $25 so I would not go hungry. I assumed that I received the scholarship because of my good grades and extracurricular activities, but now realize there were two other factors in my favour: my father was author of a pioneer book in consumer economics, *The Standard of*

Living;[4] and he and Theodore Schultz had been doctoral candidates together at the University of Wisconsin in 1927–8. Schultz used to come to our flat on Saturday afternoons to study with my father and he remembered me as a 13-year-old girl.

Watching my father work on his PhD in Madison led to my own determination to get one some day. He had often said that of course women could get PhDs, his favourite example being Jessica Peixotto in the economics department of the University of California, Berkeley.[5]

Elizabeth Hoyt (1893–1980) had come to Iowa State in 1925 after securing her PhD at Radcliffe. She had studied under Harvard professors and combined anthropology and economics to write a dissertation published as *Primitive Trade*. Her next book, written at Iowa State, was *Consumption of Wealth*, published in 1928. Hoyt's was a classical education. She knew Latin, Greek and philosophy, and had attended the Girls' Latin School in Boston. Almost every summer during her long life she returned to Round Pond, Maine, to live on the Ellis Farm, her ancestral home.[6]

I literally had two mentors at the same time at Iowa State, the second being Margaret Reid (1895–1991). Canadian born, with a BS from the University of Manitoba, Margaret Reid had taught foods and nutrition before deciding to pursue graduate work at the University of Chicago under Hazel Kyrk. She completed her PhD in 1931. When I arrived at Iowa State her dissertation had just been published as *Economics of Household Production* and I had the privilege of being in the first class in which she used her new book as the text.[7]

In the process of working on my own PhD I had an interim year at the University of Chicago where my mentor was Hazel Kyrk (1886–1957). She had taken her own PhD in economics at the University of Chicago, a rather long process because her graduate years included teaching at Oberlin and doing war work in London. Her dissertation, which won the distinguished Hart, Schaffner & Marx prize, was published as *A Theory of Consumption* in 1923. It laid important groundwork in consumption economics.[8]

4.2   KNOWLEDGE

Elizabeth Hoyt strengthened consumption economics in the curriculum of Iowa State when she was appointed to the economics faculty in 1925, but its growth as a field was made possible, not from encouragement by the economists, but from encouragement by Anna E. Richardson, dean of home economics. Dean Richardson perceived that home economics needed the principles of economics as they relate to the use of goods and services, and recognized that to a large degree home economics itself was applied consumption.[9] Dean Richardson made it possible for Hoyt to teach economics to home economics students and I strongly suspect the dean urged the economics department to hire Margaret Reid in 1930 because of her dissertation on economics of household production.

Dean Richardson's was an unusual view because home economics, ever since its creation as a field, had emphasized foods and clothing. Indeed, Ellen Swallow Richards, a chemist, invented the field of domestic science, later called home economics, in order that women scientists could find employment, because the academic world would not accept women on its faculties. Human nutrition, under auspices of home economics, was a field that hired women with PhDs in chemistry. Margaret Rossiter has written that home economics 'was the only field where a woman scientist could hope to be a full professor, department chairman, or even a dean in the 1920s and 1930s'.[10] Elizabeth Hoyt became a full professor of economics in 1931 and Margaret Reid in 1940.

Across the country in the 1930s, foods and clothing still remained a major emphasis of home economics, and I was warned by the dean of home economics of Oregon State College that, if I wanted to teach there, she would hire me only if I took some courses in foods and clothing. A PhD in economics would be insufficient. My mentors disagreed with her.[11]

At Iowa State all sophomore students, no matter what their majors, were required to take two quarters of principles of economics. The home economics students had their own classes in economics separate from the rest of the campus, but used the same principles textbook. (They also had separate chemistry classes, but I think economics and chemistry were the only segregated classes.)[12] The home economics students followed their principle of economics courses with a third quarter, in consumption economics. In this way Hoyt and Reid could encourage student interest in their new field. I taught these home economics students when I became a fellow and my $25 was raised to $60 a month.

It was handy that Margaret Hall, the dormitory where I lived, was next door to the home economics building. Hoyt and Reid's offices were in Margaret Hall, on the ground floor towards the back. The remainder of the economics faculty, all male, were in Ag Annex some distance away. There was no gender segregation in graduate courses. All graduate students across campus were required to take George W. Snedecor's statistics classes, in which he often used corn and hogs as examples. After all, this was Iowa. Snedecor's classes were tough and he gave very few As.

I took the usual economics courses: economic theory, international economics, money and banking, history of economic thought. Schultz taught the international economics course. When George Stigler joined the faculty, fresh from graduate work at the University of Chicago, I took his course on monopolistic competition.

Elizabeth Hoyt taught courses in consumption, and standards of living. Margaret Reid taught courses in economics of household production, consumer buying problems and housing. Home management majors and occasionally students in sociology, economics and other areas took Hoyt's and Reid's courses, in which there were always more women students than men. Reid was working on the regional farm housing survey and we learned about that, as well as about urban housing. My master's thesis under Reid was on credit facilities extended by the United States government for home ownership and modernization, and she made me rewrite it until it was understandable.

At the time, economics was defined as the use of scarce resources with alternative uses for attaining given ends. Hoyt was unique in that she extended this definition to the ultimate consumer, and named time and energy as resources in addition to purchasing power. I did a paper for her on capacity to consume which she thought important enough to be published and she sent it with a letter to the editor of the *AER*. It was accepted.[13]

I was the first woman student in the Iowa State economics department to attempt a PhD. It was customary for PhD students to go elsewhere for a year to gain new perspectives and to take course work unavailable at Iowa State. Margaret Reid suggested to Hazel Kyrk at the University of Chicago that I go there for my interim year; perhaps I might consider remaining there to complete my degree. Hazel Kyrk was in both the economics department and the home economics department. My appointment was in home economics. Kyrk agreed to take me but could offer only a tuition waiver. So I borrowed money to pay my room and board at Green Hall, the graduate dorm where Margaret Reid had lived a few years earlier. Sophonisba Breckinridge, the legendary figure in social work, was honorary head of the hall and her friends, Marion Talbot and Edith and Grace Abbott, also legends by that time, were frequent dinner guests. It was a privilege for students to get to know such women.

Here I digress to tell of another woman who in 1934 also came to Iowa State to study under Hoyt and Reid. Eleanor Parkhurst was a graduate of Wellesley College with a BA in English and MA in economics. When I went on to the University of Chicago, Eleanor went on also, but not in economics. She became a doctoral student in the Graduate School of Social Service Administration. Eleanor and I were good friends, with a common interest in economic matters such as family budgeting, and we had (and still have) a concern over women's place in society. At Chicago Eleanor lived in Green Hall just as I did.

I took courses from Hazel Kyrk whose appointment, as mentioned above, was both in economics and home economics. I took economic theory from Frank Knight and Jacob Viner, labour problems from Paul Douglas, anthropology from Radcliffe-Brown and philosophy from Charner Perry, editor of the international journal, *Ethics*.

Kyrk encouraged my breadth of interest, but was herself increasingly concerned with empirical facts, certainly visible in her book, *Economic Problems of the Family*.[14] I was considering doing a dissertation on evaluations of consumption in modern thought. Kyrk thought I tended to bite off more than I could chew. I later learned that Hoyt and Reid responded by saying that I managed to get all the way around any subject that I chose.[15]

Kyrk considered me very young – I was not yet 22 – and suggested that I take a teaching job for five years and then return to Chicago to finish the PhD. She promptly found me a job at Goucher starting the next autumn. But after thinking it over, I told her I preferred to return to Iowa State where I could finish fairly soon, because I was thinking of getting married. Generously, Hazel Kyrk found summer employment for me teaching consumer buying problems to home economics students at Colorado State University. So I taught at Fort Collins, to help pay my debts, and returned to Iowa State in the autumn of 1936 as a teaching fellow.

That same autumn, Virginia Britton, with a BA in economics and political science from the University of Akron (Ohio), came to Iowa State to study under Reid and Hoyt for nine months. She did a study on Iowa incomes as reported in income tax returns which was published as an agricultural experiment station bulletin co-authored with Margaret Reid.[16] Britton then went on to the University of Chicago under Hazel Kyrk where she took her master's and became Kyrk's doctoral student.

As for me, I returned to Iowa State for the academic year 1936–7, took my qualifying examinations with no special favours for being a woman and began work on the dissertation. I taught two principles of economics courses during summer school and helped Margaret Reid on her manuscript, *Consumers and the Market*.[17]

Wynne Thorne and I were married in August 1937 and he took a position in the department of agronomy at Texas A and M. I became a faculty wife and worked on my dissertation in absentia, returning to Iowa State for spring quarter 1938 to work further on it with Elizabeth Hoyt. Margaret Reid was on sabbatical, at the London School of Economics. I lived on the third floor of Margaret Hall and when it caught fire, one Saturday evening, I escaped down smoke-filled stairs carrying my dissertation materials in a stack of manila folders. Hoyt's and Reid's offices were completely destroyed. Margaret Reid never wrote the college text on housing which would have been the first in the field. All her notes were lost. I returned to Ames in December to defend my dissertation and to graduate at winter commencement. I was the only woman of 15 PhD recipients.

4.3   POWER

During my graduate years everyone assumed that the major pursuit in graduate work was knowledge. Matters of power were rarely discussed, yet we women sometimes sensed discrimination. For example, I never knew whether Hoyt and Reid regretted that their offices were in Margaret Hall, instead of over in Ag Annex where the rest of the economics faculty were. We all understood that Ag Annex was overcrowded.

Hoyt and Reid never complained about being treated as lesser, although I sensed that they wished they would be invited to be listed in *Who's Who in America*, and they knew they received less pay than men with comparable training and experience. They liked their work and their professional associations and I surmised that they were well respected. They enjoyed the discussions at departmental seminars when faculty exchanged ideas and references, and we graduate students were a part of it all. Schultz was a wonderful catalyst.

I recall a departmental seminar at which Schultz had invited a faculty wife to speak on household budgets and I was impressed with the respect that the men accorded her. Women were so outnumbered among economics graduate students that I sometimes felt myself a lesser individual, though I would not admit it. I too had my turn speaking at the economics seminar. I wrote home on 3 May 1937:

> I worked on the seminar report, the relation of consumption to economics and gave it on Thursday. It was given in the Modernistic room of the Memorial Union, where we have our seminars; a very ugly room. It went over all right, apparently, because I harangued the ag economist grad. assistants so much (to get even with remarks they have made on consumption) that they were roused to speech. And the faculty members, econ and sociology, asked lots of questions and laughed at the proper places. Once in awhile when I got stuck, Miss Reid would nod her head yes, to a question that I didn't think I could answer, and at different crucial moments, Miss Hoyt and Miss Reid each came in with a short discussion to set the people right and help me out a bit. My but they are two wonderful women.

I am uncertain just how to analyse the matter of power. The foregoing are my speculations on possible gender discrimination. Another approach is to tell how Hoyt and Reid, and Schultz, empowered me. The experience of teaching was empowering. I wrote and gave radio talks and attended consumer-oriented conferences. To have an article published in *AER* was real encouragement. I wrote a paper on the German chemical industry for Schultz's class that he sent over to the graduate dean, R.E. Buchanan, to impress him with the excellent work that graduate students in economics were doing.[18]

4.4   CARE

Strictly speaking, classical economic theory could not care less about 'care'. But Elizabeth Hoyt saw beyond classical economic theory. She was concerned about the ultimate significance of consumption and believed that people, in their consumption, reflect six basic cultural interests: sensory, social, intellectual, technological, aesthetic and empathetic. 'Caring' fits well under empathetic, and also under social.[19] Twenty years later Hoyt and Reid in their professional writing would evidence concern for social well-being in their book *American Income and Its Uses*, in which Hoyt wrote Part One, on the ethics of consumption, and Reid wrote Part Two, on distribution of income and consumption.[20] But that lay in the future.

On a personal note: Hoyt and Reid were good friends and remained so throughout their long lives. They were friends with the economists' wives and we women graduate students felt part of their circle. They belonged to AAUW (American Association of University Women) and I recall attending an AAUW social.[21]

In the spring of 1937, when I told Elizabeth Hoyt I planned to marry Wynne Thorne at the end of the summer, she said, 'Oh, shoot!', commingling her consent with regret, and made me promise that our four children would be economists. It was a time of declining birth rates and I had said in a class of hers that, contrary to the trend, I hoped to have four children some day. The remarkable thing is that, after I told Hoyt I intended to marry but not to have children until I finished my degree, she promptly went over to the library and checked out books on contraception, books which were kept under lock and key and never given out to students. The Comstock law of 1873 was still in effect and Ames was a conservative community.

Today it is hard to realize that, in the 1930s at Iowa State, men students who held fellowships had to get their department head's permission to marry because fellowships paid so little that a man could not support a wife on one. Men usually waited until they were very nearly finished with their degrees before going to ask permission. And I am willing to bet that no department head checked out those library books on contraception for the benefit of their male students.

The final point I want to make is that Margaret Reid cared about women and their lives. At the conclusion of *Economics of Household Production*, Reid spoke of the reactionary and the revolutionary, and said that in both groups emotion rather than reason dominates. But she recognized that society regarded women's position as inferior. I quote: 'Traditional husband–wife relationships have been based on the inferiority of women and superiority of men. ... Increasing scientific knowledge does not support the idea that women are inferior. To continue such an idea is to add fuel to fires already kindled.'

She spoke of sex discrimination in toys and in type of activity of children, and spoke of discrimination against hiring married women. She was well aware of gainfully employed mothers' need for child care.[22]

Margaret Reid was not an activist. The 1930s were a quiescent period between the activism of first-wave feminism and the second wave which emerged in the late 1960s, bringing not only activism but also a less sharp line between reason and emotion. Reid's concern about women's lives was apparent at the winter commencement of 1938 when I got my PhD. President Friley's commencement talk included a statement about trends of the time, and the need for women to have intellectual pursuits as well as the importance of home life. Margaret Reid wrote that talk for him. And Margaret Reid placed the hood over my head and onto my shoulders. For me, for her, and for women, it was an important moment.[23]

4.5 POSTSCRIPT: THE MENTORED

I brought Virginia Britton and Eleanor Parkhurst into my narrative because they, too, were mentored in the 1930s. Although I have highlighted my own experience, a summary of the subsequent careers of all three of us illustrates the various paths taken by women trained in economics in that era.

Virginia Britton (1914–) became a bona fide economist. She completed her PhD at Chicago under Kyrk in 1950 with a dissertation on the economic history of families. This ten-year delay came about because Britton had to earn her living, and because Kyrk could not make up her mind on the direction the dissertation should take. During most of this delay, Britton was on the economics faculty of the University of Akron and Kent State University (Ohio) (1943–51). Later she was professor of family economics at Pennsylvania State University (1954–61) and then became research family economist with the Consumer and Food Economics Research Division, US Department of Agriculture (1962–76). Britton is author of a college textbook, *Personal Finance* (1968) and of numerous articles and research reports. She has worked on three nationwide surveys of consumer expenditures and has written extensively for *Rural Family Living* and *Family Economics Review*.[24]

In contrast to Virginia Britton, Eleanor Parkhurst and I have led 'improvised' professional lives, made necessary in the beginning because of family responsibilities. Eleanor Parkhurst returned home to Massachusetts because her mother was unwell. As for me, I had babies. Over the years, however, both of us used our economics training in dealing with social issues, including concerns of women.

Eleanor Parkhurst (1909–) returned to Massachusetts and became a newspaper editor and writer. As the first woman reporter on the newspaper she was greeted with some scepticism and suspicion. Over time the men on the town board and town committees on which she reported accepted her, and the atmosphere of the meetings shifted from casual to appropriately governmental. A feminist, her articles have appeared in various places, including *Sojourner*. Eleanor Parkhurst is also a historian and poet. Her article, 'Poor Relief in a Massachusetts Village in the 18th Century' (written while at the University of Chicago), appears today in the widely-used textbook, *Compassion and Responsibility: Readings in the History of Social Welfare Policy in the United States*. Currently she is doing a short study/analysis of the gender gap of the local high school faculty where nearly all the department heads are men and the percentage of women on the faculty is small.[25]

As for Alison Thorne (1914–), my academic career was delayed not only by young children, but also by anti-nepotism rulings at Utah State University. Wynne Thorne (1908–1979) joined the USU faculty in 1939, and had a long and distinguished career, becoming head of agronomy, and then Director of the Agricultural Experiment Station and Vice-President for University Research. But administrators' spouses were not allowed on the faculty. Not until 1965, at age 51, did I become a lecturer in sociology, and also in home economics and consumer education.[26] In the meantime I held state and local elected and appointed positions. As a school board member I spoke widely on school finance. As a member of the Governor's Committee on the Status of Women I wrote on employment of women and on poverty. Organizing the Northern Utah Community Action Program during the 'war on poverty' led to an invitation from the sociology department to teach for them. In 1972, at Utah State University, I helped initiate the status of women committee and the introductory course in women's studies, which I taught for over ten years. I organized and became the first coordinator of WID (Women in International Development). Through all this, Wynne Thorne strongly supported my belief in social justice and the importance of equality for women.

As for children, we did not have four. We had five. None became economists, although three became professors. Two of these professors (born 1942 and 1949) are mothers with husbands in academia,[27] something that would have been impossible in the 1930s.

NOTES

1. I am indebted to Eleanor Parkhurst, Virginia Britton and Barrie Thorne for critical analysis of an early version of this chapter. Their suggestions were invaluable. Any errors, however, are mine. The original paper was presented at a joint History of Economics Society and International Association for Feminist Economics session at the Allied Social Science Associations, Boston, January 1994.
2. 'As feminist educators we should take heed of women's paradoxical relationship to

schooling by working to transform the material and ideological conditions under which students and teachers enter into relationships of knowledge, power, and care.' This is the final sentence of Wendy Luttrell's article, '"The Teachers, They All Had Their Pets": Concepts of Gender, Knowledge and Power', *Signs*, **18**, Spring 1993: 505–46. Although my situation in the 1930s was quite different from that of women students' schooling described by Luttrell, I believe her categories of knowledge, power and care are applicable.

3. In 1934, Theodore Schultz, at age 32, became head of the economics and sociology department because senior economists had left Iowa State to take prestigious assignments elsewhere. See Nancy Wolff and Jim Hayward, 'The Historical Development of the Department of Economics at Iowa State, 1929 to 1985' (unpublished), 3. Land grant colleges emphasized agricultural economics and rural sociology and sometimes found it convenient to have a combined economics and sociology department. My father's appointment at Oregon Agricultural College in 1915 was in the economics and sociology department.

4. Newel Howland Comish, *The Standard of Living: Elements of Consumption* (Boston: Houghton Mifflin, 1923). This was a practical book on consumer problems.

5. For a discussion of the work and professional fate of Jessica Peixotto and other social economists at Berkeley see Mary E. Cookingham, 'Social Economists and Reform: Berkeley, 1906–1961', *History of Political Economy*, **19**, Spring 1987: 47–65.

6. Elizabeth Ellis Hoyt, *Primitive Trade: Its Psychology and Economics* (London: Kegan Paul, Trench, Trubner, 1926); Economics Classics Reprint (New York: Augustus M. Kelley, 1968). Hoyt, *The Consumption of Wealth* (New York: Macmillan, 1928). For her own statement of birthdate, education and interest in culture, see Elizabeth E. Hoyt, 'Integration of Culture: A Review of Concepts', *Current Anthropology*, **2**, December 1961: 407–26

7. Margaret G. Reid, *Economics of Household Production* (New York: John Wiley, 1934). For a summary biography see Helen H. Jensen, 'Margaret G. Reid', *Newsletter*, Committee on the Status of Women in the Economics Profession, American Economic Association, Summer Issue, June 1993: 13–14.

8. Hazel Kyrk, *A Theory of Consumption* (Boston: Houghton Mifflin, 1923). For her biography see Elizabeth Nelson, 'Hazel Kyrk', *Notable American Women: The Modern Period*, Cambridge, MA: Belknap Press of Harvard University Press. 405–6.

9. Hoyt recognized the encouragement of Dean Richardson in the preface of *Consumption in Our Society* (New York: McGraw-Hill, 1938, vi). In 1987, the 116-year-old College of Home Economics lost its name and became the College of Family and Consumer Sciences (*The Iowa Stater*, June 1987).

10. Margaret W. Rossiter, *Women Scientists in America. Struggles and Strategies to 1940* (Baltimore: Johns Hopkins Press, 1982, 70, 68–9, 201).

11. When I was a graduate student at the University of Chicago, Dean Ava B. Milam of Oregon State interviewed me for a teaching position in the school of home economics. Afterwards, Hazel Kyrk assured me I did not have to take foods and clothing to be an economist on a home economics faculty. Lydia Roberts, distinguished nutrition scientist and head of home economics at the University of Chicago, concurred (Alison Comish family letters, 24 November and 8 December 1935).

12. While I was teaching economics to home economics students, Bertha Fietz (Carter) was a graduate student in chemistry assigned to teach chemistry to freshman home economics students. Appalled at first by the idea of separate classes, she found the chemistry text written by Iowa State professor Nellie Naylor to be excellent. *Introductory Chemistry with Household Applications* (1935) was also used in other colleges where separate chemistry courses for home economics students were given. Bertha Carter letter to Alison Thorne 6 January 1986.

13. Alison Comish, 'Capacity to Consume', *American Economic Review*, 26 (June 1936): 292–5. See Hoyt, *Consumption in Our Society*, ch.1.

14. Hazel Kyrk, *Economic Problems of the Family* (New York: Harper, 1929).

15. Alison Comish family letters, 19 January 1936. Also 22 February, 30 March and 4 December 1937.
16. Margaret G. Reid and Virginia Britton, 'Iowa Incomes as Reported in Income Tax Returns', *Iowa Agricultural Experiment Station Bulletin*, 236, June 1938, 224–41.
17. Margaret G. Reid, *Consumers and the Market* (New York: Crofts, 1938).
18. Alison Comish family letter, 3 April 1935.
19. *Consumption in Our Society*. ch.2.
20. Elizabeth E. Hoyt, Margaret G. Reid, Joseph L. McConnell and Janet M. Hooks, *American Income and its Use* (New York: Harper, 1954), sponsored by the National Council of Churches.
21. Alison Comish family letter, 7 October 1934.
22. Reid, *Economics of Household Production*, 378, 344, 317, 362, 364 .
23. Although my diploma calls it a PhD in consumption economics, the departmental history says it was the first in general economics. See Nancy Wolff and Jim Hayward, 'Historical Development', 6. My family letter of 26 December 1938 describes the commencement.
24. To her knowledge, Virginia Britton was the first woman ever hired onto the University of Akron economics faculty, but the pay was low. When Margaret Reid joined the University of Chicago faculty in 1951, Britton, looking around for better paying employment, returned for one quarter and lived with her. Britton's earliest research position was with the University of Vermont. Towards the end of her career she lectured at the University of Maryland, along with her government work. Her textbook, *Personal Finance* (406 pages) was published by the American Book Company, New York, 1968.
25. Eleanor Parkhurst, 'Poor Relief in a Massachusetts Village in the Eighteenth Century', *Social Service Review*, **11**, September 1937: 446–64; reprinted in Frank R. Brent and Steven J. Diner (eds), *Compassion and Responsibility: Readings in the History of Social Welfare Policy in the United States* (Chicago: University of Chicago Press, 1980), 95–113. See also Eleanor Parkhurst, 'Mush! Dogsledding to the Pole', *Sojourner*, May 1987, about the American Women's North Pole Expedition.
26. The Civil Rights Act of 1964 made academic anti-nepotism rulings illegal. The economics department would have welcomed me as part of their faculty, but I was not interested in teaching principles of economics courses and money and banking. I chose to remain less than half-time because of my community work and thus was ineligible for tenure. However, I was promoted from lecturer to professor emerita in 1985, the year in which I became the fourth woman to give the Faculty Honor Lecture: Alison Comish Thorne, 'Visible and Invisible Women in the History of Land-Grant Colleges, 1890–1940', *72nd Faculty Honor Lecture* (Logan: Utah State University Press, 8 October 1985).
27. Barrie Thorne, sociology and women's studies, University of Southern California; and Avril Thorne, psychology, University of California at Santa Cruz. The other children are Kip S. Thorne, astrophysics, California Institute of Technology; Sandra Thorne-Brown, urban forester by training, currently a fifth-grade teacher in Knoxville, Tennessee; and Lance G. Thorne, designer and builder of fine furniture, Takilma, Oregon.

5. Jane Marcet and Harriet Martineau: motive, market experience and reception of their works popularizing classical political economy

Bette Polkinghorn[1]

5.1 INTRODUCTION

Adam Smith, David Ricardo and John Stuart Mill are the traditional 'giants' of nineteenth century economic theory. Contrary to the usual impression, however, all knowledge of political economy did not come from the works of the masters. Parallel to their writings was a collection of publications by those disseminating economic theory. Most knowledge of the theories of political economy was transmitted from these original writers to readers through the work of the 'popularizers', several of whom were women. Important among these writers were Jane Marcet (1769–1858) and Harriet Martineau (1802–76) who were among the most successful pioneers in economic education. These early leaders in economic education echoed the teachings of the masters and disseminated their ideas in palatable form.

Teachers of the history of economics seldom consider the achievements of the popularizers. In addition, they fail to raise the question of how the general public acquires its understanding of economic principles. Yet this is an important question, as what people learn affects their actions.

The purpose of this chapter is to investigate the motive, market experience and reception of two nineteenth-century popularizers of classical economics. Specifically, each writer's work will be examined to determine the target market for their books and an estimate will be made regarding sales and readership. Last, comments by contemporary reviewers and other individuals will be studied to determine how their works were received.

5.2 THE WRITERS

Jane Marcet was the earliest of the writers considered here. She was a popularizer of science, having produced books on as diverse subjects as chemistry, government and geology. She wrote three books on political economy: *Conversations on Political Economy* (first published in 1816), *John Hopkins's Notions on Political Economy* (1833) and *Rich and Poor* (1851). At the time of the publication of her first book, the serious study of political economy was limited to a few scholars. Comparatively few men sought knowledge of its principles and almost no women. Yet Jane Marcet's introductory book became the best selling text of the nineteenth century. A reviewer of one of Mrs Marcet's books in a later period spoke of the atmosphere in which Marcet began a career that resulted in nearly 30 books on a variety of subjects. The reviewer wrote:

> We can distinctly call to mind a period in the history of society when it would have been scarcely less preposterous for a lady to send forth a treatise on a science so abstruse as political economy, than to have commanded a brigade, or manoeuvred a frigate. In the days of our early boyhood, we remember to have heard it predicated, that a girl, in order to be a meet companion for her lord and master, required no fictitious aid of education; that beauty, and sense enough to preserve her from the danger of falling into the fire, were all the qualifications to fit her for society. (*American Monthly Magazine*, 1833, 387)

A better known popularizer was Harriet Martineau. Her interest in political economy was temporary but intense during a two year period (1832–4) when she published 25 stories ranging in length from 100 to 200 pages. She credited Jane Marcet's *Conversations* as her inspiration. She chose the narrative form of writing and claimed to have 'chosen this method not only because it is new, not only because it is entertaining, but because we think it is the most faithful and most complete' (Martineau, 1834, Preface, XII–XIII). She criticized systematic economic treatises then available because they provided only general principles and left the reader to find illustrations of these truths in action. She wrote, 'We cannot see why the truth and its application should not go together, – why an explanation of the principles ... should not be made more clear and interesting at the same time by pictures of what those principles are actually doing in communities' (Martineau, 1834, Preface, XII–XIII). After the 1830s she never returned to the subject of political economy, but continued to write in a variety of literary forms including essays, travel journals and children's stories.

5.3   THE BOOKS

The writings of the popularizers range from entertaining stories to longer publications corresponding to present-day textbooks. The differing degrees of sophistication reflect the varied audiences for whom they were written. The most sophisticated books were intended as teaching aids for students and may have taught the teachers as well. Compilations of lectures were also published for the same market. At the lowest end of the scale were collections of stories designed to be read by the labouring class or by children. These inexpensive primers in political economy were accessible to the barely literate.

Jane Marcet's first book, *Conversations on Political Economy* (1824), was aimed at the top of the market – the most educated. In it she defined political economy as being that science that 'treats especially of the means of promoting social happiness so far as [it] relates to the acquisition, possession, and the use of the objects which constitute national wealth' (Marcet, 1824, 25). She undertook to acquaint the reader with 'a science which no English writer has yet presented in an easy and familiar form' (Marcet, 1824, 10).

Marcet's motivation in writing *Conversations on Political Economy* was economic education. In one of her letters, she gave the following explanation: 'I can assure you that the greatest pleasure I derive from success is the hope of doing good by the propagation of useful truths among a class of people who, excepting in such a popular and familiar form would never have become acquainted with them' (Marcet, 1816). Who were the people she sought to educate? It was an audience composed of both adults and young people.

Marcet's modesty and her style of writing have led scholars to the wrong conclusion about the book's intended readers. In the preface she stated that the book was intended for 'young persons'. In the text she used a dialogue between a teacher (Mrs. B) and her female pupil (Caroline) as a method of instruction.[2] Even Schumpeter came to the wrong conclusion that the *Conversations* was economics for 'high school girls' (Schumpeter, 1954, 477). Certainly, the book was read by young people of both sexes and by their teachers as well, yet there was a very substantial readership among adults that has been overlooked until now.

Many adults bought and read the *Conversations* as an easy introduction to the subject of political economy and this accounts for an important part of Marcet's sales. Marcet's correspondence reveals that many adults wrote to her expressing their thanks for providing a most helpful and readable book. Such an opinion was expressed by Lady Ann Romilly. She wrote to a friend:

> Haven't you been delighted by Mme. Marcet's book? What an extraordinary work
> for a woman! Everyone who knows the subject is astonished, and people like me
> who understand nothing about it, or next to nothing, are delighted by the knowl-
> edge they have gained from it. One of our former judges who at 83 reads every-
> thing that comes out was impressed and truly regrets that he didn't know every-
> thing this book taught him when he was still presiding on the bench. How fortu-
> nate it would be for the country if our judges, not to mention our statesmen, knew
> half of what this work contains. You may say that this is a rather bold statement,
> but I assure you this is not merely my opinion. (La Rive, 1859, 13)

Contemporary economists were also favourably impressed. Their positive
comments led to increased sales. Ricardo made suggestions about some
issues when a second edition was required and noted the fact in a subsequent
letter. He believed that 'the most intricate parts of Political Economy might
be made familiar to the people's understanding ... and a subject which
appears at first view so difficult is within the grasp of a moderate share of
talents' (Sraffa, 1952, 240–41). Subsequently, he recommended the *Conversations* to a young member of his family and was pleased with the result.

Conversations on Political Economy was also praised by Macaulay,
McCulloch and Say. Macaulay claimed that a student who read Marcet's
Little Talks on Political Economy could teach Montague or Walpole many
lessons in finance (Macaulay, 1851, 3) and McCulloch praised it saying, 'this
is, on the whole, the best introduction to the science that has yet appeared'
(McCulloch, 1845, 18). Say praised Marcet as 'the only woman who has
written on political economy and shown herself superior even to men' (Lee,
1893, 122–3). Malthus summed up what was perhaps the judgement of the
entire profession when he wrote to her in August 1816:

> I own I had felt some anxiety about the success of your undertaking, both on
> account of its difficulty, and its utility; and I am very happy to be able to say that I
> think you have overcome the first and consequently insured completely the sec-
> ond. ... I have no doubt that it will have a considerable effect in rendering the
> science much more popular than it was, and spreading it among a class of persons
> that was before totally unacquainted with these subjects. (Malthus, 1816)

Recognizing that the book was bought by adults for their own use helps
explain why sales were so large – at least 14 editions. Adults used it as a
primer when they did not want to read the originals. The essential topics were
included and could be mastered rather quickly. Apart from Martineau's
stories intended for a different market, the *Conversations* was the *only* popularization of classical economics that was notably successful as a publishing
venture (La Rive, 1859, 3).

Subsequently, Marcet wrote *John Hopkins's Notions on Political Economy*,
aimed at the labouring classes. Here also Marcet's goal was education, but

for a different group. In the early 1830s many individuals in the middle and upper classes began to fear what they thought was increasing unrest in the working classes. Suddenly, there emerged a substantial number of societies proclaiming the need for worker education in those principles of political economy which they believed determined the living conditions of the working class. In the advertisement preceeding the text of *Hopkins*, Marcet wrote that some of the stories had been published by a society interested in the 'improvement of the laboring classes' and that 'it is for that rank of life that this little work is principally intended' (Marcet, 1833, advertisement). Thus this book was fundamentally different from the *Conversations*. It is less to inform than persuade; it is more of preaching than teaching.

The *Edinburgh Review* reviewed *Hopkins* as follows:

Mrs. Marcet has resumed her valuable labours in the unpretending little volume. ... It is delightfully written, and is admirably adapted, by plain straight-forward sense, for its virtuous purpose – the improvement of the labouring classes. It is intended to do for the uneducated generally, what her well-known *Conversations on Political Economy* had before done. (*Edinburgh Review*, 1833, 2)

Another reviewer from across the Atlantic concluded:

We most earnestly recommend it to the attention of all of our readers, nor can we do better than adopt a thought, which has already been published in the columns of our daily press, – that it would give us true pleasure to learn, that every family of the working classes were provided with a copy throughout the entire union, convinced as we are that, if it did not ameliorate their condition, which is indeed beyond its province, it would at least prevent vain yearnings for a state of things, which they may promise, but practice will never realize. (*American Monthly Magazine*, 1833, 387)

Again Malthus took the trouble to communicate directly with Marcet regarding the new book. He wrote:

I have read John Hopkins's Notions on Political Economy with great interest and satisfaction and am decidedly of opinion that they are calculated to be very useful. They are in many respects better suited to the labouring classes than Miss Martineau's Tales which are justly so admired ... I think your doctrines are very sound, and what is a more essential point, you have explained them with great plainness and clearness. (Malthus, 1833)

It was never believed that the working class would purchase these books themselves, although they did purchase the penny broadsheets expressing the views of the radicals. *Hopkins* was just too expensive. Rather, capitalists and landowners would buy them to distribute. Further limiting sales was the relatively brief duration of capitalist and landowner concern about radical-ization of the labouring classes. When the fear of revolution subsided, so did the interest in educating them in the principles of political economy. Thus it is not surprising that sales of *Hopkins* were smaller than those of the *Conversations*. Where the latter went to at least 14 editions, *Hopkins* had a maximum of four – two on each side of the Atlantic. Furthermore, these were more like separate printings, as no major revisions took place between them. Using the usual number of books per edition (2000) leads to estimated sales of 8000 at most. This understates the number of those exposed to the book, however, as it was not uncommon for literate individuals to read newspapers and stories to groups of illiterate people. Thus, if we estimate the book's influence by the number of sales, *Hopkins*'s influence was far smaller than that of the *Conversations*.

Marcet's *Rich and Poor* was written as a primer on political economy for young children and it is possible that she wrote it with her own grandchildren in mind. In it she returned to the dialogue form of writing, this time using a master and a group of young boys as pupils. It was short and simple and avoided all controversial topics. The habits of saving, responsibility and charity to the deserving needy were praised. On this book, market experience and opinions agreed: both were low. There was only one British edition, but there could have been one American edition as well. Clearly, its influence was negligible.

Martineau's writing, unlike that of Marcet, was for only one market – ordinary people. While she believed that the public wanted to learn about economic principles, her initial motivation was money. As a young woman she found herself without resources or support owing to the collapse of her father's previously prosperous business. The usual occupations of teacher or governess were closed to her because she was deaf. Her mother suggested that she do needlework for a living and she took it up reluctantly. At night she wrote, hoping to sell her work. Her sewing provided the bulk of her income at first, but her writing eventually became a means to independence.

When studying at a school in Bristol, she had been fascinated by the work of Jeremy Bentham. Subsequently, she studied the *Wealth of Nations* and Malthus's *Essay on Population*. These only intensified her interest in political economy. After reading Marcet's *Conversations on Political Economy*, she proposed a series of stories explaining the principles of political economy by illustrations from daily life. Early efforts to find a publisher for her fictionalized political economy were unsuccessful. Those she approached claimed that public attention was turned to the Reform Bill and to the Cholera (1831). Still she persisted and believed that this 'work was wanted – was even craved by the popular mind' (Martineau, 1877, 122). She stood by her convictions as to the success of the book, telling prospective publishers, 'the people want this book and they *shall* have it' (Martineau, 1877, 129). Deeply discouraged,

Harriet wrote the preface and thought of 'the multitudes who needed it [education from the stories] – and especially of the poor – to assist them in managing their own welfare' (Martineau, 1877, 130). Despite the fact that James Mill predicted failure for the project, a reluctant publisher was finally found. He required that she furnish a minimum number of subscribers and this she did with difficulty.

Like some of the tales she wrote, Martineau's story had a happy ending. When the first story was published, it was an immediate success. In fact, the degree of success can hardly be exaggerated. Her conquest was total; she was financially independent and remarked afterward, 'From that hour [10 February 1832], I have never had any anxiety about employment [other] than what to choose, not any real care about money' (Martineau, 1877, 135). She calculated that she had earned approximately £10 000 from her stories on political economy, a truly exceptional amount for the time. After her first success, 24 *Illustrations* followed, totalling more than 3000 pages. She received so much mail that it was collected from the post office in a wheelbarrow (Martineau, 1877, 136)!

What was the readership? Estimates differ. The first volume sold 10 000 copies, which the publisher took to mean approximately 144 000 readers (Fletcher, 1974, 369–70). This might be compared to Mill's *Principles*, which sold 4000 copies in four years and Dickens's novels, most of which had immediate sales of 2000 to 3000 copies. Using the same ratio between pages and readers as did Martineau's publisher leads to an estimate of three million readers at the time of publication, a monumental number for the period. This estimate is probably too high.

The Society for Diffusion of Useful Knowledge bid for the publication rights to the whole series, promising any price after previously rejecting her proposal. Readers such as Princess Victoria and Coleridge anticipated the arrival of the next number. Richard Cobden publicly supported the work and the politician Peel sent a letter of congratulations. Translations were made into French, German and Spanish. Louis-Philippe ordered his educational minister to introduce the French version into the national schools and the Emperor of Russia did the same (Blaug, 1958, 130). Later, both changed their minds when an anti-monarchical story appeared.

Some economists also viewed Martineau's efforts favourably. James Mill changed his mind about whether economic principles could be explained in such a form. J.R. McCulloch had doubts about her original proposal but advised a correspondent 'that [the tales] are of extraordinary merit' (Blaug, 1958, 130). To the surprise of many, John Stuart Mill gave the *Tales* a review, although he differed with her presentation of the theory on some points. He recognized that her stories would increase the knowledge of economic principles in an audience much different from his own.

Some reviewers were less charitable. Leslie Stephen, who wrote about Martineau for the *Dictionary of National Biography*, concluded that the *Tales* were an unreadable mixture of fiction, founded on rapid cramming, with raw masses of the dismal science (Lee, 1893, 310). Her biographer, Webb, judged that 'her characters are for the most part wooden, the emotion is synthetic, and the rare attempts at humour are hopeless' (Fletcher, 1974, 372). Another writer found her stories on population quite objectionable. He wrote:

> We should be loath to bring a blush unnecessarily upon the cheek of any woman; but may venture to ask this maiden sage the meaning of the following passage: A parent has a considerable influence over the subsistence-fund of his family, and an absolute control over the numbers to be supported by the fund. (*Quarterly Review*, 1833, 6)

The writer railed,

> she was a *female Malthusian*. A woman who thinks child-bearing a *crime against society*! An *unmarried woman* who declaims against *marriage*!! A young woman who depreciates charity and a provision for the *poor*!! (*Quarterly Review*, 1833, 6)

Some later critics have been less hysterical but no more approving. Blaug, for example, thought Martineau's thinking an 'uncritical approach to economic theory' (Blaug, 1958, 130) while one biographer stated that she had a 'knowledge of economics ... [which was] superficial, impressionistic, and often ill-digested' (Pichanick, 1980).

5.4 CONCLUSION

The purpose of this chapter has been to study the motive, market experience and reception of two nineteenth-century popularizers of classical political economy. For Jane Marcet, the motive was 'doing good'. For Harriet Martineau, the primary motive was income, although she hoped also to educate the reader. Both women believed that knowledge of the principles of political economy would raise the well-being of the entire society.

When the working class became restive in the early 1830s, attention turned to educating the working class – opponents called it 'propagandizing'. Both of these writers believed that learning the laws of political economy was in the best interest of the working class. Workers would learn which conditions could be changed and which could not, so that they would concentrate their efforts where they would do the most good. For both Marcet and Martineau this meant that the working class had to understand the wages fund equation. If workers wanted higher wages, they would have to limit their numbers. Strikes and machine breaking alike would only diminish the funds available to pay them.

The books and stories which illustrated these economic 'facts of life' were remarkably popular and sales were larger than most current economists have recognized. Marcet's *Conversations* was aimed at a middle-class audience eager to learn the new science, but loath to struggle through the work of the masters. That the book was successful cannot be doubted. It went to at least 14 editions and found contemporary favour with individuals who saw them as a short-cut to the economic knowledge they desired. Certainly the *Conversations* was not just appropriate to high school girls – as Schumpeter had judged it.

The stories for the working class were a different matter. From a twentieth-century point of view, they sound more like preaching than teaching. In part this is due to a difference in literary style between the nineteenth century and the end of the twentieth. Yet these explanations of classical economic theory sold extremely well. Marcet's *Hopkins* went to three editions and Martineau's *Illustrations* went to approximately 3000 profitable pages. Each was a financial success as a publishing venture.

Many contemporary writers were also favourably impressed. Even as sophisticated an economist as Malthus took the trouble to write to Marcet quite positively on her first two books. Martineau's *Illustrations* had its detractors, but it had its supporters as well. Surely the Society for the Diffusion of Useful Knowledge would not have offered to publish the series at any price if they had not been convinced of its value for economic education.

One might speculate about why Marcet and Martineau's contributions to knowledge in our science have been so long undervalued. Some possibilities are given below.

1. Classical economics is not at present in vogue, so some think its popularization is not of current relevance.
2. Economists find it difficult to take fictionalized tales seriously.
3. Some successful economists – Schumpeter for example – misjudged the readership and failed to see this body of knowledge as economic education for adults.
4. Many popularizers were women.
5. Market sales and estimates of readership were thought to be much smaller than was actually the case.
6. Most often popularizers had done no original work; they popularized theories that had been formulated by others.

As for myself, I would favour (3), (5) and (6) above – or some combination of all of them.

It would certainly be appropriate to extend this study to other writers and examine the work of later popularizers in both the nineteenth and twentieth centuries. In the case of Marcet – and perhaps Martineau – more will be found there than was formerly believed. These books bridged the distance between scholar and society by spelling out the ideas of the masters. They educated, at a time when that was much needed. Surely Disraeli had it right when he said, 'upon the education of the people of this country, the fate of this country depends' (House of Commons, 15 June 1874).

NOTES

1. Original paper presented to a joint session of the American Economic Association and the History of Economics Society at the Allied Social Science Associations meetings, Anaheim, California, 1993.
2. The writer Maria Edgeworth's father suggested that Jane change the student from a girl to a boy, as he thought that would increase sales. Marcet refused.

REFERENCES

Allibone, S. Austin (1897), *A Critical Dictionary of English Literature*, **2**, Philadelphia: J.B. Lippincott, Co., 1218.
American Monthly Magazine (1833), **1**, 387.
Blaug, Mark (1958), *Ricardian Economics*, New Haven, CT: Yale University Press, 129–30.
Carpenter, Kenneth (1975), *The Economic Bestsellers Before 1850*, **11**, May, 3, Cambridge, MA: Kress Library of Business and Economics, Harvard Business School.
Edinburgh Review (1833), April, 2.
Fletcher, Max E. (1974), 'Harriet Martineau and Ayn Rand: Economics in the Guise of Fiction', *American Journal of Economics and Sociology*, **33**, October, 369–70.
La Rive, August de (1859), 'Madame Marcet', *Bibliothèque Universelle de Genève*, March, 3, 13.
Lee, Sydney (ed.) (1893), *Dictionary of National Biography*, XXXVI, 122–3, London: Smith, Elder and Co.
Macaulay, T.B. (1851), *Critical and Historical Essays*, London: Longman, Brown, Green and Longmans, 3.
Malthus, T.R. (1816), Letter to Jane Marcet (August), unpublished, Marcet Collection, Archive Guy de Pourtales, Etoy, Switzerland.
Malthus, T.R. (1833), 'Letter to Jane Marcet' (22 January), *American Economic Review* (1986), **76**, September, 845–47.
Marcet, Jane (1816), Letter to Pierre Prevost (21 September), unpublished, Marcet Collection, Archive Guy de Pourtales, Etoy, Switzerland.
Marcet, Jane (1824), *Conversations on Political Economy*, 5th edn, London: Longmans.
Marcet, Jane (1833), *John Hopkins's Notions on Political Economy*, London: Longman, Rees, Orme, Brown, Green & Longman.

Marcet, Jane (1851), *Rich and Poor*, London: Longman, Brown, Green, and Longmans.

Martineau, Harriet (1834), 'Preface', *Illustrations of Political Economy*, 9 vols, London: Charles Fox.

Martineau, Harriet (1877), *Autobiography*, 3rd edn, Boston: Elder & Co.

McCulloch, J.R. (1845), *The Literature of Political Economy*; reprinted London: London School of Economics, 1938, 18.

Pichanick, V.K. (1980), *Harriet Martineau*, Michigan: University of Michigan Press.

Quarterly Review, The, (1833), **XLIX** April/July, London: John Murray.

Schumpeter, Joseph (1954), *History of Economic Analysis*, New York: Oxford University Press.

Sraffa, P. (1952), *The Works and Correspondence of David Ricardo*, Vol. VII, 240–41 (6 January, 1818), Cambridge: Cambridge University Press.

Thomson, Dorothy Lampen (1973), *Adam Smith's Daughters*, Jericho, New York: Exposition-University Press.

Tregarthen, Suzanne (1987), 'Harriet Martineau', *The Margin*, November.

6. The feminist economic thought of Harriet Taylor (1807–58)

Michèle Pujol

6.1 INTRODUCTION

The difficulty in writing about Harriet Taylor is that all documentation and all that has been written about her has focused not on her but on her relationship to Mill (with the exception of Spender, 1982, and Rossi, 1970).

Very little is known about Harriet Hardy's early life. While we know a lot about Mill's youth and education and the formation of his intellect, we have very little information on the sources of Harriet Hardy's education and radical ideas. Interestingly, the paucity of information on Taylor's intellectual history is confirmed by Mill himself:

> Were it possible in a memoir to have the formation and growth of a mind like hers portrayed, to do so would be as valuable a benefit to mankind as was ever conferred by a biography. But such a psychological history is seldom possible, and in her case the materials for it do not exist. All that could be furnished is her birth-place, parentage, and a few dates, and it seems to me that her memory is more honoured by the absence of any attempt at a biographical notice than by the presence of a most meagre one.[1]
>
> Harriet Hardy was the daughter of Thomas Hardy, an austere surgeon whose relative wealth must have meant access to education for his children. She married John Taylor at eighteen, presumably to escape from her father's authoritarian control. She became part of the Unitarian Radical group of William J. Fox[2] and contributed poetry and essays to the *Monthly Repository* which he edited. (Hayek, 1951, 23–7)

Harriet Taylor and John Stuart Mill met in 1830 and developed an intense friendship characterized by intellectual collaboration and a presumably platonic romantic attachment until their marriage in 1851, two years after John Taylor's death.

Taylor's writings are still to be gathered and published on their own. Hayek reprinted three of her poems and a short essay on the tyranny of conformism and public opinion, from the *Monthly Repository* (Hayek, 1951,

271–9). Her early essay on marriage and divorce, part of a dialogue with Mill on these topics in 1832, has been published by Hayek (1951, 75–8) and Rossi (Taylor, 1970, 84–7). Her better-known 1851 essay, 'The Enfranchisement of Women' has been published both by Rossi (Taylor, 1970) and more recently (Taylor, 1983).[3] Both of these collections of essays, however, centre on Mill's *Subjection of Women*.

6.2 DEBATE ON THE COLLABORATION BETWEEN TAYLOR AND MILL

In his *Autobiography*, Mill talks at length about Harriet Taylor's influence on his ideas and unequivocally asserts her joint authorship of his published work. He describes thus in detail their intellectual partnership:

> When two persons have their thoughts and speculations completely in common ... it is of little consequence in respect to the question of originality, which of them holds the pen; the one who contributes least to the composition may contribute most to the thought; the writings which result are the joint product of both. ... In this wide sense, not only during the years of our married life, but during many of the years of confidential friendship which preceded, all my published writings were as much her work as mine.[4] (1989, 204–5)

As early as 1848, Mill wanted to give this collaboration due recognition by dedicating the first edition of *The Principles of Political Economy*

> To/Mrs John Taylor,/as the most eminently qualified/of all persons known to the author/either to originate or to appreciate/speculations on social improvement,/ this attempt to explain and diffuse ideas/many of which were first learned from herself,/is/with the highest respect and regard/dedicated.[5]

Both Mill's *Autobiography* and the published correspondence between Mill and Taylor give further evidence of their continuing collaboration: discussion of ideas and revisions for subsequent editions of the *Principles* and discussions of the plan and order in which to write and publish their ideas (Mill, 1873/1989; Hayek, 1951).

Whereas Mill emphatically attributes authorship of ideas to Harriet Taylor, and to the dynamic of intellectual interaction between them, her ideas and her contributions have been denied, ignored or derided during her lifetime and in the subsequent tradition of the Western history of ideas until feminists started questioning this erasure (Rossi, 1970; Spender, 1982; Soper, 1983; Pujol, 1992). Sexism and the malestream contruction of genius as a male attribute have been identified as the direct reason for this obliteration:

> The hypothesis that a mere woman was the collaborator of so logical and intellec-
> tual a thinker as Mill, much less that she influenced the development of his
> thought, can be expected to meet resistance in the mind of men right up to the
> 1970s. (Rossi, 1970, 36)

Mill's statements about Taylor's ideas and influence have been seen as an embarrassment, the result of 'sheer delusion' (Hayek, 1951, 15), attributed to his besotted state.[6]

Harriet Taylor's intellect has been systematically dismissed and her person discredited. Dale Spender analyses the many ways in which she was ridi-culed, 'portrayed as stupid, as an "ogling" woman', demeaned in the standard treatment given feminists to this date (Spender, 1982, 185). She was painted as having no original ideas, parroting men – from W.J. Fox to Mill – and as having bewitched Mill, the only reason why he gave her such credit and got involved in the feminist cause (Spender, 1982; Rossi, 1970).

Harriet Taylor has also been denounced as having had too much influence on Mill, the wrong kind of influence: typically, all elements of Mill's work which were found unacceptable or too challenging were attributed to her persuasion. Their intellectual collaboration is bewailed as having altered the course of Mill's thought and influenced his ideas in the wrong way.

For instance, Gertrude Himmelfarb charges that Taylor changed Mill's approach to the concept of liberty, and that he blindly accepted her mediocre influence. She deplores that this had irreversible consequences on the course of Western thought on the subject:

> It took only a shift in the weight of the argument to convert the balanced, modu-
> lated, complicated view that was distinctly his into the simple and extreme view
> that was distinctly hers [... this] marks the transition from a whiggish mode of
> liberalism, in which liberty was one of several values making for a good society,
> to the contemporary mode, in which it is the supreme and indeed the only value.
> (Himmelfarb, 1974, 272)

Elsewhere, Mill's sympathies toward socialism, feminism and cooperation were easily dismissed by conservative critics as the result of her influence. Consequently, *The Subjection of Women* never received the respectful and enthusiastic reception given his other works. As Spender points out, Taylor 'is damned for not being the intellectual influence that Mill made her out to be, but dammed for being an intellectual influence – when it suits!' (1982, 190).

The debate on Taylor's influence on Mill seems to have been entirely missed by historians of economic thought who simply do not acknowledge Taylor's existence (or Mill's feminist ideas) (Blaug, 1962; Hunt, 1979). Maurice Dobb mentions Harriet Taylor's socialist influence on Mill but is silent on her contribution to his work and on Mill's feminism (Dobb, 1973).

Feminism is clearly not one of the 'ideologies' he considers. Jacob Oser mentions Mill's 'passionate defense of the rights of women' and Harriet Taylor's influence. However, after quoting the passage from the *Autobiography* cited above, he casts doubts on its veracity (1970).[7]

It is remarkable that these writers ignored Hayek's 1951 attempt to clarify the nature of the collaboration between Taylor and Mill through their correspondence and other documents. The substantial evidence led Hayek to counter extant opinion and affirm: 'Far from it having been the sentimental it was the rationalist element in Mill's thought which was mainly strengthened by her influence' (1951, 17). Yet it is clear that Hayek's design was limited to documenting and assessing the extent of Taylor's influence on Mill, rather than identifying her as an original thinker worthy of recognition.

It is this male-centred history of ideas which is challenged by feminists. They have suggested we should follow from Mill's statements and recognize Harriet Taylor's joint authorship of all the works published as a result of their intellectual collaboration (Eisenstein, 1981; Pujol, 1992).[8] Yet the recognition of Harriet Taylor's intellectual contribution must go beyond the acknowledgement of her part in Mill's published work to the identification of her ideas, which are distinct from his and those of their contemporaries.

6.3 HARRIET TAYLOR'S IDEAS AND CONTRIBUTIONS

The specific nature of Harriet Taylor's ideas is never fully documented in Mill's writings and can only be inferred from an analysis of the writings specifically from her hand, of some of the exchange in what remains of their correspondence, and of the various changes made by Mill to the successive editions of the *Principles* during the years of their intellectual collaboration and after Harriet Taylor's death.

Utilitarianism

Utilitarian principles clearly inform Taylor and Mill's thought. While it is well known that Mill's education included a strong Benthamite element, we do not know the source of Taylor's utilitarian ideas. These ideas are clearly present, not only in *On Liberty* and in the *Principles*, Mill and Taylor's 'joint productions' (Mill, 1873/1989, 186–8) but in the essays authored solely by Taylor.[9]

Utilitarian principles were particularly put to use to support the argument for women's rights to equality, liberty and self-determination.[10] Women, as human beings, are equally capable of feelings of pleasure and pain: 'Are we not born with the *five* senses?' (M&D, 87). They are thus subject to the universal principle of utility. As no one can judge another's enjoyment or pain, men have no reasonable claim to making decisions for women and 'in their interest':

> We deny the right of any portion of the species to decide for another portion, or any individual for another individual, what is and what is not their 'proper sphere'. The proper sphere for all human beings is the largest and highest which they are able to attain to. What this is, cannot be ascertained, without complete liberty of choice. (E, 100)

An individual woman is capable of measuring her own happiness: no one can decide for her what will improve her state of being. Anything which hampers women's autonomy of decision and utility maximization is detrimental to their welfare and contrary to the goal of greatest happiness for the greatest number.

'Liberty of choice', the freedom to achieve individuality and self-development, is necessary to attain happiness. The greatest happiness for all can only be achieved if all, including women, have self-determination and are free to engage in activities they deem will bring them happiness. The ability to develop according to one's nature also yields the greatest happiness for society as a whole: the emancipation of women will eliminate sources of suffering and barriers to their enjoyment, and 'every pleasure would be infinitely heightened both in kind and degree by the perfect equality of the sexes' (E, 84–5). Additionally, and not insignificantly, it will increase the total human resources available to society and total benefits to the world (E, 101).

Customs and traditions, which are invoked by anti-feminists as reasons to keep women dependent, and conformity, by which dominant conservative opinion is internalized, are denounced for standing in the way of women's self-development (Taylor's early essay on conformity in Hayek, 1951, 275–9; *On Liberty*, 260–75; E, 98–9). Similarly, men's control over women's lives and livelihood, enforced by social rules which keep women dependent on men and deprived of any other means of economic livelihood besides marriage, is condemned as 'tyranny' or 'despotism' within the household (E, 113–16).

As we will see in the following discussion, utilitarian principles inform Taylor's approaches to issues of women's choices and opportunities.

Women's Opportunities in Life and Economic Livelihood

At the beginning of *Enfranchisement of Women*, Harriet Taylor uses the list of resolutions passed at the 1850 Worcester Convention in the United States to detail the restrictions society imposes on women's lives. In her analysis, feminists like those assembled in Worcester are questioning the privileges garnered by 'the aristocracy of sex', based on 'a distinction as accidental as that of colour, and as fully irrelevant to all questions of government' (E, 96). She denounces as 'flagrant injustice' and 'unqualified mischief' the division of humanity 'into two castes, one born to rule over the other', where the power of one caste is maintained through the exclusion of the other from most occupations and life activities. This 'flagrant injustice' arises when

> that which is interdicted includes nearly everything which those to whom it is permitted most prize, and to be deprived of which they feel to be most insulting; when not only political liberty but personal freedom of action is the prerogative of a caste; when even in the exercise of industry, almost all employments which task the higher faculties in an important field, which lead to distinction, riches, or even pecuniary independence, are fenced round as the exclusive domain of the pre-dominant section, scarcely any doors being left open to the dependent class, except such as all who can enter elsewhere disdainfully pass by. (E, 97)

The severe restrictions society imposes on women's liberty of choice and access to opportunities prevent them from maximizing their happiness and more often than not denies them any control over their own life and livelihood. Women should be freed from psychological and economic dependence on men, they should be treated as adult, autonomous human beings, they should have unhindered access to employment and free decision making in that respect. Denial of opportunities is entirely tied to a social situation in which women are made utterly dependent on marriage as their only economic option. 'Women are educated for one single object, to gain their living by marrying – (some poor souls get it without the churchgoing ...)' wrote Taylor in 1832 (M&D, 85). And, again, in 1851:

> Numbers of women are wives and mothers only because there is no other career open to them, no other occupation for their feelings or their activities. ... To say that women must be excluded from active life because maternity disqualifies them for it, is in fact to say, that every other career should be forbidden them in order that maternity may be their only resource. (E, 104)

If women are, by nature, only capable of mothering, then why should society, by denying them other options, compel them to this single activity? 'It is neither necessay nor just to make imperative on women that they shall be either mothers or nothing; or that if they have been mothers once, they shall be nothing else during the whole remainder of their lives.'[11] What is further unjust is that all women, not just those who have or have had children, are barred from all other life activity (E, 103–4). In her analysis, Taylor exposes the patriarchal design of economically coercing women into marriage and motherhood (M&D; E, 103–4).[12] 'Where the incompatibility [between mothering and other occupations] is real, it will take care of itself' – mothers will exclude themselves from other activities. The argument of incompatibility is thus 'a pretence for the exclusion of those in whose case it does not exist'. Women should instead be 'free to choose' (E, 103).

If they were to gain access to free choice, women 'would have no more reason to barter person for bread, or for anything else, than have men. Public offices being open to them alike, all occupations would be divided between the sexes in their natural arrangements' (M&D, 86). Taylor advocated complete freedom of access by women to the labour market: 'Let every occupation be open to all, without favour or discouragement to any, and employments will fall into the hands of those men or women who are found by experience to be most capable of worthily exercising them' (E, 100–101). And further: 'All who have attained the age of self-government have an equal claim to be permitted to sell whatever kind of useful labour they are capable of, for the price which it will bring' (E, 105). This application of liberal economic principles is also found in the *Principles* (P, 765). Just as liberal philosophy is used to argue in favour of women's political equality (E, 93–100), it is also used to support women's economic equality within a free competitive situation where, provided with free entry (along with access to education and training), women will offer their labour in competion with men at the going price, and the market will sort out who will get employed in what occupations on the basis of the skills offered.

This position requires abrogating not only customs, traditions and specious rationales against women's employment (E, 98–9, 103–7), but also all existing legislation which impairs their free entry. The Factory Acts, in particular, should only apply to children who have not 'attained the age of self-government' (E, 105; P, 953). The Factory Acts are denounced as patronizing: protection is no longer needed for a 'woman who either possesses or is able to earn an independent livelihood' (P, 761).

Women's free choice between alternative activities on the basis of expected returns will also greatly increase general welfare: 'the world will have the benefit of the best faculties of all its inhabitants'. At the same time, overall allocation and use of human resources will improve in comparison to the existing situation where 'arbitrary limits' on the exertion of 'the genius, talent, energy, or force of mind of an individual of a certain sex or class' is a 'detriment to society, which loses what it can ill spare' (E, 101).

Equal economic opportunities also means that women should have the same claim as men to property, to the ownership of their own earnings and to inheritance.[13] In short, women must have equal access to opportunities by participating equally in all aspects of economic and civil life: 'what is wanted for women is equal rights, equal admission to all social privileges' (E, 120).

Women's Employment and Wages

In addition to the societal prescription on women to marry and become mothers, other factors restrict their access to economic self-determination through employment: severely limited entry to occupations, restricted acquisition of skills and education, and wage levels below self-sufficiency requirements.

Taylor denounces the fact that lucrative employments are 'fenced round as the exclusive domain' of men (E, 97). She argues that, 'so long as competition is the general law of human life, it is tyranny to shut out one-half of the competitors' (E, 105), identifying a substantial exception to the law of free market competition. She reviews and criticizes three contemporary justifications for excluding women from the labour force – that employment is incompatible with motherhood, that employment will harden their character and that it will create excessive levels of competition (E, 103–7).[14] With the first, women are denied choice of activities. The second argument displays the patronization used to 'seclude them from society altogether' (E, 107). The irony of the latter argument, given the orthodox liberal extolling of the virtues and necessity of a free competitive market, should not have been missed by her readers.

According to the latter argument,[15] giving 'the same freedom of occupation to women and men, would be an injurious addition to the crowd of competitors, by whom the avenues to almost all kinds of employment are choked up, and its remuneration depressed' (E, 104). Taylor's response uses economic theory and women's right to personal and financial autonomy. What if women 'break open the employments now monopolized by men'? What if the outcome is, 'like the breaking down of other monopolies, to lower the rate of remuneration in those employments' (E, 104)? Is not the breaking down of monopolies a good thing? Analysing the worst possible scenario, where 'a man and a woman could not together earn more than is now earned by the man alone',[16] she asserts that society would still witness a net improvement as the woman would have gained access to her own earnings: she 'would be raised from the position of a servant to that of a partner' and could no longer 'be treated in the same contemptuously tyrannical manner as one who, however she may toil as a domestic drudge, is a dependent on the man for subsistence' (E, 104–5).

Taylor's position that women should have unconditional access to all activities throughout their lives is to be contrasted with J.S. Mill's mitigated support for women's access to employment. He saw unrestricted access to employment as a necessary condition for women's equality, yet he deemed employment incompatible with marriage. He felt that women could accede to equality merely by being given the option of employment: 'The *power* of earning is essential to the dignity of a woman.' But a married woman has once and for all chosen her vocation and must 'renounce' all occupations 'not consistent with the requirements' of marriage (S, 179). Mill also opposed the idea that married women should contribute on a continuing basis to the income of their families (P, 394; S, 178).[17]

Taylor's analysis of the status of women is rooted in a materialist understanding beyond Mill's grasp: women must have free choice and free access to earning their own income; a mere option for employment before marriage and a promise of equality within marriage (S, 179) will not make them autonomous from male economic rule.

Taylor believes women to be capable of entering any occupation, provided they have access to the required education and training. In *Enfranchisement*, she refuses to engage in a discussion of 'the alleged differences in physical or mental qualities between the sexes' because it would be too lengthy. She simply quotes in support of her position Sidney Smith's statement on the existing differences in the sexes' abilities being of cultural rather than natural origin (E, 101). The 'trial' of employment is what will prove women's abilities: 'women have shown fitness for the highest social functions, exactly in proportion as they have been admitted to them' (E, 102): at present their opportunities to demonstrate their capabilities are too restricted. In *Principles*, Mill and Taylor state a fact, obvious, but unacknowledged by women's detractors: 'Women are not found less efficient than men for the uniformity of factory work, or they would not so generally be employed for it' (P, 128).

But skill and ability are not limited to performance in a labour market setting. Taylor recognizes the specific skills involved in women's ability to perform a multitude of tasks: 'the varied though petty details which compose the occupation of most women, call forth probably as much of mental ability, as the uniform routine of the pursuits which are the habitual occupation of a large majority of men' (E, 111). This is developed further in *Principles*:

> There are few women who would not reject the idea that work is made vigorous by being protracted, and is inefficient for some time after changing to a new thing. … The occupations of nine out of every ten [men] are special, those of nine out of every ten women general, embracing a multitude of details each of which requires very little time. Women are in the constant practice of passing quickly from one manual, and still more from one mental operation to another, which therefore rarely costs them either effort or loss of time. (P, 127–8)

These observations definitely question the prevailing Smithian doctrine of the division of labour and insist on the importance of 'habit' or training to the achievement of efficiency. Taylor's contribution to the analysis of labour processes deserves due recognition, particularly as it contradicts the dominant discourse of the past two centuries on women's skill and productivity. It brings to this issue an analysis grounded in the observation of women's experience of productive and reproductive labour.

Although they suggest no clear remedy, Taylor and Mill discuss at length, in *Principles*, the issue of the inferior wages women receive in occupations open to them. They identify three causes for this situation: (1) the prejudicial 'custom' of seeing women as economically dependent on men, (2) the crowding of women into few employments and (3) the dichotomy between paying women 'the pittance absolutely requisite for the sustenance of one human being', while men's wages must 'be at least sufficient to support himself, a wife, and a number of children adequate to keep up the population' (P, 394–6). Taylor and Mill thus see in wage inequality another mark of patriarchy: not only do men have claim to most of the labour market, they receive a 'family wage' which assumes and reinforces the dependent status of women and allows them dominant status in the home.

In *Enfranchisement*, Taylor does not deal specifically with wages, except to denounce the tyrannical power derived by men from control over them, and to state her belief that 'the regulation of the reward of labourers mainly by demand and supply' should stop being the rule in the future (E, 105). The latter statement relates to her beliefs in some form of socialism and cooperation.

Sexual Division of Labour and Power Relations

Taylor engages in a review of the origins and manifestations of the sexual division of labour and sex roles in society through history and cultures for the purpose of supporting her argument for sex equality (E, 108–9).[18] Her analysis leads her to the conclusion that sex roles are not natural but socially developed, and coerced upon women either by force or, in the society of her time, 'by sedulous inculcation of the mind' (E, 108). She also establishes the economic nature of this coercion when women are denied any form of economic support other than by being a man's wife and mothering his children (E, 103–5).

Taylor questions the ideology used to justify the sexual division of labour, through which

> the world [is] still persuaded that the paramount virtue of womanhood is loyalty to men. ... in practice self-will and self-assertion form the type of what are designated as manly virtues, while abnegation of self, patience, resignation and submission to power ... have been stamped by general consent as pre-eminently the duties and graces required of women. (E, 108)

This ideology is used to convince women that their self-denial is a virtue, 'that the greatest good fortune which can befall them, is to be chosen by a man' to 'bring up *his* children, and make *his* home pleasant to him', and that no other law but those of 'nature and destiny' have closed all other careers to them (E, 107).[19]

Taylor uncovers the power relations behind this ideology: 'power makes itself the centre of moral obligation, ... a man likes to have his own will, but does not like that his domestic companion should have a will different from his' (E, 108). She challenges these power relations, asking 'whether it is right and expedient that one half of the human race should pass through life in a state of forced subordination to the other half' (E, 107). Hence it is not nature and destiny which have placed women in a position of servitude towards men, but men's power: the existing division of labour works for the exclusive benefit of men, and through it their needs are serviced and their power further reinforced. 'When ... we ask why the existence of one-half the species should be merely ancillary to that of the other ... the only reason which can be given is, that men like it. It is agreeable to them that men should live for their own sake, women for the sake of men' (E, 107).

Here again, Taylor uses a standpoint based on her analysis of women's material position to see through the ideology which justifies women's dependence and powerlessness. Here too, her position can be contrasted with Mill's. Mill adheres to the necessity for a sexual division of labour where women's 'natural task' will be to 'adorn and beautify' life rather than 'support' it (Mill, 1869/1970, 75), to 'contribute' within the family rather than outside it (S, 178), where women can 'share' the occupations and interests of her husband rather than have her own (1869/1970, 77). It is clear that Mill did not 'share' Taylor's analysis of the sexual division of labour, its link to power relations between the sexes and the ideology used to entrench it.

Marriage and Women's Economic Status

This difference in analysis is carried into Taylor's and Mill's diverging approaches to marriage. Mill idealizes his 'communion of equals' relationship with Taylor (from his perspective, no doubt) into a model where love and equal rights are all that is required for a fair treatment of women. For Taylor, it is very clear that marriage is both the end and the means of a socioeconomic arrangement which maintains the subservience of women. Marriage, given the denial of legal rights (property, divorce), economic rights (property, employment, inheritance, any alternative means of economic sufficiency) and political rights (means to change existing laws) to women, is their only viable option.

Taylor denounces the powerlessness of women in a situation where the husband 'is judge, magistrate, ruler, over their joint concerns; arbiter of all differences between them ... the only tribunal, in civilized life, in which the same person is judge and party' (E, 113). This position, and the lack of any recourse for women, lead to abuses of power, where the man 'becomes either the conscious or unconscious despot of his household' (E, 114). The argument of male 'brutality and tyranny' within the home is used to challenge the opponents to women's rights, for whom women's welfare is adequately maximized by their husbands.

Unlike Mill, who justifies resorting to divorce only in the most extreme cases (Mill, 1970, 77–84), Taylor advocates unconditional rights to divorce on demand: 'would not the best plan be divorce which would be attained by any without any reason assigned, and at small expense' (M&D, 85)?[20]

In a society where women have complete equality and access to economic self-sufficiency, Taylor predicts that the institution of marriage would be cast off: 'I have no doubt that when the whole community is really educated, though the present laws of marriage were to continue they would be perfectly disregarded, because no one would marry' (M&D, 85). 'What evil,' she asks, 'could be caused by, first placing women on the most entire equality with men, as to all rights and privileges, civil and political, and then doing away with all laws whatever relating to marriage?' (M&D, 86). For Taylor, then, marriage exists only because women are kept dependent on men. Legal equality alone would not change this condition. Yet access to full economic independence would remove for women the need to marry. We can identify here again the divergence between Mill's idealist approach, which is based on and would maintain male privilege, and Taylor's economic materialism, grounded in her own experience of marriage.

Women's Education

Women's economic and social autonomy is also at the centre of Taylor's position on women's access to education and on the nature of such education. Women need education, not only to gain access to occupations, but also to develop independent thought and gain control over their lives.

Reviewing the contemporary situation, Taylor finds women 'perfectly uneducated', or 'educated for a single object, to gain their living by marrying' (M&D, 84–5). But this does not imply that they are given any prior knowledge of what marriage entails: 'girls enter what is called a contract perfectly ignorant of the conditions of it, and that it should be so is considered absolutely essential to their fitness for it!' (M&D, 86). Thus women's 'utter dependence' upon marriage and powerlessness within it are carefully constructed and reinforced by depriving them of education.

Femininity is socially inculcated: women are 'told from infancy that thought, and all its greater applications, are other people's business, while theirs is to make themselves agreeable to other people' (E, 112). They are not encour-

aged to develop independent thought. Furthermore, any criticism or rebellion
of their condition is impressed upon them as unfeminine:

> They are taught to think, that to repel actively even an admitted injustice done to
> themselves, is somewhat unfeminine, and had better be left to some male friend or
> protector. To be accused of rebelling against anything which admits of being
> called an ordinance of society, they are taught to regard as an imputation of a
> serious offence ... against the proprieties of their sex. (E, 118)

Women's dependence and their acquiescence in their oppression is engi-
neered through the indoctrination which they suffer from childhood. They are
not allowed to have their own thoughts. Their dependence on men is pushed
to an extreme where they must even rely on them to express any grievance
they might somehow elaborate about their own condition.

Women must have access to education and, for Taylor, this means an
education on equal terms with that received by men. She engages in a passionate argument against those (including Mill) whom she calls 'the moderate reformers ... who would maintain the old bad principles, mitigating their
consequences', those who support women's education for the sole purpose of
providing men with better companionship (E, 111).[21] This would only impart
'superficial information on solid subjects' (E, 112), maintain women's dependent situation and solely benefit men. These 'modern, and what are regarded as the improved and enlightened modes of education for women' are
not acceptable: 'High mental powers in women will be but an exceptional
accident, until every career is open to them, and until they, as well as men,
are educated for themselves and for the world – not one sex for the other' (E,
112–13). This is a clear and uncompromising message: women's education
should satisfy their own needs and give them the knowledge and skills
necessary to enter all occupations. It must be an instrument to their economic
independence, but also to their intellectual autonomy. Education should 'form
strong-minded women' rather than 'prevent them from being formed' (E,
112).

Education was seen by the utilitarians as one of the means of social
reform, and it is clear that Taylor wanted women to be fully included in that
project: focusing on improving men's education and/or improving women's
education for men's needs would only preclude their sharing in the increased
social welfare and limit the benefits available to 'the world'. Similarly, improving women's education but keeping them excluded from employment
would only contribute to their oppression and be detrimental to society (E,
101).

Social Change

Taylor's rationalism and her adherence to the age of enlightenment ideology of social improvement inspire her optimistic view of social change. She observes an 'improvement in the moral sentiments of mankind', increased commonality of tastes and behaviour among men and women, decreases in violent behaviour and 'intemperance', except in 'the very poorest classes' (E, 110, 105). She sees education, reason, improved standards of living and women's influence as 'civilizing'. In a discussion which anticipates modern feminist thought, she associates social progress with the merging of the public and the private spheres. There will be limits to women's influence and social improvement if they are kept separate, in the subordinate position which has been theirs (E, 110). This position is strongly reiterated at the end of her essay: 'What is wanted for women is equal rights, equal admission to all social privileges; not a position apart, a sort of sentimental priesthood' (E, 120).

Women's access to education, employment and equality is also seen as part of the solution to the problem of population growth. In *Principles*, Mill and Taylor linked unregulated fertility and population growth to the subjection of women and advocated education on birth control methods (P, 368–72). Interestingly, in *Enfranchisement*, Taylor links excessive population growth to the harsh competitive conditions of the capitalist labour market:

> With respect to the future, we neither believe that improvident multiplication, and the consequent excessive difficulty of gaining a subsistence, will always continue, nor that the division of mankind into capitalists and hired labourers, and the regulation of the reward of labourers mainly by demand and supply, will be for ever, or even much longer, the rule of the world. (E, 105)

For her, change towards a more socialist arrangement is both necessary and imminent. In his *Autobiography*, Mill summarizes their common belief: 'The social problem of the future we considered to be, how to unite the greatest individual liberty of action with a common ownership of the raw material of the globe, and an equal participation of all in the benefits of combined labour' (1873/1989, 175). But neither Taylor nor Mill elaborate for their readers how they see these changes coming about.[22]

In the section 'On the Probable Futurity of the Labouring Classes' in *Principles*, which Mill specifically refers to as having been written on the basis of Taylor's ideas (Mill, 1873/1989, 186–7), the class and power relations in capitalism are also denounced: 'I do not recognise as either just or salutary, a state of society in which there is any "class" which is not labouring ... So long ... as the great social evil exists of a non-labouring class, labourers also constitute a class' (P, 758). The poor are maintained dependent, 'the lot of the poor [is] regulated *for* them, not *by* them'; 'while yielding passive and active obedience to the rules prescribed for them, they may resign themselves … to a trustful *insouciance*, and repose under the shadow of their protectors' (P, 759, emphasis in original). The relationship between the rich and the poor is compared to the relationship between men and women (P, 759).[23] Mill and Taylor argue that relationships of inequality between the classes and the sexes, reinforced by the idealized paternalistic tradition of 'loyalty on the one side, chivalry on the other', should not persist 'where there are no longer serious dangers from which to protect' (P, 760–61). The argument of a need for protection is incompatible with the freedom and autonomy which the labour market should provide all: 'No man or woman who either possesses or is able to earn an independent livelihood, requires any other protection than that which the law could and ought to give' (P, 761).

Laws, therefore, and not individuals, should be the sole protection of autonomous citizens. Mill and Taylor point out that lack of autonomy, being 'under the power of someone … is now … the only situation which exposes to grievous wrong'. And here reference is specifically made to 'the brutality and tyranny … of husbands to wives' (P, 761). Laws must also enhance rather than hamper autonomy. The Factory Acts, for instance, are obviously part of the old system of protection and paternalism and should be repealed, except in the case of children who do not have full control over their labour force participation (P, 953; E, 105). Similarly, for Taylor, all laws controlling or restricting women's decisions with respect to marriage, divorce and employment should be repealed, leaving the field completely open for them to act according to their own best interest (M&D; E, 103).

Taylor's specific suggestions for legal reform show a libertarian tendency, where the focus is on abrogating repressive or unnecessary legislations, rather than on elaborating new ones, a position opposite to utilitarian approaches of effecting social change through the passage of legislation (Boralevi, 1987, 163, 167). Taylor's analysis of patriarchal power may have led her to distrust the state and its institutions as avenues for social change, at least until women have more input into law making and enforcement. Yet one may wonder whether the use of reason and persuasion to impress upon men in society at large the necessity of women's full equality would provide a more successful approach. The immediate proof of the tenuousness of her beliefs is Mill's failure to understand, fully adopt and retain into his late writings Taylor's analysis.

Ideology, False Consciousness and Feminist Standpoint

In *Enfranchisement*, Taylor generates an insightful analysis of the nature of patriarchal hegemonic ideology. She shows how women are made to internalize this ideology and argues against those who use this as evidence of their acquiescence in their social position: 'the alleged preference of women for their dependent state is merely apparent, and arises from their being allowed no choice' (E, 118).

As we saw earlier, Taylor identifies the social conditioning women are subjected to from infancy, which makes them compliant to their assigned feminine role. She compares this process to that of the subjection of colonized people, tenants and labourers (E, 117, 118). It is a strategy of the ruling classes or castes to generate among their subjects, not only the acceptance of their lot, but active participation in maintaining the status quo: 'the qualities and conducts in subjects which are agreeable to rulers, they succeed for a long time in making the subjects themselves consider as their appropriate virtues' (E, 107). The manufacturing of false consciousness among oppressed groups does not, however, imply that group utility is maximized by the perpetuating of their oppression. Their apparent acquiescence is only a survival mechanism: 'Custom hardens human beings to any kind of degradation, by deadening the part of their nature which would resist it' (E, 117–18). Besides, the indoctrination of women into accepting their state is backed up by legal coercion: if 'women's preference [for their dependent state] be natural, there can be no necessity for enforcing it by law' (E, 118).

The concepts of femininity and 'the proprieties of their [women's] sex' are thus denounced by Taylor as patriarchal ideological constructs which purport to deny women any agency and disempower them from taking action in their own personal, economic and political interest. A belief in women's right to autonomy, in their individually separate claim to economic well-being and to physical and intellectual liberty is a persistent theme in Taylor's writings. Women must have access to all freedoms: freedom of education and occupation, freedom of thought and freedom of disposing of their own person without putting someone else's interests first. To attain this goal, women must have access to the means to exert these freedoms. In particular, 'education should form strong minded women rather than prevent them from being formed' (E, 112), and all laws which restrict women's freedoms should be abolished. Society has to treat women as fully responsible persons capable of identifying their own interests and making decisions accordingly.

Taylor's feminist standpoint is influenced by her liberal and utilitarian beliefs, but mostly it is firmly grounded in her own experience as a woman. This allowed her to elaborate a ground-breaking analysis of gendered power relations, sex roles and the sexual division of labour, and of the mechanisms, economic, political, legal and ideological, which maintain the material subjection of women.

Her standpoint is also grounded in her class position: even though she uses her analysis of the power and economic relations which affect the working class to illustrate her argument on the oppression of women, she exposes her prejudice against that class which she stereotypes as brutal and coarse (E, 105, 110). Her bias prevents adequate recognition of the strength and greater economic independence of working-class women, and of the model it could present for middle-class women.

6.4 CONCLUSION

Taylor's understanding of the material nature of women's oppression is what distinguishes her from the thinkers of her day (except Barbara Bodichon, Anna Wheeler and William Thompson)[24] and what makes her analysis much more advanced than that of John Stuart Mill.

The contrasts between the ideas of Harriet Taylor and John Stuart Mill give us insights into the male bias present in patriarchal liberal thought, even in the most 'pro-feminist' of its proponents, where existing gender roles, the separateness of the sexes and the bases of male privilege are maintained. Mill's approach limits women's access to the public realm on the basis of their 'primary duty' to be wives and mothers. It reinforces the construction of the private realm as a place of privilege for men where they get their needs met, where their power is unchallenged, where women 'adorn and beautify', meet men's needs and provide intellectual companionship and a 'refuge' from the harshness and competition of the public realm.[25]

Taylor correctly perceived that this vision is not liberating for women, that it reinforces their powerlessness and economic dependence and that the enfranchisement of women requires more than a promise of equal treatment within the private sphere and conditional access to the public sphere. She perceptively analyses how women's exclusion from the public realm reinforces their confinement to the private realm and their seclusion into economic dependency. She exposes male agency in the exclusion of women from the economic realm to ensure their availability in the private realm (E, 107). She criticizes the reforms proposed by the most enlightened liberal thinkers as meaningless because they do not come from a woman's perspective, but from that of the 'rulers' over women, who, at best, only want to soften the impact of their rule. By applying a (pre-Marxian) class analysis to the power relations between the sexes, she can establish that the rulers will never emancipate those whose lives they control, because it is against their interests.

It is this materialist analysis that distinguishes Taylor from Mill's idealist and male-centred position. There cannot be any doubt that Taylor stands on her own as an original and insightful feminist thinker and as an economist and political theorist.[26] Her ideas were well ahead of her times and recog-

nition of her contribution to economic analysis and to feminist theory is long
overdue.

NOTES

1. From a 1870 letter to Paulina Wright Davies (quoted by Hayek, 1951, 15). This statement
   is indeed curious, given Mill's detailed documentation of his own intellectual history. One
   can only speculate on his reasons for not contributing to a record of her life: control over
   her public image, construction of Harriet Taylor as a mythical woman, or reluctance to
   document her genius as self-made rather than the product of a controlled education?
2. For more on the Unitarian Radicals, the Philosophic Radicals, utilitarianism and the ideas
   of and relationships between these two radical groups, see Mineka (1944), Hayek (1951),
   Rossi (1970) and Mill's *Autobiography* (1989).
3. This essay was initially published anonymously in 1851 in the *Westminster Review*.
   Harriet Martineau, thinking it was written by Mill, wrote in amazement at the possibility
   that a man could so well understand the position of women – not so surprising once
   Taylor's authorship was subsequently clarified. Mill never put his name on anything quite
   as radically feminist.
4. In his *Autobiography*, Mill identifies Taylor's collaboration on *The Principles of Political
   Economy* (written between 1845 and 1847, editions: 1848, 1849, 1852, 1857) and on *On
   Liberty* (1859/1977) 'more directly and literally our joint production than anything else
   which bears my name'; *The Subjection of Women* published in 1869 does not completely
   reflect her ideas and influence.
5. This dedication was not printed, however, out of consideration for John Taylor. In the
   Collected Works of J.S. Mill, it was not restored to its proper place but buried in a
   footnote, in an appendix on the Mill–Taylor correspondence (1965, 1026).
6. 'Was all this sheer delusion? Some of Mill's friends evidently thought so and their views,
   especially Carlyle's, have largely determined the opinions of later generations. Yet even if
   it had been nothing more it would not only present us with a curious psychological puzzle,
   but also leave open the question how far Mill's ideas, and especially his changes of
   opinion at a critical juncture of European thought, may have been due to this delusion. Yet
   it is not altogether easy to accept the view that so eminently sober, balanced and disciplined a mind, and a man who chose his words as deliberately and carefully as Mill,
   should have had no foundation for what he must have known to be unique claims on
   behalf of any human being' (Hayek, 1951, 14–15). Mill's words are still not taken
   seriously. See, for instance, Bladen, the editor of Mill's collected works, describing Mill's
   'account of the part played by Harriet Taylor' as 'generous, perhaps overgenerous' (1965,
   lxii).
7. 'He tried to persuade the world that his whole intellectual development (other than his
   competence in economics) was due to Mrs Taylor. He called his writings both before and
   after their marriage the joint product of their minds, claiming that her share constantly
   increased as the years advanced' (Oser, 1970, 120).
8. In the *Autobiography*, Mill details the works 'in which her share was conspicuous' (1989,
   186–98). Beyond these, Eisenstein also suggests joint authorship of *The Subjection of
   Women*, about which Mill explains 'in what was of my own composition, all that is most
   striking and profound belongs to my wife, coming from the fund of thought which had
   been made common to us both' (Mill, 1989, 197–8). He also clarifies that 'it was enriched
   with some important ideas of my daughter's, and passages of her writing' (197). Joint
   authorship should then also include Helen Taylor. I am myself reluctant to fully attribute
   to Harriet Taylor the authorship of some of the more conservative ideas of Mill which
   appear in *The Subjection*.
9. The works of Harriet Taylor and John Stuart Mill will be referred to as follows: E =
   Taylor's 'Enfranchisement of Women', 1970 (1851); M&D = Taylor's essay on Marriage

and Divorce, 1970 (1832); P = *Principles of Political Economy*, 1965 (Vols II and III of *Collected Works of John Stuart Mill*); S = Mill's 'The Subjection of Women', 1970 (1869).

10. See Boralevi (1987) for a discussion of the links between utilitarianism and feminism.

11. See also, in the *Principles*: 'the least which justice requires is that law and custom should not enforce dependence ... by ordaining that a woman, who does not happen to have a provision by inheritance, shall have scarcely any means open to her of gaining a livelihood, except as a wife and mother' (P, 765).

12. In *The Subjection of Women*, Mill also makes the link between the restriction of women's employment and their subservient position in the home: 'I believe that their disabilities elsewhere are only clung to in order to maintain their subordination in domestic life; because the generality of the male sex cannot yet tolerate the idea of living with an equal' (S, 181).

13. Access to equal opportunity should start early: 'Fathers would provide for their daughters in the same manner as for their sons' (M&D, 86).

14. It is of interest to note that these three arguments seemed to have been endorsed to some degree by John Stuart Mill.

15. Mill stated his position in his 1832 essay: 'It is not desirable to burthen the labour market with a double number of competitors' (Mill, 1832/1970, 74–5). Alice Rossi points out that this issue seemed to have been contentious between Taylor and Mill, the argument of unwanted competition being used by Mill in support of his opposition to married women's employment. Rossi comments: 'Harriet took this point by the horns and demolished it' (Rossi, 1970, 42). The issue of monopoly rent received by male workers is not addressed in the *Principles*, even though it could have been an extension of Mill and Taylor's theory of non-competing groups. This further points at a disagreement between them (Pujol, 1992, 26).

16. Taylor here alludes to the wage-fund argument that total wages paid are fixed, no matter how many workers are employed. Belief in such a theory would inform the fear that entry of women in the labour market will generate a decrease in men's wages.

17. The case of working-class women is discussed – intermittently – in the *Principles*: 'It cannot, however, be considered desirable as a *permanent* element in the condition of the labouring classes, that the mother of the family ... should be under the necessity of working for subsistence, at least elsewhere than in their place of abode' (P, 394). This passage has a curious history; it was deleted from the 1852, 1857 and 1862 editions and reintroduced in the 1865 and 1871 ones, a result presumably of Harriet Taylor's influence, which did not survive her death. The case of middle-class women is discussed in *Subjection*: 'When the support of the family depends, not on property, but on earnings, the common arrangement, by which the man earns the income and the wife superintends the domestic expenditure, seems to me in general the most suitable division of labour between the two persons' (S, 178).

18. This discussion rests on stereotypical and Eurocentric views of the sexual division of labour and social relations among Australian and American Aboriginal peoples, and among the 'somewhat more advanced' Asian cultures, where evolutionary periodization and classification of cultures points to the 'superiority' of Western social relations where ideology has replaced brutality and enslavement as modes of patriarchal rule (E, 108).

19. In a passage with similar overtones, Mill and Taylor condemn the Factory Acts in *Principles*: 'If women had as absolute a control as men have over their own persons and their own patrimony or acquisitions, there would be no plea for limiting their hours of labouring for themselves, in order that they might have time to labour for the husband, in what is called, by the advocates of restriction, *his* home' (P, 953).

20. Interestingly, Taylor is closer than Mill is to Bentham's position on divorce: he strongly supported the concept of women's legal autonomy and saw access to divorce as a necessary guarantee to protecting the separateness of women's interests from men's (Boralevi, 1987, 165, 170).

21. Using a reverse standpoint, Taylor pointed out the lack of reciprocity in such a proposition: 'they do not say that men should be educated to be the companions of women' (E, 111).

22. Kate Soper points out, however, that the 'More "socialist" vein of comment' of *Enfranchisement* is absent from Mill's *Subjection* (Soper, 1983, x).
23. This was added in the 1857 edition.
24. See Bodichon (1987), Lacey (1987) and Thompson (1825/1970).
25. See Mill's *Subjection*. For a detailed discussion of liberal feminist thought, see Eisenstein (1981).
26. Having reviewed Taylor's ideas, one wonders how she was ever accused of 'parroting' men's words.

REFERENCES

Bladen, V.W. (1965), 'Introduction', Vol. II, *Collected Works of John Stuart Mill*, J.M. Robson ed., Toronto: University of Toronto Press.

Blaug, M. (1962), *Economic Theory in Retrospect*, Homewood, IL: Richard D. Irwin.

Bodichon, Barbara Leigh Smith (1857), *Women and Work*, English edn, London: Bosworth and Harrison; reprinted in Candida Ann Lacey (ed.) (1987); American edn, with introduction by Catharine M. Sedgwick, New York: C.S. Francis & Co, 1859.

Boralevi, Lea Campos (1987), 'Utilitarianism and Feminism', in Ellen Kennedy and Susan Mendus (eds), *Women in Western Political Philosophy*, Brighton, Sussex: Harvester Wheatsheaf, 159–78.

Dobb, Maurice (1973), *Theories of Value and Distribution since Adam Smith; Ideology and Economic Theory*, Cambridge: Cambridge University Press.

Eisenstein, Zillah (1981), *The Radical Future of Liberal Feminism*, Boston, MA: Northeastern University Press.

Hayek, F.A. (1951), *John Stuart Mill and Harriet Taylor, Their Correspondence and Subsequent Marriage*, London: Routledge and Kegan Paul.

Himmelfarb, Gertrude (1974), *On Liberty and Liberalism, the Case of John Stuart Mill*, New York: Alfred A. Knopf.

Hunt, E.K. (1979), *History of Economic Thought, a Critical Perspective*, Belmont, CA: Wadsworth Publishing Co.

Lacey, Candida Ann (ed.) (1987), *Barbara Leigh Smith Bodichon and the Langham Place Group*, New York and London: Routledge & Kegan Paul.

Mill, John Stuart (1832/1970), 'Early Essay on Marriage and Divorce', in Alice S. Rossi (ed.) (1970), *Essays on Sex Equality*, Chicago: University of Chicago Press, 67–84.

Mill, John Stuart (1859/1977), *On Liberty*, in *Collected Works of John Stuart Mill*, Vol. XVIII, ed. J.M. Robson, Toronto: University of Toronto Press.

Mill, John Stuart (1869/1970), *The Subjection of Women*, in Alice S. Rossi (ed.) (1970), *Essays on Sex Equality*, Chicago: University of Chicago Press, 123–242.

Mill, John Stuart (1873/1989), *Autobiography*, edited with an introduction by John M. Robson, London: Penguin Books.

Mill, John Stuart (1965), *Principles of Political Economy, with some of their Applications to Social Philosophy*, Volumes II and III of the *Collected Works of John Stuart Mill*, ed. J.M. Robson, Toronto: University of Toronto Press.

Mineka, Francis E. (1944), *The Dissidence of Dissent*, Chapel Hill: University of North Carolina Press.

Oser, Jacob (1970), *The Evolution of Economic Thought*, 2nd ed., New York: Harcourt, Brace & World.

Pujol, Michèle A. (1992), *Feminism and Anti-Feminism in Early Economic Thought*, Aldershot: Edward Elgar.

Rossi, Alice S. (ed.) (1970), 'Introduction', John Stuart Mill and Harriet Taylor Mill, *Essays on Sex Equality*, Chicago: University of Chicago Press.

Soper, Kate (1983), 'New Introduction', John Stuart Mill, *The Subjection of Women*, and Harriet Taylor Mill, *The Enfranchisement of Women*, London: Virago.

Spender, Dale (1982), 'Harriet Taylor (1807–1858)', *Women of Ideas (And What Men Have Done to Them)*, London: Pandora.

Taylor, Harriet (1832/1970), 'Early Essay on Marriage and Divorce', in Alice S. Rossi (ed.), *Essays on Sex Equality*, 84–7, Chicago: University of Chicago Press.

Taylor, Harriet (1851/1970), 'Enfranchisement of Women', in Alice S. Rossi (ed.), *Essays on Sex Equality*, 89–121, Chicago: University of Chicago Press.

Taylor Mill, Harriet (1983), *Enfranchisement of Women*, in Kate Soper (1983).

Thompson, William (1825/1970), *Appeal of One Half of the Human Race, Women, Against the Pretensions of the Other Half, Men, To Retain Them in Political, and Thence in Civil and Domestic, Slavery, in reply to a paragraph of Mr Mill's celebrated "Article on Government"*, New York: B. Franklin.

7. Barbara Bodichon and the women of Langham Place

William D. Sockwell

7.1 INTRODUCTION

No story of women in economics could be complete without exploring the pioneering role of Barbara Bodichon and the women at Langham Place. While they wrote about economic issues, their major importance was in initiating in Britain during the 1850s and 1860s a movement to gain economic independence for women. This group played a significant role in agitating for women's property and marriage rights, in pushing for more and better-quality education for women, and in breaking down barriers in the workplace and helping women find jobs, and they were among the earliest promoters of suffrage for women.

It is not possible, in one chapter, to do justice to the myriad of activities of the Langham Place group, so this chapter is necessarily selective. It concentrates on the early years of the movement and in particular Barbara Bodichon, who was the inspirational, if not always actual, leader of the group. Particular attention is afforded to *A Brief Summary* and *Women and Work* (1857), the latter of which is her major written contribution to economics. Other women and their activities are mentioned, principally to give some indication of the breadth of their activities, though the discussion is necessarily brief. While the two subjects are clearly intertwined, most attention is devoted to activities geared towards giving women economic rather than political independence.

7.2 BARBARA BODICHON: EARLY LIFE AND ACCOMPLISHMENTS

Barbara Bodichon (1827–91) had an early life that was anything but conventional.[1] Bodichon was the eldest daughter of the common law marriage of Annie Longden and Benjamin Smith. Her mother died when she was seven

103

and responsibility for her upbringing fell to her father, Benjamin Smith, who was a wealthy landowner and member of Parliament from Norwich (1838–47) where he actively supported free trade and repeal of the Corn Laws. The Smith household 'was a centre for radical … politicians, visiting American abolitionists … and political refugees from Europe' (Matthews, 1983, 90).

Benjamin Smith had an abiding interest in education. In 1818, he collaborated with Henry Brougham, James Mill and others to set up the infant school at Brewer's Green, which was the first infant school in London and was patterned on Robert Owen's infant school at New Lanark.[2] When many of the original subscribers gave up with the infant school, Benjamin Smith built a new building at Vincent Square and until 1839 paid the salary of the teacher, James Buchanan. It was said that many of the original participants lost interest in the project because of the strange methods of Buchanan. Smith, however, had so much confidence in him that he not only continued to pay his salary, but also sent his children to school there, and had Buchanan serve as their tutor, despite the fact that many of the children attending were from the poorest classes (Herstein, 1985, 11–14; Stewart and McCann, 1967, 245–54).[3] Stewart and McCann note (1967, 254) that later in life, when Barbara Bodichon started her own school (see below), 'Buchanan's spirit pervaded the school of his former pupil.'

Another unusual aspect of Bodichon's upbringing was that her father always treated his daughter and sons equally. When she turned 21 her father gave her an income of £300 a year; 12 years later, she was receiving £1000 a year. As Herstein notes, this financial independence allowed her a certain 'liberty and eccentricity' that was certainly not available to most women of the period (1985, 21).

At age 22, she used her financial independence to attend the newly formed Bedford College for women. Bedford was a non-sectarian alternative to the only other college for women, Queen's College. Both were aimed primarily at providing a better education for governesses. Despite the few facilities and generally low standards, spirits were high, since women were excited to attend any college. At Bedford women were even involved in the management of the college – something almost unheard of at the time. Bodichon attended Bedford with her aunt, Julia Smith, who was a friend of Mrs Reid, the founder of the college. Her aunt had also introduced her to Harriet Martineau, and Herstein suggests that it was Bodichon and a group of her friends that revolved around Martineau that gave the college its character (1985, 19). Bedford provided Bodichon with many contacts and helped her understand the importance of education for women.

Bodichon's work for women began in 1854. Her father gave her title to the infant school he had supported at Westminster Square, and she started her own school. Bodichon rented new quarters at Portman Hall, hired Elizabeth

Whitehead (later Malleson) as the first teacher and opened its doors on 6 November 1854. Bodichon's ideas about education were mainly influenced by her former tutor, James Buchanan, and by George Combe and William Ellis (Stewart and McCann, 1967, 315). She had read Combe's *Moral Philosophy* when she was only 17, had been influenced by his philosophy of health and had concluded that 'gaining knowledge is a moral duty' (Burton, 1949, 14–15).[4] She had met and become friends with William Ellis at social gatherings at the house of George Chapman, and she considered Ellis's Peckham school, which was just one of Ellis's Birkbeck Schools, to be the most advanced school in London. When opening her own school, Bodichon had Elizabeth Whitehead spend time at the Peckham school observing the methods of its master, William Shields (Burton, 1949, 50; Herstein, 1985, 60; Stewart and McCann, 1967, 315–16).[5]

The major distinguishing characteristics of the school were that it was coeducational, it mixed together different social classes, it was tolerant of different races and it had non-denominational religious teaching (Stewart and McCann, 1967, 311). Bodichon also strongly agreed with Buchanan in having no punishments, no uniform and no creed (Burton, 1949, 49). At first Bodichon, her friends and her relatives did much of the teaching (Stewart and McCann, 1967, 310). In addition to reading, writing and mathematics, lessons were given in English, French, drawing, physiology, music, health, and cleanliness and order (Burton, 1949, 51: Herstein, 1985, 63).

Bodichon was directly involved in the school for only about three years, but it continued to have her support during its entire ten-year life. During this time, in 1859, Bodichon provided written testimony concerning the deficiencies of education for middle-class women and girls. The next year, she presented a paper on the subject to the National Association for the Promotion of Social Sciences, which was printed in the *English Woman's Journal* later in the year (Herstein, 1985, 63). Her school and these later activities demonstrated the viability of coeducational schools and schools that mixed different races and social classes, and the importance of giving women a voice in their education. This laid the groundwork for the more inclusive public system that was created in 1870.

7.3   BODICHON'S *BRIEF SUMMARY* AND *WOMEN AND WORK*

In 1854 Bodichon wrote a pamphlet, *A Brief Summary, in Plain Language, of the Most Important Laws Concerning Women*, that created quite a sensation. This pamphlet was a short and direct explanation of the legal status of women in England, primarily with respect to property and marriage. At that time single women had the same property rights and paid the same taxes as men, but had fewer inheritance rights and could not vote for members of Parliament. Married women, however, were virtually without property rights. A husband had absolute legal control over all his wife's property and earnings. As Bodichon notes,

> A man and wife are one person in law; the wife loses all her rights as a single women, and her existence is entirely absorbed in that of her husband. He is civilly responsible for her acts; she lives under his protection or cover, and her condition is called coverture.
>
> A women's body belongs to her husband; she is in his custody and he can enforce his right by a writ of *habeas corpus*. (Bodichon, 1854, 25)

To make matters worse, divorce could not be attained through legal means except by an Act of Parliament, in which the expenses were six to seven hundred pounds (Bodichon, 1854, 28). Obviously, divorces were only for the rich and even then they were rarely obtained. If the divorce was granted, the father maintained custody of the children.

Bodichon's solutions to women's legal problems were quite simple. All that was necessary was to erase the laws that were restraining women. In making these arguments in her *Brief Summary*, she 'clearly reflect[s] a strong belief in an individualistic, noninterventionist mode of government' (Herstein, 1985, 73). She asserts:

> Philosophical thinkers have generally come to the conclusion that the tendency of progress is gradually to dispense with law – that is to say, as each individual man becomes unto himself a law, less external restraint is necessary. And certainly the most urgently needed reforms are simple erasures from the statute book. Women, more than any other members of the community, suffer from over-legislation. (Bodichon, 1854, 30–31)

She continues:

> A woman of twenty-one becomes an independent human creature … But if she unites herself to a man, the law immediately steps in, and she finds herself legislated for, and her condition of life suddenly and entirely changed. … She is again considered as an infant – she is again under '*reasonable restraint*' – she loses her separate existence … she is absorbed, and can hold nothing of herself, she has no legal right to any property; not even her clothes, books, and household goods are her own, and any money which she earns can be robbed from her legally by her husband. (Bodichon, 1854, 31)

Bodichon carefully notes that not all or perhaps even very many men act as brutishly as the law might allow, but she rejected that rationale as a justification for the existing laws:

It is always said, even by those who support the existing law, that it is in fact never acted upon by men of good feeling. That is true; but the very admission condemns the law, and it is not right that the good feeling of men should be all that a woman can look to for simple justice. (Bodichon, 1854, 31)

J.S. Mill made similar statements in *The Subjection of Women* (1869):

I readily admit ... that numbers of married people even under the present law... live in the spirit of a just law of equality. ... But persons even of considerable moral worth, unless they are also thinkers, are very ready to believe that laws or practices, the evils of which they have not experienced, do not produce any evils ... and that it is wrong to object to them. It would, however, be a great mistake in such married people to suppose ... that the same is the case with all other married couples. To suppose this, would be to show equal ignorance of human nature and fact. The less fit a man is for the possession of power ... the more does he ... exact its legal rights to the utmost point which custom ... will tolerate. ... What is more; in the most naturally brutal and uneducated part of the lower classes, the legal slavery of women ... causes them to feel a sort of disrespect and contempt towards their own wife which they do not feel towards any other ... human being. (Mill, 1869, 161–2)

Elsewhere Mill compared the position of the wife to that of Greek and Roman slaves. He noted that there were many instances of good masters in which the slave would willingly die for them. On the other hand, many were known to treat their slaves cruelly. He asks:

Who doubts that there may be great goodness, and great happiness, and great affection, under the absolute government of a good man? Meanwhile, laws and institutions require to be adapted, not to good men, but to bad. (Mill, 1869, 150–51)

Consistent with Mill's analysis, Bodichon argued that the same laws regarding property rights apply to both men and women.

Bodichon expressed concern about the plight of women and their loss of identity at the young age of 22 when she read with great interest John Stuart Mill's *Principles of Political Economy* (1965). She was critical of him for neglecting the laws concerning women. As Lacey (1987, 4) notes: 'She had been disappointed that "one who carries so much weight" failed to mention "the injustice of their [men's] laws to women and the absurdity of the present Laws of Marriage and Divorce."' Her *Brief Summary* was meant to rectify that inadequacy. She hoped that, if she pointed out the injustices, the outrage of the general public might elicit some change.

Bodichon was certainly not the first to call attention to the legal problems of married women. Caroline Norton, for example, gained notoriety in the 1830s by writing numerous passionate pamphlets publicizing her problems in trying to retain profits from her books and custody of her children after she had separated from her husband (Strachey, 1928, 34–40). Nevertheless, there was no organized movement for change until Bodichon organized the Married Women's Property Committee in December 1855. The committee collected over 24 000 signatures to a petition asking for property rights for married women, with Bodichon collecting 3000 signatures. With the help of the Law Amendment Society, a bill was presented in Parliament in 1857 that eventually led to the passage of the Marriage and Divorce Bills of 1857 and 1858. These bills did not give Bodichon and her committee all they wanted, but they made divorce more accessible and gave women the right to separate with their children and the right to keep any future earnings or inheritance (Strachey, 1928, 73–6; Burton, 1949, 66–71; Herstein, 1985, 78–93). It would be another 36 years 'before the demands of the original 1857 Married Women's Property Bill were met in full' (Lacey, 1987, 5). But 'it may be said that all the subsequent Married Women's Property Acts were based on Barbara's petition and *Brief Summary*' (Matthews, 1983, 97).

Bodichon next turned to women's problems in the workplace, writing her most important pamphlet concerning economics, *Women and Work* (1857).[6] Despite being poorly arranged, the essay raised important points and presented one of the earliest accounts of the overcrowding theory of women's pay.[7]

Women's status in the workplace had been the subject of some debate since at least the early 1850s: The 1851 census revealed that 'the number of females of marriageable age, in Great Britain, will always exceed the number of males of the same age to the extent of half a million' (Lacey, 1987, 10; Parkes, 1860b, 177), which suggested that a significant number of women would be forced into the workplace. For those unmarried as well as those married women who were forced into the workplace, the working conditions were grim, as noted by several Commissions. Bodichon was one of the first actively to promote change, and *Women and Work* was the first part of her campaign.

Bodichon suggested that 'Women want work both for the health of their minds and bodies. They want it often because they must eat and because they have children and others dependent on them – *for all the reasons that men want work*' (1857, 63). Yet she indicated that many positions were closed to women because they were poorly trained and unskilled. Parents, she argued, should see that their daughters were educated and trained equally with men (1857, 64).

Many parents had beliefs that led them not to adequately provide for their daughters' training. First, Bodichon suggested that too many parents simply thought that their daughters would be provided for when they married. She listed a number of problems with this belief: a woman 'will make a better wife' after serious training both because she will be able to enhance house-hold income and because she will possess what would be referred to today as improved self-worth; a daughter may never marry; she may take a long time to find a husband; her husband may die or abandon her, leaving her with dependent children; her husband may be poor, so that the family needs extra income. Bodichon noted that for 'women at the age of twenty and upwards, forty-three out of the hundred in England and Wales are unmarried' (1857, 40).[8]

She also argued that it was wrong to think of women as less feminine if they worked:

> To think a woman is more feminine because she is frivolous, ignorant, weak, and sickly is absurd. ... If men think they shall lose anything charming by not having ignorant, dependent women about them, they are quite wrong. The vivacity of women will not be injured by their serious work.
> None play so heartily as those who work heartily. (Bodichon, 1857, 44)

Still another problem was the common prejudice against women working for money.[9] Bodichon warned against the belief that only women of the lower classes worked for money and that all others should work for nothing, primarily for charities. She wrote:

> It would be well if all should part with what they make, or what they do well for money; they will then know that some really want what they produce ... and you gain a power of sending a child to school, of buying a good book to lend to the ignorant, of sending a sick person to a good climate, etc. We may give this power up to another whom we consider can use it better than we, but money is a power which we have not the right to lightly reject. It is a responsibility which we must accept. (1857, 62)

Another fallacy she noted was the common belief that ladies should not take the bread out of the mouths of the poor working man or woman by selling in their market. She refutes this fallacy in the best tradition of Say's Law: supply creates it own demand:

> The riches and material well-being of the country consist in the quantity of stuff in the country to eat and wear, houses to live in, books to read ... etc. Anyone who puts more of any of these things into the country, adds to its riches and happiness. The more of these things, the easier it is for all to get. Do not think of money until you see this fact. This is why we bless steam-engines; this is why we would bless women. Steam-engines did at first take the bread out of a few mouths, but how many thousands have they fed for one they have starved! (Bodichon, 1857, 62–3)

This argument, along with liberal economic arguments that suggested that barriers to employment should be removed, gave women powerful persuasive tools to open the job market. Caine (1992, 33) suggests that 'Liberal economic arguments were continually used to argue against the barriers women faced in employment and against any attempt to restrict their hours or conditions.' She also cites Millicent Fawcett, who would later argue 'that the demand for the removal of the barrier that excluded women from higher education was only a "phase of the free trade argument"'.

The exclusion of women from jobs and education created a situation in which women were poorly trained for the workforce, but were then thrust into it by necessity or by their own desires. Because they were poorly trained and because of societal prejudice, few jobs were open to women and competition for these jobs was intense. Naturally, this caused the wages in those occupations to be abysmally low. As Bodichon put it:

> there are fewer paths open to [women], and these are choke full. We are sick at heart at the cries that have been raised about distressed needlewomen, and decayed gentlewomen, and broken-down governesses. ... There is no way of aiding governesses or needlewomen but by opening more ways of gaining livelihoods for women. It is the most efficacious way of preventing prostitution. ... At present the language practically held by modern society to destitute women may be resolved into Marry – Stitch – Die – or do worse. (Bodichon, 1857, 44)

A final fallacy that Bodichon noted was that of not placing a high enough value on women's work in the home.

> Women who act as housekeepers, nurses, and instructors of their children, often do as much for the support of the household as their husbands; and it is very unfair for men to speak of supporting a wife and children when such is the case. When a woman gives up a profitable employment to be governess to her own family, she earns her right to live. (Bodichon, 1857, 41)

This was an instance in which patriarchal attitudes, which considered women as dependants and did not recognize the value of their contribution to the household, actually caused women who stayed at home to be less productive than they might have been. Bodichon argued that even if women stayed at home they should be educated so they would be a more satisfied and productive member of the household. Herstein suggests (1985, 128):

> By recognizing the monetary value of the duties of wife and mother, she redefines their status as nonworkers, making the first written declaration that women's traditional role is work with a quantifiable market value of economic significance within the family financial unit.[10]

In the American edition of *Women and Work* (1859), Bodichon was somewhat more optimistic about the prospects for women in the workplace.[11] She noted that, 'in the United States the want of professional training for women is almost as much felt as in England', but added that there is a 'greater ease in gaining a livelihood' and some better pay, particularly in the teaching profession. 'But,' she noted, 'all these teachers do not teach well, or teach because it is the profession they like best, they are teachers because, in America as in England, teaching is almost the only means of gaining bread, open to women.' In fact, she argued, 'at this present time, I believe there is in America as strong a public opinion against women working for a livelihood as in England'. Nevertheless, she expressed greater hope for change in America:

> evils do not go on for ever dragging their slow length as in England. ... The ideas of human liberty and justice are too widely spread in America for any state of things in direct opposition to these principles, to endure for ever. We believe Europe will never move forward on this question until America goes ahead and clears the way. (Bodichon, 1859, 18, 20)[12]

A slightly different case was one in which an occupation was open to women, but they were paid a lower wage for equal work. Both Mill and Bodichon believed that this condition was again at least partly the result of the oversupply of women willing to work. In the American edition of *Women and Work*, Bodichon reported a case in which women working in the Philadelphia mint received half or less than half of the wages men earned for the same work. She cited this as evidence of the 'lamentable amount of competition among women, even in the United States, for any work which is open to them' (1859, 17). Mill agreed with this notion of oversupply. He wrote:

> In occupations in which employers take full advantage of competition, the low wages of women as compared with the ordinary earnings of men, are a proof that the employments are overstocked: that although so much smaller a number of women, than of men, support themselves by wages, the occupations which law and usage make accessible to them are comparatively so few, that the field of their employment is still more overcrowded. It must be observed, that as matters now stand, a sufficient degree of overcrowding may depress the wages of women to a much lower minimum than those of men. (Mill, 1965, 395)

Economic theory leads us to suspect that, if women were being paid less for equal work, employers might be able to earn additional profits by continually hiring women at cheaper wages until the wages of men and women were equal. Mill's answer to this was

> when the efficiency is equal, but the pay unequal, the only explanation that can be given is custom; grounded either in a prejudice, or in the present constitution of society, which, making almost every woman, socially speaking, an appendage of some man, enables men to take systematically the lion's share of whatever belongs to both. (Mill, 1965, 395)

Strachey (1928, 226) suggests that another reason women were paid less during this period was that they were relatively docile and glad to have a job, any job, no matter what the pay. Nevertheless, one would still expect that, as prejudice abated and customs changed, employers would tend to hire more and more women or be able to hire better quality women at the same wage. According to Strachey this is precisely what happened in many fields. She quotes (227–8) an official of the Post Office who openly declared in 1871: 'We get a better class of women for the same pay ... they are more patient under routine, less liable to combine, and leave often on marriage when their pay would be increasing.'

Lown (1990, 213) notes still another reason why women's wages remained lower than those of men in equivalent positions: 'The spread of a market economy based increasingly on individual wage labour instead of household production fuelled male fears of competition from women and a loss of patriarchal status.' She suggests that capitalists, in particular, were faced with a conflict. On the one hand, to improve profits they wanted to hire cheap female labour, but this might tend to bid up wages and give women greater independence. On the other hand, they generally approved of patriarchal familial relationships and wanted to make sure these were maintained. Employers resolved this conflict by establishing two career paths, with women not eligible for positions of authority or high wages. Thus many mill owners were able to fight for women's right to work, while maintaining low wages. In addition, many mill owners favoured laissez-faire on the part of the government, but insisted that it was their duty to look out for the welfare of the women workers.

Suffice it to say that there were many complex and interrelated reasons for many jobs being closed to women and most others paying abysmally low wages. Bodichon and the Langham Place circle sought to explode the fallacies in arguments limiting women's work potential. Throughout *Women and Work*, Bodichon noted numerous occupations women could profitably and easily pursue with the proper training. Aiding women in this task turned out to be a major task of Bodichon and the women at Langham Place in the years ahead. While Bodichon was certainly an inspirational leader in all their activities, she was not always in the forefront.[13] The next section details some of the other activities that Bodichon and the others at Langham Place were involved in during the 1850s and 1860s.

7.4   THE WOMEN OF LANGHAM PLACE

Before the 1850s, there were certainly individuals who wrote about economic issues concerning women. As noted previously, however, the Married Women's Property Committee was probably the first *formally* organized move-ment that actively worked to improve the status of women. For that reason it is sometimes referred to as the 'beginning of the Women's Movement' (Burton, 1949, 66; Herstein, 1985, 55; Strachey, 1928, 64, 71; Folbre, 1994, 148). The activities of the Committee and other interested women gradually 'coalesced around the office of the [*English Woman's*] *Journal*', which was located at Langham Place (Herstein, 1985, 134).[14] The women who worked at Langham Place should be recognized as the first group in England actively to promote women's issues. They wrote about reform, but their major legacy was the agencies they created to seek change.

The women at Langham Place focused their efforts on activities that would enhance the independence of women. Of major importance was securing educational opportunities and improving job opportunities for women. The major outlet for their views was the newly formed *English Woman's Journal*. The *Journal* was started by Barbara Bodichon and her friend, Bessie Rayner Parkes (1829–1925) and began publication in 1858.[15] By this time Bodichon was spending six months of every year in Algeria, so she provided seed money and inspiration, while Parkes (Madame Belloc) ran the day-to-day operations and was joint editor with Mary Hays (Herstein, 1985, 126, 134–5; Parkes, 1864, 218). The *Journal* ceased publication in 1864, but Emily Davies, who had become its editor in 1862, carried on the work when she became editor of the new *Victoria Magazine* in 1865 (Herstein, 1985, 144).

For a short time the *Journal* was very successful as the major outlet for feminist writings. It should be noted, however, that, as might be expected, the women of Langham Place had many critics. They had to support 'each other in the face of jibes and taunts from the press and public' and were subject to ridicule and mockery. Though 'their "reputations" were besmirched and they were called strong-minded *and* foolish, they decided "duty was more important than reputation"' (Strachey, 1928, 94, quoted by Spender, 1983b, 413).

It should also be noted that, despite the hostility of some critics, the feminist writings in the *English Woman's Journal*, or the writings of the Langham Place group in general, were certainly not radical by today's stand-ards. Burton notes (1949, 102) that, as editor, Bessie Parkes tried hard not to cause offence, which made the *Journal* dull to some. Even Barbara Bodichon, who was probably the most radical of the group, 'unconsciously accepted the contemporary image of the feminine nature' (Herstein, 1985, 129). In *Women and Work* she clearly differentiated between men and women when she discussed appropriate jobs for women. She concluded by suggesting women will naturally prefer some work to others. She indicated that 'it is not likely' that many women will enter politics, go to sea or become barristers:

women will rather prefer those nobler works which have in them something congenial to their moral natures. Perhaps we may say that women will only enter those professions which are ... consistent with the highest moral development of humanity. ... The arts, the sciences, commerce, and the education of the young in all its branches – these will most strongly attract them. (Bodichon, 1857, 64)

Soon after the *Journal* was launched, women began to come by its offices to inquire about jobs at the *Journal* or leads for jobs elsewhere. To meet the demands for jobs, the women at Langham Place founded the first employment bureau. Bessie Parkes first started a simple employment registry for women, but Jessie Boucherett (1825–1905) soon took over the leadership of this activity and, along with Adelaide Anne Proctor and Barbara Bodichon, formed the Society for the Promotion of the Employment of Women in 1859.[16] One of its first successes was in training women in the printing profession, which was greatly facilitated by Emily Faithfull (1835–95) who, in addition to helping form the Society and serving as its secretary, founded the Victoria Printing Press in 1860, which printed the *English Woman's Journal* as well as training women compositors and helping place them in other printing jobs.

Other activities started by the Society included a law engrossing office that trained women to copy legal documents. This office was begun by Maria Rye (1829–1903), who had been the secretary to the Committee formed to promote the Married Women's Property Bill and who was a member of the Society for Promoting the Employment of Women. In addition, Rye helped Isa Craig (1831–1903) form a Telegraph School to teach women how to work in that emerging field. In 1860, the Langham Place group opened a business school for young women to help them attain the training necessary for many business-related jobs that had been closed to them. The Employment Society and its related affiliates were successful at finding many other jobs for women and eventually opened branch offices across England. In 1861, Maria Rye and Janet Lewin even founded the Female Middle Class Emigration Society to give women information about emigration and to encourage them to consider it as an option if suitable work were not available. 'For the next eight years [Rye] helped countless women settle in Australia, New Zealand and Canada' (Uglow, 1982, 404).

Many of the women at Langham Place were also members of the National Association for the Promotion of Social Science, which was founded in 1857 by Henry Brougham. This society 'quickly became the mainspring of the Humanitarian movement' in England (Strachey, 1928, 87). One of its novelties was that from the start it admitted women and allowed them to make speeches and to participate in the meetings. 'The formation of this body... gave a tremendous impetus to the activities of public-spirited women' (Strachey, 1928, 87). Isa Craig became the assistant secretary of the Association, and the women at Langham Place were frequently able to find patrons for their projects among its members or at least a friendly forum in which to present their ideas.

The National Association was particularly important as an advocate of middle-class education. Throughout the 1850s there was a growing awareness of the importance of educating both the middle and lower classes. The National Association 'gave the initial impetus to, and provided a forum for, the advocates of an organized middle-class education' (Stewart and McCann, 1967, 278). The Langham Place group had also begun to devote much of its attention to education for middle-class *girls*. The National Association also 'had links with [this] contemporary and parallel agitation for raising the status and improving the educational provision for women' (Stewart and McCann, 1967, 278). Thus, when Bodichon wrote 'Middle-Class Schools for Girls' (1860) it was first presented to the National Association for the Promotion of Social Sciences before being reprinted in the *English Woman's Journal* (1860); this was to become a frequent pattern.

Bodichon advocated non-secular private schools for children whose parents could afford them, but felt there were many problems with existing schools of this type. She called for investigations of schools to see what was being taught, what materials were being used, and so forth. After visiting several private schools she felt that, while there were problems with the system of government aid to education and with the National and British schools, other existing private schools were 'inferior in every respect to the education given in the National and British Schools' (1860, 75). She did note exceptions, such as 'the Birkbeck Schools established by Mr. William Ellis [which] admirably supply the want as far as they go'. The main problem was that 'they are not specially for girls' and this was what the country was most in need of (1860, 77); 'The fact that most of the girls will probably have to work during some years for their own livelihood must not be lost sight of.' For that reason she felt that girls should be taught the 'advantages and disadvantages of different employments for women ... and the principles of social and political economy', as well as 'independent habits, quickness to help themselves in emergencies, and an intimate acquaintance with the countries they may visit' so they might be prepared to be emigrants (1860, 82).

Bodichon suggested the most needed changes to enhance education for middle-class girls were greater endowments and better training for the headmistresses of the private schools that taught middle-class girls. Furthermore, she suggested that the Cambridge examination system be opened up for non-students of Cambridge to ensure that all students, and especially prospective teachers, be adequately qualified. She also suggested that these schools would need to be supported by charity, should be open to inspection and should be affiliated to the Queen's College 'and similar London societies' (1860, 78–80, 83).

Once parents realized there was a good probability that their daughters might work at some point in their life, the next step was to emphasize that if they were better educated they would have more job opportunities. As had Bodichon, others working at Langham Place emphasized this connection between work and education. Parkes wrote four articles in 1859 and 1860 that emphasized the wider job market for educated women and discussed various job opportunities. She conceded that most women might eventually marry, but 'the miseries which befall a penniless woman are so great, that if the opposing chances were but as one in a hundred, the parent should provide against it' (1859a, 147). She indicated that many women were educated, but that their education was inferior to that of men. She suggested (1859a, 149) that fathers should feel morally bound to provide *adequate* training for their daughters, attain enough savings to provide for them during hard times, or provide them with insurance in case of their death.

Her later articles (1859b, 1860a, 1860b) on this subject recommended various occupations that might be most suitable for women. She suggested that women might be most profitably employed in social institutions, including 'Sanitary [hospitals], Educational, Reformatory, and Penal' (1859b, 151). She also felt that mature women might be able to provide superintendence in workhouses or factories or, if nothing else, might consider emigration (1859b, 155–60). One article focused on occupations suitable for educated women of the middle class; a later article (1860b, 184), written with the knowledge gained from the results of the Langham Place employment bureau, concluded that:

> for young people living at home with their parents, and for single women not possessing a high stamp of education and having only themselves to support ... the semi-mechanical arts – such as that of working the telegraph, printing, law-copying, managing sewing-machines, etc. are profitable, and will supply with bread and meat and clothes; and that it is highly desirable to extend and encourage such occupation in every way.

Again, the conservative nature of the recommendations can be noted. The women at Langham Place professed that certain occupations were more suitable for women and only pressed for those to be opened, rather than taking the more radical position that all occupations should be open to women.

Prior to the 1860s there were very few colleges for women. The ones that did exist, such as Queen's College and Bedford College, which were created in 1848 and 1849, respectively, were primarily geared towards training women to be governesses or teachers of children (Strachey, 1928, 124–6; Levine, 1987, 32–4). Many of the women that attended were poorly prepared for college, so the standards and expectations were low. By the 1860s the women of Langham Place came to believe that the time was right to press for more and better higher education for women. Many of them also joined in 1865 the Kensington Society, whose primary goal was to open education to women (Spender, 1983b, 417).

Although many of the women of Langham Place were involved, 'in all matters relating to education the chief arbiter of tactics and the chief organiser of campaigns soon came to be Emily Davies' (Strachey, 1928, 131). In 1862, Davies (1830–1921) helped form and became secretary of a committee to work for allowing girls to take the admission exams for Oxford and Cambridge. Cambridge allowed 91 women to take a trial exam in 1862. The women reportedly 'did fairly well in some subjects, but failed wholesale in arithmetic' (Strachey, 1928, 133; also see Stephen, 1933, 9; Levine, 1987, 35–6).

In 1864, Davies succeeded in getting the Schools Enquiry Commission to include girls' education in their study. Their 1868 report confirmed the 'deplorable state of female education', but it did not recommend any extreme changes (Strachey, 1928, 138). The report was still important, because it called attention to the plight of female education. Stephen notes (1933, 10):

> the Commission's report on girls' education was most fruitful and far-reaching in its results, supplying a powerful stimulus to the movement which brought about the great reformation in girls' schools, without which the work of the women's Colleges could not have been accomplished.

As a result of her involvement in girls' education, Davies was asked to testify before the Schools Enquiry Commission. This brought her 'into contact with a number of schoolmistresses, who, she found, had been working in isolation, and were anxious for opportunities of co-operation and exchange of ideas with other women teachers'. Davies organized the London Schoolmistresses' Association for them and was later rewarded when many of these women became involved in Davies's most important project, Girton College (Stephen, 1933, 10).

It was Davies's meetings with the schoolmistresses that confirmed her idea that higher education was sorely needed for women. The biggest problems facing women were that they were poorly prepared for college, and the colleges that admitted women did not rigorously prepare them to take subsequent exams. Davies resolved to solve these problems by starting her own college. The new college would be rigorous enough for women to compete with men on the exams and for future schoolmistresses to have the knowledge to teach future generations of scholars.

Once again, it should be noted that the mainstream women's movement tried not to upset the status quo any more than necessary and was thus quite conservative in many ways. As noted previously, when agitating for more job opportunities for women they believed that women were more suited for certain types of jobs, so they did not encourage women to pursue a number of occupations. Davies was certainly very concerned that her college might be perceived as being too revolutionary. To conciliate the public she wrote that, in addition to the expected subjects, periodic examinations would be given in 'Modern Languages, Music, Drawing, and other subjects which usually form part of the education of an English lady' (Stephen, 1933, 14). As further evidence of her conservative inclination (or at least her inclination to appease a conservative society), when the college's executive committee was formed in 1867 she asked that Barbara Bodichon, who was considered to be the most radical of the Langham Place women, not be a part of the committee even though she was working closely with Davies and had agreed to contribute the largest sum of money to the project (Stephen, 1933, 12–19).[17] Also, in 1869, Davies rented the Benslow House in Hitchin as the original site of the new college; this site, which was several miles outside Cambridge and safe from the temptations of male students, was chosen to mollify potential critics.[18] To protect the reputation of the students and the college, she also required the women to be chaperoned at all times.

Even so, Davies would settle for nothing less than ensuring that women received as rigorous an education as men and that women took the same set of college exams as men. She resisted attempts to establish separate exams for women college students, assuming that women could not be perceived as equal until they met the same standards as men.[19] She insisted that her students ready themselves for the Cambridge Tripos examinations. When her first three students were ready to take these exams in 1872, Cambridge would not agree to let them sit for the exams. Davies, however, persuaded several examiners to grade them privately and all three women passed. Burton maintains that it was Davies's insistence that women sit for the Cambridge Tripos that

> set Girton apart from all previous foundations for higher education of women, foundations like Queen's College and Bedford College, and the contemporary Newnham. And it was this which gave Girton the right to claim for itself the title of the first University College for women. By insisting that girls were quite capable of taking the same University courses as men, Emily achieved a far earlier admittance of women to the Universities than would otherwise have been the case. (Burton, 1949, 175)

Women continued to gain more access to higher education, but progress was slow. Until 1880, females were not allowed to take the exams on equal footing with men; this changed after one of the Girton women scored the equivalent of Eighth Wrangler on the Maths Tripos, which had traditionally been the weakest subject for the women (Stephen, 1933, 55–6, 74–5). They were not admitted to Cambridge on equal status with men, however, until 1947 (Burton, 1949, 175). Nevertheless, the work of the women at Langham Place was instrumental in setting in motion the process of gaining equal access for women to higher education.

Economics and politics cannot be separated fully but, while Bodichon and her colleagues contributed in significant ways to the women's suffrage movement, neither space nor focus permits a full discussion of the contributions or the relationships between the suffrage movement and the other activities of these women. Similarly, many women other than the ones mentioned above participated in the activities of the Langham Place group, but space does not permit a full discussion of their contributions. Lacey (1987) cites writer and social reformer Frances Power Cobbe (1822–1904), Elizabeth Blackwell (1821–1910), the first women to gain a medical degree in the United States, and Elizabeth Garrett (1836–1917), who was the only woman member of the British Medical Association from 1873 to 1892, as other major members of the group. While others might be mentioned, the important point is that Barbara Bodichon's Married Women's Property Committee spawned a women's movement encompassing a large network of women who were involved in numerous different activities. Strachey (1928, 94) suggests they 'dealt with everything which could be connected with the Women's Movement with a moderation, a seriousness, and tact which deserved the utmost praise'. Levine (1987, 15) maintains that the

> feminism of these women was more of a life-style than merely a form of organized political activism. ... Feminists in all areas of the country not only knew of but chose to mix socially with one another. Their diaries and letters tell of teas and soirees and at-homes, as well as close sustained friendships.

7.5   CONCLUSION

Barbara Bodichon and her cohorts based their economic arguments and justified their activities principally on the simple principles of laissez-faire, Say's Law, and the simple equitable concept that females should be able to own and dispose of property to the same extent that males could.[20] In this they were very comfortable with the ideas of the classical economists, such as John Stuart Mill, in whose Parliamentary election they campaigned vigorously.[21] Bodichon best exemplified this view in *Women and Work*, arguing that, if only the impediments preventing women from working and attaining an education could be removed, women and society would be enhanced as productivity and output increased. Along with Mill, she developed the notion of overcrowding of women, arguing that there was a surplus of women workers that drove down their wages, but only because of the laws, rules and customs that restricted women's entry into the workforce. Consistent with these views, she and her colleagues concentrated on ensuring that women were able to own property and had access to better education and thus more jobs.

As noted, the work of this network is often considered to be the starting-point of the Women's Movement in England, but the network was more than a starting-point. The close working relationships of these women allowed them to sustain their momentum over a number of years. Herstein (1985, 145) maintains, 'the Langhamites remained a loosely connected circle for decades [after the 1860s], meeting one another in a variety of new feminist committees, each with roots in Bodichon's Married Women's Property Committee of 1856'. Although their later activities were increasingly centred around obtaining the vote for women, they continued to write about and participate in activities designed to promote economic independence for women; in doing so, they created a legacy that survives even today.

NOTES

1. Her unconventional life has been well documented. The most extensive treatments, and the ones from which this chapter are mostly drawn, are in Herstein (1985) and Burton (1949).
2. For a discussion of this early infant school, see Stewart and McCann (1967, 241–67). It should also be noted that the Smith family had a history of supporting educational experiments. Benjamin's father, William, had joined Henry Brougham in helping establish the Royal Lancasterian Institution in 1808 (Herstein, 1985, 10).
3. Stewart and McCann note that part of the strangeness of Buchanan was due to his association with the New Church and Swedenborgian principles. They suggest that it is possible that Buchanan was introduced to Swedenborgian principles by Benjamin Smith.
4. Stewart and McCann (1967, 280) consider Combe to be the 'father figure' of the progressive Scottish educational renaissance of the 1830s and 1840s. Among other things, he is noted as an advocate of equal educational opportunity for women.
5. For more information about William Ellis and the Birkbeck Schools, see Sockwell (forthcoming).
6. *Women and Work* first appeared on 7 February 1857 in the *Waverly Journal*. It was reprinted as a pamphlet in April 1857 (Herstein, 1985, 125–6). For further discussion of the conditions of women in the workplace and for statistics on the percentages of women in various occupations, see Frader (1987, 309–34).
7. Pujol notes (1992, 94) that, although F.Y. Edgeworth is frequently given credit for developing the overcrowding theory of women's pay, credit should go to J.S. Mill (1848), Barbara Bodichon (1857) and Millicent Garrett Fawcett (1892, 1918).
8. More extensive statistics from the 1851 census that buttressed Bodichon's claims regarding the number of women who needed jobs are provided by Parkes (1860b, 174–9).
9. Lown notes that the uncertainties created by the economic transformations due to industrialization led many to believe that women should not compete with men for jobs and therefore should not perform paid work unless they were destitute. This question of whether women should engage in work for pay came to be known as the 'Woman Question' (Lown, 1990, 1–2).

10. Of course, acknowledging and quantifying the value of women's work in the home is still a subject that economists are grappling with. Some attempts are being made to add the value of housework to the gross domestic product, but this work is far from complete.
11. The American edition of *Women and Work* is similar to the British edition, but it was shortened, better arranged, and some was material added or altered to make it more relevant to the American readership.
12. Offen (1987, 351–2) asserts that 'the most successful initial efforts to organize took place ... in the United States', but that soon after many equivalent organizations sprang up in Western Europe and were mostly led by 'upper middle-class women who were well connected to the governing male elites. The epitome of such a feminist activism blossomed in England'.
13. While Bodichon could not possibly have led all the activities, she was involved in a large number of them. Her efforts are quite remarkable considering that, after 1857, when she married Eugene Bodichon, she began spending half of each year in Algeria. Among her many talents, she was an accomplished painter who seemed to have no trouble selling her work. She used her time in Algeria to pursue her art. For an assessment of Bodichon as a painter, see Crabbe (1981, 311–13).
14. The offices of the *English Woman's Journal* were originally located at Cavendish Square, but moved to Langham Place in 1859 (Herstein, 1985, 140).
15. Parkes had been a long-time friend of Bodichon's. They created something of a sensation in 1850 when they took an extended unchaperoned trip together through Europe (Herstein, 1985, 56; Burton, 1949, 31). Obviously, both Parkes and Bodichon possessed a degree of independence that was unusual at the time. They almost bought the *Waverly Journal* in 1857 as an outlet for their views, but abandoned that idea to start their own journal.
16. Boucherett's experiences with the Employment Society also prompted her to write several articles advising women about job prospects. See, for example, Boucherett (1862).
17. In 1868, Bodichon gave £1000 of the £2000 collected for the college. She contributed another £10000 upon her death (Burton, 1949, 169, 180). Stephen notes (1933, 17) that Bodichon's 'influence proved, however, so valuable as to outweigh this consideration, and she joined the Committee formally in February, 1869'. Burton suggests that another reason Bodichon was left off the original committee was that she had been ill (1949, 165–6).
18. The college was moved to its permanent location at Girton, still two and a-half miles from Cambridge, in 1873.
19. The rival Newnham College was established in 1871 because of a disagreement with Henry Sidgwick, Millicent Fawcett and others over this issue and whether the college should be located in Cambridge (Stephen, 1933, 49–51; Strachey, 1928, 162–3).
20. This is a useful, albeit simplistic, way of viewing the economic content of the work of the women of Langham Place. It should be noted, however, that many modern writers stress the complexity and diversity of feminist writing. Caine suggests: 'Victorian domestic ideology, centring as it did on the notion of separate spheres for women and men, on the intellectual, moral, and emotional differences between men and women, and on moral superiority of women, was at least as important in the formulation of feminist thought as was liberal political and economic theory' (1992, 2–3).
21. Mill was held in high esteem by many feminists, mainly because he was the 'most eminent man publicly to identify himself with the cause'. His ideas about women were not, however, considered to be novel by most of the women and he was not regarded as their leader (Caine, 1992, 35).

REFERENCES

Bodichon, Barbara Leigh Smith (1854), *A Brief Summary, in Plain Language, of the Most Important Laws Concerning Women: Together with a Few Observations Thereon*; reprinted in Lacey (1987), 23–35.

Bodichon, Barbara Leigh Smith (1857), *Women and Work*; reprinted in Lacey (1987), 36–73.

Bodichon, Barbara Leigh Smith (1859), *Women and Work*, American edn, New York: C.S. Francis.

Bodichon, Barbara Leigh Smith (1860), 'Middle-Class Schools for Girls'; reprinted in Lacey (1987), 74–83.

Boucherett, Jessie (1862), 'On the Choice of a Business', *English Woman's Journal*; reprinted in Lacey (1987), 258–67.

Burton, Hester (1949), *Barbara Bodichon*, London: John Murray.

Caine, Barbara (1992), *Victorian Feminists*, Oxford: Oxford University Press.

Crabbe, John (1981), 'An Artist Divided: The forgotten talent of Barbara Bodichon, a very remarkable Victorian', *Apollo*, **113**, May, 311–13.

Fawcett, Millicent G. (1892), 'Mr. Sidney Webb's article on women's wages', *Economic Journal*, **2**, March, 173–6.

Fawcett, Millicent G. (1918), 'Equal pay for equal work', *Economic Journal*, **28**, March, 1–6.

Folbre, Nancy (1994), *Who Pays for the Kids?*, London and New York: Routledge.

Frader, Laura Levine (1987), 'Women in the Industrial Capitalist Economy', in R. Bridenthal, C. Koonz and S. Stuard (eds), *Becoming Visible: Women in European History*, 2nd edn, 309–34, Boston, MA: Houghton Mifflin.

Herstein, Sheila R. (1985), *A Mid-Victorian Feminist, Barbara Leigh Smith Bodichon*, New Haven, CT: Yale University Press.

Lacey, Candida Ann (ed.) (1987), *Barbara Leigh Smith Bodichon and the Langham Place Group*, New York and London: Routledge & Kegan Paul.

Levine, Philippa (1987), *Victorian Feminism, 1850–1900*, Tallahassee, FL: Florida State University Press.

Lown, Judy (1990), *Women and Industrialization: Gender and Work in 19th Century England*, Cambridge: Polity Press.

Matthews, Jacquie (1983), 'Barbara Bodichon: Integrity in Diversity', in Spender (1983a), 90–123.

Mill, John Stuart (1848), *Principles of Political Economy, with Some of their Applications to Social Philosophy*, London: J.W. Parker.

Mill, John Stuart (1869), *The Subjection of Women*; reprinted in Stefan Collini (ed.) (1989), *J.S. Mill: On Liberty and other writings*, 117–217, Cambridge: Cambridge University Press.

Mill, John Stuart (1965), *Principles of Political Economy*, Vol. II of the *Collected Works of John Stuart Mill*, ed. J.M. Robson, Toronto: University of Toronto Press.

Offen, Karen (1987), 'Liberty, Equality, and Justice for Women: The Theory and Practice of Feminism in Nineteenth-Century Europe', in R. Bridenthal, C. Koonz and S. Stuard (eds), *Becoming Visible: Women in European History*, 2nd edn, 335–74, Boston, MA: Houghton Mifflin.

Parkes, Bessie Rayner (1859a), 'The Market for Educated Female Labour'; reprinted in Lacey (1987), 141–9.

Parkes, Bessie Rayner (1859b), 'What Can Educated Women Do? (I)'; reprinted in Lacey (1987), 150–62.

Parkes, Bessie Rayner (1860a), 'What Can Educated Women Do? (II); reprinted in Lacey (1987), 163–73.

Parkes, Bessie Rayner (1860b), 'Statistics as to the Employment of the Female Population of Great Britain'; reprinted in Lacey (1987), 174–9.

Parkes, Bessie Rayner (1864), 'A Review of the Last Six Years'; reprinted in Lacey (1987), 215–22.

Pujol, Michèle A. (1992), *Feminism and Anti-Feminism in Early Economic Thought*, Aldershot: Edward Elgar.

Sockwell, W.D. (forthcoming), 'William Ellis: Contributions as a Classical Economist, Economic Educator, Economic Popularizer, and Social Economist', *Research in the History of Economic Thought and Methodology*.

Spender, Dale (ed.) (1983a), *Feminist Theorists: Three Centuries of Key Women Thinkers*, New York: Pantheon Books.

Spender, Dale (1983b), *Women of Ideas (And What Men Have Done to Them)*, London: Ark Paperbacks.

Stephen, Barbara (1933), *Girton College, 1869–1932*, Cambridge: Cambridge University Press.

Stewart, W.A.C. and W.P. McCann (1967), *The Educational Innovators, 1750–1880*, London: Macmillan.

Strachey, Ray (1928), *The Cause: A Short History of the Women's Movement in Great Britain*, London: G. Bell and Sons; reprinted London: Virago, 1978.

Uglow, Jennifer (comp. and ed.) (1982), *The Macmillan Dictionary of Women's Biography*, London: Macmillan.

8. The economics of Charlotte Perkins Gilman

Mary Ann Dimand[1]

8.1 INTRODUCTION

In Charlotte Perkins Gilman's lifetime, her reputation (and some of her notoriety) was based firmly on her first prose book, *Women and Economics* (1898a). A reviewer at the time stated in the *Nation* that this work was the most important on the subject since John Stuart Mill's *The Subjection of Women* (1869/1970). Andrew Sinclair (1965, 272) called her 'the greatest writer that the feminists ever produced on sociology and economics, the Marx and Veblen of the movement [who] always asked the brutal question, and was never satisfied by the easy answer'. After her death in 1935, Gilman's work 'disappeared' from public consciousness,[2] although her short story, 'The Yellow Wallpaper' was anthologized at least twice. Since the reissue of *Women and Economics* in 1966, however, Charlotte Perkins Gilman has experienced a renaissance as a feminist theorist. Selections from *Women and Economics* have been anthologized in Schneir (1972, 230–46) and Rossi (1973, 572–98). Other selections from her essays appear in Kraditor (1968). Kraditor (1965) and Spender (1982) have discussed her theories. Selections of her short stories have been edited by Ann J. Lane and Lynne Sharon Schwartz. This attention focuses on Gilman as a feminist, as a writer of feminist utopias and, to a lesser extent, as a sociologist (which is what she usually considered herself). Her contributions to economics have been ignored, with the exception of Margaret O'Donnell (1985), who considered only *Women and Economics* and Gilman's autobiography.

Much of the sociological groundwork of Gilman's thought derives from the 'gynaecocentric' theory of Lester Ward, whom she met in 1896. (She may have been introduced by her friend Edward Ross, who was Ward's nephew.) This theory considered women, rather than men, as the 'race type' and thus source of evolutionary 'progress'. Her work also bears the stamp of his belief that human purpose could guide evolution despite the randomness of natural variation (Hofstadter, 1944, 67–84). Gilman acknowledged Ward's influence lavishly. Her characters recommend Ward's work in much of her fiction, and she cited Ward frequently in her non-fiction. In 1903, Ward complained in *Pure Sociology* that his theory had not received the attention it deserved. Gilman wrote to him, mentioning *Women and Economics*, which he said he had read and enjoyed. Yet several years later he claimed that his theory had no advocates. (Gilman then wrote to him again. He hastily answered, agreeing that her work continued his. This was not a public letter.) It would seem that more recent sociologists also fail to admit Gilman to their ranks. Although two of her works appear in the bibliography of their radical analysis of North American sociology, Schwendinger and Schwendinger (1974) lambasted Ward for 30 pages without mentioning Gilman. Ward was frequently mentioned in Bottomore and Nisbet (1978) and received three pages of discussion (although his gynaecocentrism was not alluded to) but Gilman again went unmentioned.

Gilman's works are now recognized as feminist documents, yet not considered as economics. Ann J. Lane, who stated that 'Gilman had an enormous reputation in her lifetime', identified her work as 'anthropology, history, philosophy, sociology, and ethics' (1979, ix) – not economics. Carl Degler (1956) exhumed Gilman's work and introduced the 1966 reprint of *Women and Economics*. In his introduction, he referred to her as 'one of the leading intellectuals of the women's movement' (1966, xix) and discussed the book as a 'reform tract', but not as economics. Aileen Kraditor called Gilman 'the most influential woman thinker in the pre-World War I generation in the United States', originator of 'the only systematic theory linking the demand for suffrage with the long sweep of history' (1965, 82), yet gave little attention to her economic theories. The American Economics Association's *Index of Economic Journals* lists no articles about her work as such. The *Journal of Economic Literature* lists only Margaret O'Donnell (1985). Caroline Hill did, however, publish a 12-page review article on *The Home* (1903) in the 1904 *Journal of Political Economy*. Although *The New Palgrave* (1987) published a brief entry on Gilman, it did little more than list her major works and associate her with Ward.

Gilman has been examined as an economic theorist only by Michael Barratt Brown (1984). Brown's discussion of *Women and Economics* was extremely superficial. He mentioned only Gilman's recognition that household work by women would be quite expensive if salaried and that, where men are employed on the market and women are not, women depend on men. This reading of Gilman is so fragmentary as to amount to misrepresentation. Not only was Gilman's discussion of women's economic status more complex and arresting than Brown indicated, but her treatment of externalities and the function of the market was novel.

The general neglect of Gilman as an economist may be partly due to her lack of conventional academic qualifications. Not necessarily, however. At least one of her associates, Helen Campbell, has shared the same fate. Although she studied under Richard Ely and won an American Economic Association award for her monograph, 'Women and Wages', she never held a full-time academic job and is now forgotten by the profession.[3]

8.2   BIOGRAPHY

Born Charlotte Anna Perkins[4] in 1860, Gilman was related to the Beecher family. She was raised almost solely by her mother. They moved fairly frequently and Gilman's formal education consequently occupied only a few years. (Hill, 1980, said that records indicate that Gilman was good at English and only fair at mathematics.) She attended the Rhode Island School of Design for a few years, but did not receive a degree. She married the artist Walter Stetson in 1884, only to find that confinement to housekeeping and child-raising made her ill. She and Stetson separated in 1888, when she moved from the east coast to California. They divorced amicably in 1894. (Gilman wed her distant cousin, Houghton Gilman, happily in 1900.) In California Gilman initially ran a boarding-house to support herself, her mother and daughter. She was nonetheless able to mingle with California intellectuals. These included Campbell, the literary radical Hamlin Garland, a number of others she joined in fighting the monopoly of the Southern Pacific Railroad, and the then economist Edward A. Ross. She was later to meet and talk with Jane Addams, Elizabeth Cady Stanton, John Dewey, the Webbs and G.B. Shaw, among others.

In 1890, Gilman began to speak publicly on social questions: by 1891 she was highly enough regarded to be invited to give a lecture in honour of Susan B. Anthony's seventy-first birthday. In 1892, she read her prize essay on the labour movement before the Trades and Labor Unions of Alameda County. Gilman helped to plan, as well as speak at, the California Woman's Congresses in 1894 and 1895. In 1896, Gilman spoke at Susan B. Anthony's request at the Woman's Suffrage Convention in Washington. From 1890 to 1900, Gilman travelled extensively to speak in the United States and England, earning the bulk of her income by this means. She continued to speak publicly through World War I. Speaking engagements dropped off in the 1920s, with a decline in demand for lecturers. She spoke in favour of women's suffrage, but also on broader questions affecting women's rights and conditions, which she felt would not be ameliorated by the vote.

Gilman was active in many fields of literature from the mid-1880s until the end of her life. 'By the end of 1890, Charlotte had produced a rather impressive array of subversive writings' (Hill, 1980, 185), a number of which were published by the *Women's Journal*. Her magazine pieces throughout her life included poems, stories and essays. She helped to edit and wrote for the populist paper the *Impress* from 1894 to 1895. In 1896, after a trip to England on which she met, approved of and was approved by several prominent Fabians, she was invited to become a contributing editor to the *American Fabian*. Her first book, the poetry collection *In This Our World*, was published in 1893. The themes of that volume are primarily political and social in nature, as they are in all of her literary output, and her tone makes it clear that Gilman's intent is persuasion. Her verse is competent and amusing when it is not sentimental, but would not now be considered valuable as poetry. Gilman's novels differed from those of Harriet Martineau and Jane Marcet in advancing revolutionary economic theories, rather than expounding received economic doctrine. They differed from Edward Bellamy's *Looking Backward* in employing economic arguments extensively.

In the 1898 *Women and Economics*, Gilman spelled out her views on the productivity and rewards of women more explicitly and at greater length, arguing that reforms which gave women more choices would increase society's output and welfare. Her discussion of women's past, present and future condition in the economy and society, which will be discussed below, rests on concepts of surplus extraction, the causes and effects of the institution of the home and social externality.

From 1909 to 1917, Gilman produced the magazine *The Forerunner* (since reprinted by Greenwood Reprint Corporation, 1968). Apparently begun partly because of the number of manuscripts Gilman had sitting idle, *The Forerunner* was entirely written and published by her. A reader wrote in after the first year to ask why Gilman was not setting the type as well! A complete novel and a complete non-fiction work by Gilman were published in parts in each of the seven volumes. Each issue also contained short stories, essays, poems and criticism. It is a commonplace to say that Gilman's later works merely elaborate her position in *Women and Economics*. Examination of *The Forerunner*, however, shows that, as well as discussing the status of women, Gilman had innovative views on physical and social externalities. She also proposed a solution to the problem of monopoly which prefigures (oddly, for one who considered herself a socialist)[5] Chicago School ideas. Gilman's tone is always that of a propagandist: she hoped to initiate the evolutionary change of institutions which seemed beneficial and inevitable to her. Her work is nevertheless usually quite carefully reasoned, although she did not use mathematical analysis. Few academic economists at the time did so (Baumol, 1985, 8–9). As literature, her works are not masterpieces. Her prose is better than most in contemporary periodicals, though, and holds up well in comparison with American reform writings of the period.[6] While Lane (1979) felt that Gilman seldom wrote funny material, I have found most of her essays and quite a few short stories, as well as the novel *Herland* (1979), intentionally and successfully diverting.

8.3   GILMAN ON WOMEN

A theme of *Women and Economics* (W&E) and many of Gilman's essays was the attempt to define the conventionally housebound and unpaid woman's role in the economy. Gilman's analysis established that that role was neither partner nor employee, and that women were not paid for their output of house service or children. Gilman concluded that unpaid housewives received their livelihood as a pure transfer, although she sometimes forgot this.

Gilman approached the question of women's role by a careful analysis of claims that, although unpaid, they earned their keep.

> We are confronted by the commonly received opinion that, although it must be admitted that men make and distribute the wealth of the world, yet women earn their share of it as wives. This assumes either that the husband is in the position of employer and wife as employee, or that marriage is a 'partnership', and the wife an equal factor with the husband in producing wealth. (W&E, 10)

Public acknowledgment of women's productivity in the home did not mean that women were partners entitled to share in joint household income:

> when the woman, left alone with no man to 'support' her, tries to meet her own economic necessities, the difficulties which confront her prove conclusively what the general economic status of women is. ... The claim that marriage is a partnership, in which the two persons married produce wealth which neither of them, separately, could produce, will not bear examination. ... [While a wife can make the earning male more comfortable, so could others, and] those ... who make him happy are not therefore his business partners, and entitled to share his income. (W&E, 10–11)

The difficulty is that men and their female family are not economically independent, and that the role of women in the family is ill-defined. Gilman defined economic independence as the voluntary exchange by individuals of the products of their labour. This relationship does not typically hold between male and female family members:

> But the salient fact in this discussion is that, whatever the economic value of the domestic industry of women is, they do not get it. The women who do the most work get the least money, and the women who have the most money do the least work. Their labour is neither given nor taken as a factor in economic exchange. (W&E, 14–15)

Thus women are not employees of their husbands or fathers. It may be said that women

> earn all they get, and more, by house service. ... The labour of women in the house, certainly, enables men to produce more wealth than they otherwise could; and in this way women are economic factors in society. But so are horses. ... But the horse is not economically independent, nor is the woman. (W&E, 12–13)

In the absence of a market for the services they provided, the productivity of women gave them neither economic independence nor earnings. They were not employees of their family.

Gilman confronted the argument that women are employed and earn as mothers. If this were true, women without children have no economic status. She noted, moreover, that if women are remunerated for maternal functions it is odd that payment is not linked to the mother's efficiency in this role or to the number of her children. Just as women with the most spending money do the least housework, they have the fewest children and do the least mothering (W&E, 15–17). Women with a comparative disadvantage in motherhood or housework are not competed out of the market, since no such market exists. Gilman asked

> what remains to those who deny that women are supported by men? ... that the function of motherhood unfits a woman for economic production, and, therefore, it is right that she should be supported by her husband. ... Does the human mother, by her motherhood, thereby lose control of brain and body, lose power and skill and desire for any other work? (W&E, 17, 19)

She argued that the economic dependence of human females is unnatural: 'in other species of animals, male and female alike graze and browse, hunt and kill, climb, swim, dig, run, and fly for their livings' (W&E, 18). If women were incapacitated for other work by motherhood, they would resemble the queen bee, 'modified entirely to maternity ... unfit for any other exertion, and a hopeless dependant' (W&E, 19). This clearly does not obtain.[7] A typical mother works hard for her husband, brothers, father, mother, sisters and church, not just for her children. Her work is simply unpaid and she is 'denied independence on the ground that motherhood prevents her working' (W&E, 20–21). In this circumstance, 'the female of genus homo is economically dependent on the male. He is her food supply' (W&E, 22).

Gilman could not define the role of women in economic society clearly: she argued cogently that it was not what it had been called. Women were not employees of men, not partners of men and were not remunerated for their reproductive powers. Part of the thrust of her plans for a better society lay in letting women, like men define themselves as architects, mathematicians or janitors, rather than as women per se. She described the contemporary status of woman as characterized by male appropriation of her produced surplus. Not only did men coopt women's work, but women could not be said to be paid for it at all. Since payments to women by their husbands (or fathers) did not depend on the quantity or quality of their work, and could be withheld at will, those payments were pure transfers. All of the products of the labour of women in the traditional home were surplus and extracted.

Gilman maintained that the economic dependence of women meant that they were supported by men: a change in home relationships was necessary to alter this position. Suffrage would be a move in that direction, but not sufficient for full reform. Gilman made this argument in response to Dr Anna Shaw's contention that women earned their keep and should therefore be given suffrage, in a debate sponsored by the Women's Trade Union League in 1909, and soundly lost the ensuing audience vote (Kraditor, 1965, 97).

Gilman occasionally lost track of her conclusion that housewives's receipts were transfers. In the light of her recognition of the unpaid and dependent role of most women, it is curious that Gilman stated that, 'when a man marries a housemaid, makes a wife of his servant, he alters her social status; but if she continues in the same industry he does not alter her economic status ... that of domestic service', for what she earns is her wage as housemaid. Anything she receives above that is given her 'without any economic equivalent' (Gilman, 1898b, 177). It seems clear that a husband need not transfer as much to his wife as he would pay his housemaid, and that she is less mobile in seeking a new employer after her marriage.

Gilman's treatment of alimony stemmed from concern with changing the institutions which have defined women as men's family members. She wrote in *The Forerunner* (VII) that there are no grounds for alimony upon divorce, unless a woman's previous work in her husband's house had injured her for future work or enjoyment. In that case she should be able to sue him as his workman. Implicit in this view is her rejection of the classification of women as wives who are automatically injured when they lose this status. Alimony, an institution which demarcates marriage as women's 'job', impedes women from defining themselves individually.[8]

The subordination of women confines not only their economic condition, but all their choices. Gilman's utopian heroine Ellador remarks to her husband, after viewing the society of the world outside Herland, that she

'can see that these women are dull ... But then – if they do things differently there are penalties, aren't there? ... If the women innovate and rebel the least that happens to them is that the men won't marry them – isn't that so?'

'I shouldn't think *you* would call that a penalty, my dear ...'

'Oh, yes it is; it means extinction – the end of that variety of woman. You seem to have quite successfully checked mutation in women; and they had neither education, opportunity, or encouragement in their variation.' (*With Her in Ourland* (WHO), 71–2)

Gilman contended that the family is not a human institution but a natural one, since animals also have families. Humans, unlike animals, have altered the form and function of the family:

> Like all natural institutions, the family has a purpose ... which is the care and nurture of the young. ... When a natural institution becomes human it enters the plane of consciousness. We think about it; and in our strange new power of voluntary action we do things to it. We have done strange things to the family; or, more specifically, men have. ... What man has done to the family, speaking broadly, is to change it from an institution for the best service of the child to one modified to his own service, the vehicle of his comfort, power and pride. (*Our Androcentric Culture* (OAC) II, 19)

She claimed that men confined women to domestic production[9] in a period when all production was domestic, assigning wives and daughters to the role of personal service to the husband. Having achieved this capture, men consider women theirs and jealously restrict women by customs, from foot-binding to enforced ignorance (OAC, II, 21).

In this framework, women have been educated by their mothers, while men were formally educated to train them for life outside the home: 'To be a woman was to be ignorant, uneducated; to be wise, educated, was to be a man. Women were not men, visibly; therefore they could not be educated, and ought not to want to be' (OAC, VIII, 19). Not only would teaching women 'unsex' them, but teaching women was held to be bad for men: 'Mr. Barrett Wendell, of Harvard, solemnly [claims] that teaching women weakens the intellect of the teacher' (OAC, VIII, 20). While the influence of men was assumed to be normal and human, the influence of women on men 'effeminizes' them.

Gilman felt that the barriers set up against women's progress had an adverse effect, not merely on the women themselves, but on their husbands and children. The husband, as a household despot, does not learn the values of justice, freedom, human rights, self-control or consideration – a lack which impoverishes both him and society (OAC, II, 22). Children with subordinate mothers thus lose half their 'social inheritance' (OAC, II, 21).

What was even worse, from Gilman's point of view, women whose only opportunity for a livelihood is marriage compete for husbands. This was unnatural, since in other animal species, the male competes for the female's attentions. She felt that monogamy was wholesome, but that women were not good at competing for mates. This competition led to a hypertrophy of sexual differentiation, encouraging women to become 'oversexed', tiny and weak.

Such mothers retard the evolutionary progress of the species (W&E, 30–32, 45–6).

A further difficulty lies in the high male valuation of 'innocence' in a prospective wife. A woman's 'whole life's success is made to depend on her marrying; her health and happiness depends on her marrying the right man. The more "innocent" she is, the less she knows, the easier it is for the wrong man to get her' (OAC, IX, 18). Gilman was not only concerned that 'innocent' women would marry feeble, race-depleting men. She feared that women might unwittingly marry men with venereal diseases. Men did not suffer the same hazard, since women who 'misstep' lose their value while men enjoy sexual license: 'it is his shop – not hers' (OAC, IX, 18). Gilman was not a eugenicist who would have prescribed desirable and proscribed undesirable matings. She felt, however, that the incentive for women to maintain their innocence deprived them of information on which to make marital choices.

Gilman's account of the origins of the conventional household have scarcely been mentioned above. This story derives from Lester Ward's belief in women, not men, as the race type, and from a postulate that men, unlike women, lack an instinct for constructive work.[10] The theory of evolution Gilman attached to it is biologically faulty. Unlike Ward, but like a number of her contemporaries, she seems to confuse Lamarckian with Darwinian theories and to believe that women could be more evolutionarily retarded than the male children they bear. This does not, however, invalidate the bulk of her analysis.

In short, Gilman asserted that women have been confined to the ownership of men who support them, and thus limited to being mothers and providers of 'house service'. Since neither form of production is linked to remuneration, inappropriate quantities are produced. One result of the traditional household roles is that men living with their families may not voluntarily choose their consumption of household services at the market price. Women in a male-headed household also have no opportunity cost of consuming household services. With an artificially imposed price of zero for household production, people tend to overconsume house service. Hence the institution of the traditional home leads households to suboptimal consumption choices. Gilman did not analyse the welfare effects of the conventional household in this language, but she was aware that 'too much' household service was consumed under traditional institutions. Gilman did not note that free disposal seldom holds in this case: one can throw dinner out of the door, but discarding children or a clean house are costly. Therefore excessive production yields excessive consumption directly.

She was also very much alive to the inefficiencies of non-market household production as such, an issue discussed in the next section. Since household production is not linked to income, women with a comparative disadvantage in 'domestic industry' are nonetheless trapped in it, and unable to turn to tasks they could excel at. Gilman supported women's suffrage as a change of institutions which should help women to escape the house and enter the human race, but she felt that a change in home relationships was necessary. She suggested that the traditional home could be changed, not by legislation, but by the power of the market.

The burden of Gilman's message in her non-fiction was addressed to women who provided house service and were not formally employed, and to men. Her fiction makes it clear that she was well aware of the existence of working women: as a polemicist, she addressed parties who were doing less than working women to better women's lot. And this was a substantial population. Bergmann (1986, 20) gives female participation in the labour force as only 17 per cent of the labour force in 1890 and 18 per cent in 1900. (Amott and Matthaei, 1991, 316, agree with the latter figure.) Gilman's fiction also makes it clear that she felt that women workers had little control over their conditions, and that a market which gave them the opportunity of better boarding at reasonable prices would be preferable. Gilman addressed those parties whose actions might yield better conditions for women by providing a public market for household services, whether on the supply or on the demand side.

8.4   THE IMPARTIAL AND MIGHTY MARKET

In a story in a late number of *The Forerunner*, Gilman made clear why she thought the traditional home relation was inefficient and detrimental to both spouses, by means of a parable. Mary, a young widow with a child, runs a profitable boarding-house to support the two of them. One of her tenants is a young working woman, Jane. After a few years, Jane says, 'Mary, I love you. Let us live alone together. I will support you, and you will keep house only for me.'[11] Since Mary also loves Jane, she agrees. Mary now no longer has an income. Jane's income must support two adults and one child. Furthermore, Mary can no longer achieve economies of scale or pecuniary economies in her housekeeping expenditures. (Gilman remarked on the wastefulness of one or more women waiting on one man throughout her work, noting the household as a bastion of sub-capacity capital use as well.) Jane finds herself obliged to work longer hours to support the three of them, and yet their joint income is lower than it was before. The result is crossness and tiffs, as well as direct welfare loss through forgone income.

Gilman felt that household income was lowered by the wife's bondage to unpaid house service. In an individual case this is clearly true: even if house service is necessary to the production of the companion doing marketed work, such house service could be provided commercially if the household companion ran a boarding-house, or if the two working companions lived in one. On a nationwide basis this should also hold, since it is hard to see how a couple's real wage could fall with both working. Beyond this, individual house service could not achieve economies of scale and pecuniary economies which Gilman was sure existed. As a former boarding-house keeper, she had at least casual empiricism on her side. She is not without support: 'Boarding was a very common solution to the problem of finding an affordable home that could be managed without the cost of servants' (Shapiro, 1986, 171–2).

Boarding-houses were the leading example of market-provided house services at that time. Gilman proposed a more radical alternative to private households: the utopian centralized house service of *Herland* (1979) and *Moving the Mountain* (1912). The success of kitchenless apartment houses and meal delivery in prosperous periods makes it clear that market provision of house service is potentially viable (Hayden, 1981). Such changes go far beyond those recognized by O'Donnell (1985, 187), who claimed that Gilman's plans 'were not dramatic alterations in the economic system, but were mostly cosmetic changes designed to eliminate waste and reduce pressure on the overworked female'.

Specialization and the division of labour fuelled the industrial revolution, resulting in the efficient removal of many types of production from the home. Gilman argued that similar gains existed in household production. She also felt that, if market provision of house service existed, women might not be implicitly viewed as a source of free labour, and could specialize to their and their families' advantage. With an explicit price on them, optimal amounts of household service would be consumed. Women unskilled in house service could turn their efforts to activities in which they held a comparative advantage.

Gilman's novel, *What Diantha Did* (1910–116), abounds in examples of unexploited comparative advantage. Diantha's mother is good at accounting. Her father lacks this ability and does not employ his wife's, making him a perennial bankrupt. The architect Isabel Porne and her sympathetic husband thought she could continue her profession at home after marriage. The domestic help she hires is inefficient and she is frequently between cook-generals: her workshop grows dusty while she does the housework badly. Isabel laments, 'If I were an abler woman! ... I am able enough – in my own work! Nobody can do everything' (WDD, IV, 14). There is a shortage of servants at the going price, and the institutions which govern their hiring also lead to inefficiency. As Diantha says in a scandalous speech to the Orchardina Club, the fact that celibacy is demanded of domestics leads to constant turnover, and to low skill in the domestic, who may be trained only to be lost. The reserve army of unemployed women who had only the alternatives of domestic work and school teaching kept the wage low. Pujol (1992) discusses the crowding of women into a few occupations as an institution keeping women's remuneration low, attributing this theory to J.S. Mill, Barbara Bodichon and Millicent Garrett Fawcett.

What Diantha Did is a tale of the value of professionalizing household work. Diantha was initially a school teacher, but she loathed the work and resigned after a few years. She is engaged to a man who will not be financially able to marry her for a number of years. He is supporting his widowed mother and four sisters in wasteful idleness by running his deceased father's grocery store inefficiently, to the detriment of his desire to do biological research. Diantha decides to strike out and earn enough for them to marry, but first she must escape her own parents.

To argue for her right to leave, she draws up an accounting of the value of what she has received from her parents and of the value of her labour to them, evaluated at market prices. This is interesting of itself, as a calculation using the opportunity cost of hiring house service (which included, to her father's surprise, the value of her mother's labour on her behalf). Gilman has assumed that, if Diantha's (and her mother's) labour had not been available at zero cost, it would have been hired. She also, unfortunately, failed to include an interest rate in totting up over about 20 years. However, Diantha's accounts are of interest as an early example of cost–benefit analysis, although the Austrians had defined opportunity cost earlier. Gilman's unnamed opportunity cost is not equivalent: she is working out what service would have cost had it been paid for. This is identical to Austrian opportunity cost only if the same amount of service would have been consumed at the market price.

Having proved that she owed her parents nothing but affection, Diantha goes to Orchardina to begin her career and, coincidentally, the professionalization of domestic labour. She specifies a probationary period in which she will undertake the Porne household for $7 a week (and, implicitly, room and board), before the parties recontract with fuller information. This verbal contract is unusual only in that it is the cook-general who asks a probationary period, but Diantha startles Isabel in one respect: when asked her name, she replies 'Miss Bell'. In an era when a female servant was called by a given name (whether or not it was her own), requesting an honorific was surprising and a move towards establishing housekeeping as a profession. Diantha's great comparative advantage in housekeeping swiftly makes life at the Porne house smoother and less expensive. At the end of the probationary period, Diantha writes a 'proposition as to her staying with' her employers for six more months. This document is worth quoting at some length.

The ordinary rate for labour in this state, unskilled labour of the ordinary sort, is $2.00 a day. This is in return for the simplest exertion of brute force, under constant supervision and direction, and involving no serious risk to the employer.

Household labour calls for the practice of several distinct crafts, and ... requires thorough training and experience. Its performer is not only in a position of confidence ... but the work itself, in maintaining the life and health of the members of the household, is of most vital importance.

In consideration of existing economic conditions, however, I am willing to undertake these intricate and responsible duties for a seven day week at less wages than are given the street-digger, for $1.50 a day. ...

In further consideration of the conditions of the time, I am willing to accept part payment in board and lodging instead of cash. Such accommodations as are usually offered with this position may be rated at $17.00 a month. (WDD, V 15–16)

Diantha also stipulates that her work day is ten specified hours: she will charge for working more, but is accommodating in rearranging her personal time in advance.

By writing a specific contract, Diantha has changed the status of domestic labour in at least one household, since the Pornes accept her terms. An explicit written contract was uncommon, and placed her employment on a more formal level. Servants typically had no specific hours of work, and could be required to labour for indefinite amounts of the day. By setting the market value of room and board received, Diantha does more than remind the Pornes of the true cost of hiring her. Mr Porne remarks that employers usually think themselves kind for boarding the cook, rather than seeing this as part of her salary. Citing the payment of unskilled labour is more than just an invidious comparison: it is true opportunity cost for Diantha, despite her sex. Hiley (1979, 42) noted an 1866 case in which a woman impersonated a man for six years strictly in order to get better pay. This was discovered only because she was arrested for her garments. She intended to resume trousers if, as she expected, she could not get a reasonable income as a woman. It is notable as well that Gilman did not feel that considerations of justice overrode those of supply and demand. She felt that in the longer run women's economic independence would transform supply and demand conditions.

After her next six months with the Pornes, Diantha begins the next stage of her project, establishing and managing maid and food order-in services. Gilman avoided the problem of how a woman could borrow money by having Diantha bankrolled by a wealthy woman, who also employs her as housekeeper in this period. (The woman subsequently informs Diantha that she gets a higher return on *this* investment than on her others.) As her project advances, Diantha establishes a laundry, a boarding-house for employees, publicly offered sandwich luncheons at the boarding-house, and a House Worker's Union for her employees. Diantha later finds it profitable to separate most of these industries, put some under other managers and hire her mother as an accountant. It is well within the context of Gilman's economics that there are gains from greater scale, but diseconomies of scope, in the provision of house service. When Diantha's fiancé can bring himself to realize that Diantha's business 'was not the freak of an eccentric individual, but part of an inevitable business development, going on in various ways in many nations' (WDD, XIII, 13), they at last marry.

It has been argued that women cannot do intellectual work because of stupidity or their 'emotional nature', and that they are too weak to do physical labour. While Gilman, herself a writer and speaker, did not feel that this was true, her appraisal of the benefits of market supply of house service evaded this critique. Few would argue that women cannot execute the house services that they already provide. Commercial provision of such services by women would decrease their cost. It might be claimed that some women would be unable to gain employment in the new commercial sector owing to relative inefficiency. Yet even in households where this occurred, the cost of living would decline, in Gilman's view, so that the household would be better off. Although Gilman's view of the home as a workhouse for dependent women roused more social terror than any of her other views,[12] she did not expect women to desert the home. She thought that housekeeping would be provided largely or entirely by women, but women who were paid and efficient. Similarly, she thought that individual child care and education at home was inefficient for much the same reasons, and that child care provided through the market would be superior for children and their parents:

> First, not every woman is born with the special qualities and powers needed to take right care of children: she has not the talent for it. Second, not every woman can have the instruction and training needed to fit her for the right care of children: she has not the education for it. Third, while each woman takes all the care of her own children herself, no woman can ever have the requisite experience for it. (W&E, 293)

To Gilman, the necessary key to women's economic independence was a fully established market for house service. With housekeeping as a respected and paid activity, home production would occur at lower cost, real family incomes would rise, and both men and women would be better off economically. Furthermore, Gilman suggested in both *Herland* and *Moving the Mountain* that men would find women more agreeable and conversable when marriage and housekeeping were not women's only concerns.

Gilman apparently encountered a particular argument about the results of female economic independence often:

A FREQUENT QUESTION

If women become economically independent, their husbands will stop working –
and depend on them.

Oh, no, they won't.

How do you know they won't?

Because that kind of man will not succeed in getting that kind of woman to
depend on when women are wiser.

What's to prevent the man from becoming a burden on her afterward?

The marriage contract.

You propose a new kind of marriage contract, do you?

Why not? Marriage may be made in Heaven, but the contract is drawn up by
mere men. These – and some women to help them – may easily make a better one.
Why not? (*Forerunner*, I, 13)

The proposed more overt, enforceable marriage contract Gilman counsels
would also remedy a common concern in the late nineteenth and early twentieth centuries: 'The fear exhibited that women generally, once fully independent, will not marry, is proof of how well it has been known that only dependence forced them to marry as it was' (W&E, 91). With such a contract,
marriage would no longer be as it was.[13]

In fact, Gilman thought that creation of large markets for house service and
child care was so clearly efficient and desirable that it was inevitable in the
fairly short run. It is odd that she both noticed, and did not notice, some of the
obstacles to this revolution. Diantha's food order-in service and maid service
in Orchardina were patronized by those in the community who cared about
skilled and inexpensive provision of house service. Gilman stated that women
who liked being the mistress of the house and ordering women about, however, did not use the service: it did not provide what they wished in household relations. Yet she seems not to have seriously considered that men might
relish their domestic monarchy more than could be compensated by efficiency and household income gains. And while she was well aware of 'Antis',
women who opposed universal suffrage, Gilman seems not to have recognized that their sentiments would be as effective in keeping house service out
of the market as in delaying suffrage.

It might be claimed that Gilman would be satisfied with the existence of
fast-food outlets and maid services today. This would be a mistake. Gilman's
hope was that households would assume that house service and meals would
be purchased on the market, just as motor cars are. This has not occurred.
Women are still often expected to do the bulk of domestic work where maid
service is not heavily used. The advent of appliances has brought hopes
which have proved largely false. A number of surveys have indicated that
women spend as much time in the kitchen with 'labour-saving devices' as
they did without (Cowan, 1983). Strasser (1982, 80, 268) implied that vacuum
cleaners merely made the yearly task of spring cleaning weekly, and said that

automatic laundry washers 'restructured rather than reduced laundry time. ... Eventually, by allowing women to wash "whenever you get a load", the automatic washer, the dryer, and the synthetic fabrics that ended ironing probably increased the weekly household laundry load.'

Gilman also felt that, while individuals might be concerned about not having their private tastes, especially in food, catered to owing to mass production, they would swiftly learn to prefer the professional service. In Diantha's food service and the universal food service of *Moving the Mountain*, while it is possible for people to specify what dishes they want, they seldom do so. Here I think Gilman simply failed to understand the strength of most people's preferences, although she wrote:

WE EAT AT HOME

We eat at home; we do not care
Of what insanitary fare:
   So long as Mother makes the pie,
   Content we live, content we die,
And proudly our dyspepsia bear.

Straight from our furred forefather's lair
The instinct comes of feeding there;
   And still unmoved by progress high
                   We eat at home.

In wasteful ignorance we buy
Alone; alone our food we fry;
   What though a tenfold cost we bear,
   The doctor's bill, the dentist's chair?
Still without ever asking why
                 We eat at home. (*Forerunner*, I, 9)

A number of dining clubs and food services existed from about 1885 to 1925 in the United States, and some kitchenless houses and apartments were built. Dolores Hayden (1981) gives an excellent account of these enterprises, from which I draw. Dining clubs and food services tended to be patronized by the affluent, and dining clubs had more success in small towns, while cooked food service was more flourishing in large cities and their suburbs (Hayden, 1981, 209). These institutions tended to be economically viable only as long as food prices remained on the low side and, as Hayden noted,

if a housewife's labor was never timed or counted, then it was very difficult to persuade husbands, or the community at large, that kitchen workers should receive wages comparable to the wages of a valued 'professional' worker, or that experiments which placed a cash value on cooked meals should continue. (Hayden, 1981, 214)

The National Household Economics Association advocated a communal kitchen for small communities, and Mary Coleman Stuakert's plans for such a community were exhibited at the 1896 World's Fair (Hayden, 1981, 186–7). However, no such communities came into existence outside the final pages of *What Diantha Did*.

As 'We Eat at Home' suggests, Gilman had strong feelings about adulterated foodstuffs being imported into the home. This concern is most reasonable for the period. Upton Sinclair's *The Jungle* (1906) had revealed the lack of abattoir sanitation to many Americans. Dr Chase (1875), a reformed grocer, exposed the addition of plaster dust to flour and the substitution of sulphuric acid for honest vinegar. Gilman felt that, just as larger scale for home production would lower the cost of output, it would improve the quality of output. A large buyer would have more incentives to get appropriate information on the inputs purchased (see 'Kitchen-Mindedness', *Forerunner*, I, 4; *Moving the Mountain*, 4).

Gilman's concerns about food adulteration and the cost of meal preparation are far from incongruous for an educated woman of her period. Helen Campbell and Ellen Richards were pioneers in the new field of home economics. Richards earned, though under the regulations of the time she did not receive, an MA in chemistry from MIT in the 1870s. Trained women with degrees in economics or chemistry were allowed employment in this new field as they were not in their areas of study (Shapiro, 1986). Unlike Campbell and Richards, Gilman did not think that separate spheres for men and women were inevitable, and that women's status could be improved only by the professional apparatus of microscopes and nutritional tables within her sphere. For Gilman, the professionalization of housekeeping would free most women for work in other fields than housekeeping as scale increased.

Gilman also felt that market competition was an effective cure for monopoly. 'The Women Selling Eggs' (*Forerunner*, IV, 2, 54) details the factual activities of women who were concerned with oligopolists' egg storage, which was used to corner the market and badly deteriorated the quality of available eggs. To combat the oligopolists, Massachusetts housewives combined to purchase and market eggs direct from chicken farmers who were then highly dispersed. They outcompeted the incumbents with respect to both price and quality, and broke up the egg ring. Most of Gilman's active concern about monopoly seems to have related to the food industries, which she felt were subject to undue manipulation (see WHO, *passim*). Her early experience as an opponent of the monopoly of the Southern Pacific Railroad presumably had little effect on her solution, as the Southern Pacific Railroad was a natural monopoly by virtue of its capital. Gilman was confident that, in markets without natural monopolies, not only could consumers organize to provide a competitive yardstick, but the monopoly rents were so high that organization costs would be covered and the consumers could turn at least a small profit.

Gilman recognized the possibility of market failure in the case of geographically trapped consumers. 'Wanted, a Railroad Cafeteria' (*Forerunner*, VII, 1, 33) and 'Our Sleeping Cars' (*Forerunner*, IV, 9, 231–2) compare the cost of a meal and a bed on railways unfavourably with the cost of such amenities in cities, where there is competition.

While Gilman had considerable faith in the market's rewards for efficiency, she acknowledged some of the handicaps of the market. She realized that the determination of liability in the case of capital which produced negative externalities could be done by neither the market (for insurance) nor the courts. Similarly, she felt that the market for medical attention did not operate efficiently from the point of view of society ('Private Morality and Public Immorality', *Forerunner*, I). Indeed, she typically ignored the market as a solution for problems of externality. (See next section.) Her faith in the market was nonetheless clearly excessive, as even she found that the market does not necessarily reward quality.[14]

Gilman felt that the commercialization of domestic industry would diminish the incentive to confine women to unpaid housework and make it more difficult to exploit their labour. In an era when antitrust legislation was promoted to control monopolies, she was unusual in recommending consumer organization and competition as a yardstick. She was correct not to apply this solution to situations of natural monopoly or to cases of externality. However, her belief in the ability of the market to reward efficiency and quality was excessive and due to an underestimation of the taste for discrimination.

8.5   GILMAN ON EXTERNALITY

In 'Reasonable Resolutions' for January 1910, Gilman stated:

> ... while we, Socially, behave as badly as we do, we individually can accomplish little.
> Says the wiseacre – 'Ah! but if each of us was individually perfect Society would be perfect!'
> ... you can't learn to work together by trying to be perfect separately ...
> We need collective aims, collective efforts, collective attainments.
> Let us collectively resolve:
> That we will stop wasting our soil and our forests and our labour!
> That we will stop poisoning and clogging our rivers and harbors.
> That we will stop building combustible homes.
> That we will *now – this year –* begin in good earnest to prevent all preventable diseases.

That we will do our duty by our children and young people, as a wise Society should, and cut off the crop of criminals by not making them. (*Forerunner*, I, 3, 1)

Her statement of the social externalities of private actions was not unlike that of John Stuart Mill, who recognized poverty, ignorance and disease as private causes of social evil which it would benefit society, though not necessarily each individual, to remedy. She recognized a greater number of externalities, however, including the tragedy of the commons in soil conservation, water pollution and fire hazard from others' homes. The only externality she listed which she felt an increase in the number of markets would cure was the waste of women's labour in household work.

Gilman suggested two cures for most externalities. Firstly, as the 'Reasonable Resolutions' suggest, she believed that a greater social consciousness would decrease or eliminate negative externalities. While she did not explicitly discuss common property as a cause of externalities, this recognition lies behind the categories of externality she lists. She was not unusual in her lack of explicit notice of property rights. As Richard Ely (1917, 9) noted, 'heretofore there has been a general failure to appreciate the significance of property-relations as a necessary foundation of conservation'.

For Gilman, social consciousness was the best remedy. In each of her two utopias, *Herland* and *Moving the Mountain*, she detailed a means by which this could be achieved. In *Herland*, a biological quirk of history accomplishes an increase of moral sentiments which is implicit in the culture examined. It is a civilization deprived by war and disease of all its men, isolated by jungle-surrounded mountains. Initially, the women assumed that their society would die out with them. After a few years, however, during which the women worked together to put off this fate, one women gave birth by parthenogenesis. All the women of later generations derived from this first mother. Although they should all have been genetically identical, Gilman apparently did not know this, or thought that environment would differentiate them, for their talents, interests and intelligence vary considerably. One feels that it is because all the women were as closely related as possible that members of their society could so easily act together.

A parthenogenetic solution is not terribly feasible for most communities. In *Moving the Mountain* the cause of increased social sentiment is slightly more plausible. In 1910, a new religion arose in the United States, led by an overwhelming mass of women. The new religion, simply called Life, had just one basic tenet: social responsibility and respect for productivity. This alone sufficed to bring about new regimes in employment, child care and education, land stewardship, pollution and information publication, which became totally honest.

Gilman's second prescription for negative externalities, necessary in the first stages of social change in *Moving the Mountain*, was legislation. Publishers were held responsible for the contents of their publications. Criminals were incarcerated in physical and moral hospitals to be cured. Those found incurable were liquidated – Gilman does not seem to have found this too repugnant. The results of tests for venereal disease were open to all, so that people would not ignorantly marry those with venereal disease. Moreover, those found diseased were not permitted to have children.

In the case of many resource externalities, the utopians of *Moving the Mountain*, like those of *Herland*, depend entirely on social responsibility. This leads them to grow more fruit and nut trees to hold the soil while providing crops, and to encourage birds which devour insect pests. Mammal pests (wild animals) are completely destroyed. In *Moving the Mountain*, new soil is artificially created not, as one would expect, by composting, but by crushing stone and mixing it with 'nutrients'.

Gilman's glancing comments on conservation are in line with those of Ely (1917) in the policies of soil and water stewardship recommended. Unlike Ely, she is unfamiliar with the work of L.C. Gray and does not discuss property rights in any overt way.

In advocating legislation to achieve lump sum reductions of negative externality, Gilman followed in Mill's footsteps. Mill recommended the legislation of some minimum schooling for all children, to be tested by the government. He also felt that some public expenditure in the case of financially incapable parents would be desirable (Hollander, 1985, 699–720). The method of legislation cannot in general achieve an optimal level for any externality, but both Mill and Gilman seem to have thought along the lines of elimination rather than optimal quantity. As very early writers on externality, it is perhaps not surprising that they failed to recognize the tax-subsidy solution of Pigou (1932) or the bargaining solution of Coase (1960). Gilman did not accord the government a very large role, and certainly the classical economist Mill did not. Gilman might well have felt that the difficulty of assigning property rights and responsibilities in many cases defied the bargaining solution. Gilman's early appreciation of the existence of externalities, however, is worthy of note.

8.6   MILL? VEBLEN? MARX?

As mentioned at the beginning of this chapter, Gilman has been compared to Mill (with respect to *Women and Economics*), Marx and Veblen. Gilman's discussion of the status of women bears more similarities to Harriet Taylor Mill's 'Enfranchisement of Women' (1851/1970) than to J.S. Mill's 'The

Subjection of Women' (1869/1970).[15] Like Pujol (1992, 23–37), I feel that Harriet Taylor Mill was the better economist as well as the better feminist of the two Mills in analysing women's status. H.T. Mill, like the later Gilman, contended that 'There need be no fear that women will take out of the hands of men any occupation which men perform better than they' since the market would reward comparative advantage, and that the loss of women's skills outside the home was injurious to them and detrimental to society (H.T. Mill, 1970, 101). Mill argued against confining women to the occupation of motherhood, since women unable to be mothers and perform another job would not attempt such a hopeless task (H.T. Mill, 1970, 103–4). In a time of scandalous child labour, Mill also perceived a benefit to women's work outside the home which Gilman did not discuss. Even if women merely replaced sweated children, children would be freed to invest in education to the benefit of society (H.T. Mill, 1970, 105).

J.S. Mill (1869) agreed with his wife and Gilman that women's capacities had been constrained in the home, that society would be better off with more freedom for women, and that men should not be concerned about being outcompeted in industries at which they had comparative advantage. The tone of his essay is quite different from theirs, however – he clearly thought of himself as contending with men, whether hostile or undecided. The structure of his argument, like Gilman's, was historical. Rather than trying to establish an evolutionary trend, though, Mill followed the standard model of appeals to the classics to prove the soundness of his remarks. Furthermore, while Mill mentioned social losses from the shackling of female human powers, he devoted much more space to holding that men would be better off if women were allowed the full educational rights which would make them more equal companions. For Harriet Taylor Mill, this argument led to a state of affairs

> very agreeable to [men] no doubt, but unfortunately the reverse of improving. ... High mental powers in women will be but an exceptional accident, until every career is open to them, and until they, as well as men, are educated for themselves and for the world – not one sex for the other. (H.T. Mill, 1970, 112–13)

Gilman neither made nor evaluated the companionship argument.

Gilman's similarities to Veblen are evident. Both were institutionalists of a high order, who considered the origins, effects, disamenities and eventual passing of traditional customs. *Women and Economics*, although published a year before *The Theory of the Leisure Class* (1899b), had correspondences to it in Gilman's comparisons of humans with other animal species. Gilman read *The Theory of the Leisure Class* on the recommendation of Edward Ross, and found it 'clear and impressive, and though rather stiff and laboured in part, illuminated by the most brilliant penetrating satire I ever saw'

(Dorfman, 1961, 194, 196). *Our Androcentric Culture* (1910–11a) used arguments even more like those of Veblen, who was cited. *What Diantha Did* contains a distinct and unacknowledged swipe from Veblen in the description of Mr Warden's funeral festivities: 'the conspicuous "lot", the continual flowers, the monument (not wholly paid for yet …) – all that expenditure to do honor to the man they had worked to death' (WDD, I, 18). While her tone was never as acerbic as Veblen's, especially the early Veblen's, her use of humour was not unlike his. Lane (1990, 299) states that Gilman 'expressed an intellectual debt' to Veblen.

It seems unlikely that Veblen influenced *Women and Economics*. Diggins (1978, 159–60) concluded that 'there is no evidence that either Gilman or Veblen was influenced by the other's writings' in the 1890s. Veblen's papers, 'The Instinct of Workmanship and the Irksomeness of Labor' (1898) and 'The Barbarian Status of Women' (1899a) which had appeared in the *American Journal of Sociology* (in which Gilman later published) would have been relevant, but appeared too late to influence Gilman's first book.

Gilman was less like Marx than like the Mills or Veblen. She discussed the exploitation of women and their deprivation of pay for the surplus they produced. Like Marx, she considered social change an evolutionary process impelled by inevitable revolutions. Yet, though she called herself a socialist, her socialism bears little resemblance to Marxism. She was very much concerned with the incentives ownership gives (just as Mill was, at least in some editions of the *Principles*). She advertised *What Diantha Did* as 'a solution to the housekeeping problem – NOT by cooperation' throughout the first year of *The Forerunner*. Neither of her utopias contain publicly owned firms. John Roberts, a visitor from the past, observes agricultural workers in the reborn United States:

> … I was surprised at their eagerness. 'They look as busy as a lot of ants on an ant heap,' I said.
> 'It's their heap, you see,' Owen answered. (*Moving the Mountain*, 222).

Thus Gilman advocated worker ownership of some industries, but not the nationalization of production or non-market cooperative efforts.

8.7   CONCLUSION

Gilman's economic ideas have an insufficiently recognized importance, and indeed bear comparison with those of the Mills and Veblen, if not of Marx. She was a rare writer on the status of women bound to the home, with an analytical framework encompassing exploitation and surplus value. She was unusual in recommending an increased number of active markets to prevent such exploitation, as well as to curb monopoly. Her writing on externalities was earlier than that of anyone but John Stuart Mill and Edwin Chadwick, and embodied features unrecognized by them. Gilman deserves recognition as an economist and attention from the profession which she has not previously received.

NOTES

1. I would like to thank Robert W. Dimand for many helpful comments and some useful quotations. I am grateful for useful suggestions to Samuel Hollander and participants in his workshop in history of economic thought at the University of Toronto. The original paper was presented at a History of Economics Society and International Association for Feminist Economics joint session at the Allied Social Science Associations meetings in Washington, January 1995.
2. Degler (1966) attributed this process to the fact that Gilman did not concentrate on women's suffrage, while the history of the women's movement shrank to that issue. Spender (1982) attributes the disappearance and misrepresentation of many women's writings to male control of information. She cites the shrinkage of the feminist tradition noted by Degler, giving many instances of distortion and ridicule of such women's writing as was not erased.
3. Economists of that period did not necessarily have economics degrees, advanced degrees or any degrees at all. Carroll D. Wright, US Commissioner of Labor and later president of Clark University, held no degree and had never taken a course in economics or statistics. Four of the first five presidents of the AEA 'never had more than one undergraduate course in political economy, [and] never earned more than a four year degree' (Parrish, 1967). Marshall, Keynes and Hawtrey held only one earned degree: in mathematics.
4. The surname question is a problem here, as Gilman changed her name upon each of her marriages. Unlike Lane (1979), I elect to refer to Gilman by that name throughout this chapter.
5. Gilman's lyrics, 'Long have we lived apart,/ Women alone' were sung 'year after year ... enthusiastically' by the Women's Trade Union League, but it did not do much concrete good (Foner, 1979, 470–71).
6. For example, Bellamy's *Looking Backward*, Dreiser's *Sister Carrie*, Sinclair's *The Jungle* and the works of Lincoln Steffens.
7. At the time, however, 'Physicians ... with claims to knowledge encompassing all of human biological existence ... were the first to pass judgment on the social consequences of female anatomy and to prescribe the "natural" life plan for women' (Ehrenreich and English, 1978, 4). The 'natural' life plan barred women from any work but housework and childrearing.
8. Gilman herself neither asked for nor received alimony and supported her child herself until Stetson's imminent remarriage made it eligible to send Katharine to him.
9. 'The term "domestic industry" does not define a certain kind of labour, but a certain grade of labour. Architecture was a domestic industry once – when every savage mother set up her own tepee' (OAC II, 21). Gilman's remarks in other essays indicate that domestic production is non-market production.
10. It is small comfort that Gilman backed off slightly from the story of how 'Mr. Man gets into the saddle': this is a mystery that not even the superwoman Ellador can explain, though she has named it 'The Great Divergence' (WHO, 291).
11. In this proposal Jane is unusually forthright. Gilman noted repeatedly that women typically accept marriage proposals which include no explicit mention of household or market

work. They find out only subsequently that they have accepted a set of household duties which were never bargained for, and which typically leave no time for their paid employment. See *What Diantha Did* (WDD), IV.

12. It is of interest that, around the turn of the century, *Architectural Record* editors 'expressed *concern* that many women found industrial, charitable, social, or intellectual pursuits more interesting than domestic life' (Hayden, 1981, 194: emphasis added).

13. Gilman published an article criticizing traditional marriage in the *Union Labor Advocate* (Foner, 1979, 316).

14. When she began publishing *The Forerunner*, Gilman wrote a few amusing advertisements and printed them at the back. From her later account, it would seem that these advertisements (for a fountain pen, a chocolate, 'runless' stockings, and so on) were published without charge for a trial period. In subsequent issues, she printed a list describing (without name) products she would like to advertise since she knew their value. She requested that readers let companies know when their purchases were due to advertisements in *The Forerunner*, hoping that advertisements would support the low price (US$1.00 a year) of the magazine. Later, having given up advertisements, she instituted a commission to subscribers for signing up others, in the belief that the magazine would be even better (fewer pages lost to advertisement) if enough people subscribed to cover costs. Although Gilman was sure that her advertisements and her text were of unusual value, neither paid off. She dropped the attempt to find advertisers after a few years. When she terminated the magazine in 1917, she indicated that such a magazine, not supported by the market to the extent of covering costs, should not be continued.

15. Pujol's 'The Feminist Economic Thought of Harriet Taylor (1807–58)' in this volume reveals further similarities in Taylor's and Gilman's thought.

REFERENCES

Amott, Teresa and Julie Matthaei (1991), *Race, Gender and Work*, Montreal and New York: Black Rose Books.

Baumol, William J. (1985), 'On Method in U.S. Economics a Century Earlier', *American Economic Review*, **75**, (6), December 1–12.

Bergmann, Barbara R. (1986), *The Economic Emergence of Women*, New York: Basic Books.

Bottomore, Tom and Robert Nisbet (eds) (1978), *A History of Sociological Analysis*, New York: Basic Books.

Brown, Michael Barratt (1984), *Models in Political Economy: A Guide to the Arguments*, Harmondsworth, Middlesex: Penguin.

Chase, A.W. (1875), *Dr. Chase's Recipes; or, Information for Everybody*, Ann Arbor, MI: R.A. Beal.

Coase, Ronald H. (1960), 'The Problem of Social Cost', *Journal of Law and Economics*, **3**, (1), 1–44.

Cowan, Ruth Schwartz (1983), *More Work for Mother: The Ironies of Household Technology from the Open Hearth to the Microwave*, New York: Basic Books.

Degler, Carl (1956), 'Charlotte Perkins Gilman on the Theory and Practice of Feminism', *American Quarterly*, **8**, (1), 21–39.

Degler, Carl (1966), 'Introduction to the Torchbook Edition of *Women and Economics*', New York: Harper & Row.

Diggins, John P. (1978), *The Bard of Savagery: Thorstein Veblen and Modern Social Theory*, New York: The Seabury Press.

Dorfman, Joseph (1934/1961), *Thorstein Veblen and His America*, New York: Augustus M. Kelley.

Eatwell, John, Murray Milgate and Peter Newman (eds) (1987), *The New Palgrave: A Dictionary of Economics*, London: Stockton Press.

Ehrenreich, Barbara and Deirdre English (1978), *For Her Own Good: 150 Years of the Expert's Advice to Women*, New York: Anchor Press/Doubleday.

Ely, Richard T. (1917), 'Conservation and Economic Theory', in R.T. Ely, R.H. Hess, C.K. Leith and T.N. Carver, *The Foundations of National Prosperity*, New York: Macmillan.

Foner, Philip S. (1979), *Women and the American Labor Movement*, New York: The Free Press/Macmillan.

Gilman, Charlotte Perkins (1898a/1966), *Women and Economics: A Study of the Economic Relation Between Men and Women as a Factor in Social Evolution*, New York: Harper & Row.

Gilman, Charlotte Perkins (1898b), 'Economic Basis of the Woman Question', *Woman's Journal*, 1 October; reprinted in Kraditor (1968).

Gilman, Charlotte Perkins (1903/1970), *The Home: Its Work and Influence*, New York: New York Source Book Press.

Gilman, Charlotte Perkins *The Forerunner* (1909–17), a periodical of works by Gilman, published in seven volumes, New York: Charlton Co.

Gilman, Charlotte Perkins (1910–11a/1970), *Our Androcentric Culture, The Forerunner*, I, New York: New York Source Book Press; quotations in text are from the original publication.

Gilman, Charlotte Perkins (1910–11b), *What Diantha Did, The Forerunner*, I.

Gilman, Charlotte Perkins (1912), *Moving the Mountain, The Forerunner*, II.

Gilman, Charlotte Perkins (1914/1979), *Herland*, New York: Pantheon Press; first printed in *The Forerunner*, VI.

Gilman, Charlotte Perkins (1916), *With Her in Ourland, The Forerunner*, VII.

Hayden, Dolores (1981), *The Grand Domestic Revolution: A History of Feminist Designs for American Homes, Neighborhoods, and Cities*, Cambridge, MA: MIT Press.

Hiley, Michael (1979), *Victorian Working Women: Portraits from Life*, Boston, MA: David R. Godine.

Hill, Caroline (1904), 'The Economic Value of the Home', *Journal of Political Economy*, **12**, (3), 408–19.

Hill, Mary A. (1980), *Charlotte Perkins Gilman: The Making of a Radical Feminist, 1860–1896*, Philadelphia: Temple University Press.

Hofstadter, Richard (1944), *Social Darwinism in American Thought*, Boston, MA: Beacon Press.

Hollander, Samuel (1985), *The Economics of John Stuart Mill*, Vol. II, *Political Economy*, Toronto: University of Toronto Press.

Kraditor, Aileen S. (1965), *The Ideas of the Woman Suffrage Movement 1890–1920*, New York: Columbia University Press.

Kraditor, Aileen S. (ed.) (1968), *Up from the Pedestal: Selected Writings in the History of American Feminism*, Chicago: Quadrangle Books.

Lane, Ann J. (1979), 'Introduction' to *Herland*, New York: Pantheon Press.

Lane, Ann J. (1990), *To Herland and Beyond: the Life and Work of Charlotte Perkins Gilman*, New York: Pantheon.

Mill, Harriet Taylor (1851/1970), 'Enfranchisement of Women', in Alice S. Rossi (ed.), J.S. Mill and Harriet Taylor Mill, *Essays on Sex Equality*, Chicago: University of Chicago Press.

Mill, John Stuart (1869/1970), '*The Subjection of Women*', in Alice S. Rossi (ed.) J.S.

Mill and Harriet Taylor Mill, *Essays on Sex Equality*, Chicago: University of Chicago Press.

O'Donnell, Margaret (1985), 'Charlotte Perkins Gilman's Economic Interpretation of the Role of Women at the Turn of the Century', *Social Science Quarterly*, **69**, (1), March, 177–92.

Parrish, John B. (1967), 'The Rise of Economics as an Academic Discipline: The Formative Years to 1900', *Southern Economic Journal*, **34**, (1), 1–16.

Pigou, A.C. (1932), *The Economics of Welfare*, 4th edn, London: Macmillan.

Pujol, Michèle A. (1992), *Feminism and Anti-Feminism in Early Economic Thought*, Aldershot: Edward Elgar.

Rossi, Alice S. (ed.) (1973), *The Feminist Papers: From Adams to de Beauvoir*, New York: Columbia University Press.

Schneir, Miriam (ed.) (1972), *Feminism: The Essential Historical Writings*, New York: Random House.

Schwendinger, Herman and Julia R. Schwendinger (1974), *The Sociologists of the Chair*, New York: Basic Books.

Shapiro, Laura (1986), *Perfection Salad*, New York: Henry Holt and Co.

Sinclair, Andrew (1965), *The Emancipation of the American Woman*, New York: Harper & Row.

Sinclair, Upton (1906), *The Jungle*, New York: Signet Classics.

Spender, Dale (1982), *Women of Ideas (and What Men Have Done to Them)*, London: Ark Paperbacks.

Strasser, Susan (1982), *Never Done: A History of American Housework*, New York: Pantheon Books.

Veblen, Thorstein (1898), 'The Instinct of Workmanship and the Irksomeness of Labor', *American Journal of Sociology*, **4**, (4).

Veblen, Thorstein (1899a), 'The Barbarian Status of Women', *American Journal of Sociology*, **4**, (6).

Veblen, Thorstein (1899b), *The Theory of the Leisure Class*, New York: Macmillan.

9. Mary Paley Marshall, 1850–1944

Rita McWilliams Tullberg[1]

9.1 INTRODUCTION

When Mary Paley Marshall died in 1944, 94 years old, she had known and been known by several generations of economists in Britain and overseas. Her life story was the subject of a lengthy obituary by no less than John Maynard Keynes, who first met her during his Cambridge childhood. Her own memoirs, *What I Remember*, were published after her death. Yet despite this apparent notoriety, Mary Marshall remains an extraordinarily shadowy figure. It is difficult to analyse her work as an economist because she published so little herself. Her contribution to Alfred Marshall's writing seems to have been that of a secretary, nurse, translator, housekeeper and very junior research assistant – a general dogsbody perhaps, but one who had the satisfaction of knowing not only that she was totally indispensable, but also that her husband and most of their friends and professional acquaintances recognized the vital part she played in helping Marshall live a productive life.

The tantalizing and unanswerable question remains: if Marshall's character had been other than it was, could this have been a Webb, a Bosanquet or even a Myrdal-type partnership, with the partners contributing equally to the intellectual output of the team? Is there any evidence that Mary Marshall could have contributed or wanted to contribute more or differently to the Marshall partnership? This chapter sifts through the meagre stock of evidence which remains to us on her life with this question in mind, at the same time highlighting her own considerable talents and successes, for which she can be remembered and admired.

The discussion covers her childhood and education, her career as a teacher, her written work and significant interests besides academic economics. There are some concluding remarks.

9.2 THE RECTORY CHILD AND THE CAMBRIDGE STUDENT

Mary Paley was born on 24 October 1850 in Ufford, daughter of Thomas Paley and Ann Judith Wormald. He was from Halifax, Yorkshire, son of a doctor and grandson of Archdeacon Paley, the author of works on theology which sought to prove the existence of God with reference to the order and complexity of nature.[2] Thomas Paley studied at St John's College, Cambridge, was well placed in the competitive examination for the mathematical degree and became a college fellow.[3] Mary Paley's mother, Ann Judith, was also born into a Yorkshire family of some substance.[4] In the year of their marriage, 1847, Thomas Paley was presented by his college to the rectory of Ufford, a small village about five miles from the nearest market town of Stamford and about 40 miles north-west of Cambridge.

The area is dominated by Burleigh, the house and lands of the Marquis of Exeter. There was not a lot of social intercourse between the rectory and the 'big house' or the other 'better' families of the district; the strictness of Thomas Paley's political and religious views was said to have prevented this.[5] His daughter describes him as a 'staunch Radical', at odds with his aristocratic and exclusive neighbours over such issues as fox-hunting and horse-racing. While at Cambridge, he had been drawn to the teaching of Charles Simeon and was said by Mary Paley to be a 'strict Evangelical' with such a horror of anything even remotely reminiscent of High Church ritual or doctrines that there were few of the neighbouring clergy with whom he could be on intimate terms.[6] In an early manuscript draft of her memoir, *What I Remember*, she comments: 'So no wonder he was unpopular and that it was difficult for us to be on intimate terms with the neighbouring clergy and gentry and /were practically cut off from/ did not see much of young people of our own age' (Newnham Notes, ch. 1).[7]

It is an interesting coincidence that both Mary Paley's and Alfred Marshall's fathers have been described as 'strict Evangelicals'. While they may have shared the same views on such matters as the dangers of ritual, Thomas Paley does seem to have been more tolerant and progressive, with a better understanding of the importance of play and intellectual stimulation for his children. Where John Maynard Keynes describes William Marshall as a harsh and domineering man who kept his son at his books until late at night and who permitted no recreation, Mary Paley Marshall talks of a father who not only encouraged his children to learn foreign languages, but read story books with them and permitted the keeping of pets, lively games and play-acting.[8] She writes: 'We had a father who took part in work and play and who was interested in electricity and photography, and a mother who was full of initiative and always bright and amusing' (M.P. Marshall, 1947, 8–9). This can only be contrasted with Marshall's upbringing, where chess was forbidden and cricket discouraged, since it might have brought him into contact with 'unsuitable companions', mathematics was detested and women were to be kept strictly and subordinately in place (Newnham Notes: Talk, 1; Keynes, 1985b, 162–4).

It is also clear that the two family backgrounds were very different; the Paleys were a clerical, academic and professional family of some minor prominence and wealth, comfortably assured of their status which permitted small privileges, the most important of which was the luxury of radical views and behaviour. Marshall's family, on the other hand, as graphically presented in two biographical pieces by Coase, had seen better days and was trying, on William Marshall's small salary as a clerk at the Bank of England and the generosity of others, to claw its way back up the ladder of respectability (Coase, 1984, 1990).[9] Such family circumstances can be a breeding ground for intolerance and conservatism.

Mary Paley was educated at home and lessons began in earnest at the age of nine with the arrival of a lively German governess. Four years later, the governess married a local farmer and regular lessons stopped. Mary and her sister were then sent once a week to a 'select school ... kept by two maiden ladies' in Stamford which seems to have required little academic work of its students.[10] Their formal schooling was completed and, for the next few years, the girls 'read and did much as [they] chose', taught Sunday school, practised the hymns for the church services and visited the sick in their small village (M.P. Marshall, 1947, 8). Mary Paley found life very dull, the more so when her sister, who was two years older, married in 1868. She cites boredom and the practice of marrying young as the reason for her engagement to a young officer in the Engineers, who immediately left for a three-year tour of duty in India. Interestingly, we get here a glimpse of both her own independence of spirit and her father's tolerance and understanding of human nature. He disliked the engagement and never sanctioned it but, instead of forbidding the relationship, he distracted his clearly strong-willed daughter by encouraging her to study for the Cambridge Higher Local Examinations for Women over Eighteen which had recently been set up to test standards among women entering the teaching profession.[11] Some subjects she studied by herself, mathematics and divinity were studied with her father and languages with her former governess. Taking different groups of subjects in 1870 and 1871, she received distinctions in both divinity and German. She was awarded a scholarship on condition that she came to Cambridge and took advantage of a 'Lectures for Women' scheme which had started there in the Easter Term, 1870, whereby Cambridge lecturers offered teaching in the subjects of the Cambridge Higher Local Examination for Women. Her father was proud and pleased by her success and, although her mother objected strongly to the plan, he agreed to let her go to live in Cambridge with Ann Jemima Clough who had been invited by Henry Sidgwick to take charge of a house of residence for students coming to Cambridge to attend the women's lectures (Newnham Notes, ch. 2). Mary Paley described this scheme, whereby young, single women lived apart from their parents in Cambridge and followed lectures given by male university lecturers, as 'an outrageous proceeding' and this was undoubtedly what all but the most progressive people thought about it at that time.

Five young women were 'in residence' in Cambridge. One, Mary Kennedy, a talented woman four years older than Mary Paley, had boarded in the town with a private family and had already followed the lectures for two terms. She became Mary Paley's close friend and responsible for turning her interests towards economics:

> When I first arrived, I attended lectures for 'general cultivation', such as Latin, literature and history etc., but [Mary Kennedy] insisted on my going with her to a Political Economy lecture.[12] I said that I knew all about it, for it had only to do with wages, etc. which everyone understood. However, she was determined, so I went, and went to stay. (M.P. Marshall, 1940, 50)

The two young women studied the Moral Science subjects for Group D of the Higher Local Examinations in 1872, passed with a First Class and divided the Group D exhibition and the Marshall essay prize between them.[13] Mary Paley had gained distinctions in Logic and Political Economy.

Alfred Marshall was a member of the General Committee of Management for the Lectures for Women from the scheme's inception in January 1870 and had lectured in political economy for candidates to Section D of the Higher Locals from the first term. He saw no objection to women pursuing advanced studies and persuaded his two best women students, Mary Paley and Mary Kennedy, to study for the Moral Sciences Tripos, at that time the degree examination which included papers in political economy (Phillips, 1988, 3). Special teaching arrangements were made for the two women Tripos candidates. The lectures of Fawcett, the Professor of Political Economy, and Birks, the Knightsbridge Professor of Philosophy, were open to them and they were coached by Marshall, Foxwell, Sidgwick, Venn and others in the Tripos subjects, coaching being the normal form of teaching in Cambridge at this time.

Mary Paley sat her Tripos examinations, on an informal basis, in December 1874 (examinations were taken after ten terms at that time). The Tripos examiners, Herbert Foxwell, W.S. Jevons, P.G. Gardiner and J.B. Pearson, who had been persuaded to look over her papers, were unable to agree whether to place her in the First or Second Class and, in the absence of a chairman to cast a deciding vote, she was 'left hanging between heaven and hell' (M.P. Marshall, 1947, 17). A young John Neville Keynes noted in his diary for 15 December 1874 that: 'Two examiners put her in the first and two in the second class and neither seems disposed to give way. I suppose Pearson and Gardiner were the corking individuals who wanted to put her in the 2nd.'

Mary Paley's achievement was astonishing when compared with that of many of the male students taking honours degrees at that time. Not only did women students lack the disciplined habits of study and practice in writing examination papers in which most men students had been drilled since their earliest schooldays, but society persistently fed women negative signals as to the wisdom, propriety and need for them to study beyond an elementary level. Clearly, the companionship of like-minded women and the encouragement of their male teachers was of enormous importance and helped to combat social and often family disapproval of their thirst for knowledge or a professional qualification. However, they lacked the all-important role-models of successful women who had tried and succeeded in the quest for academic recognition. Thus Mary Paley's first and probably most important contribution to women academics in general and to women economists in particular was to show that formal qualifications could be attained by a woman, and with distinction.

By 1874, there were 27 women in residence in Cambridge and more wanting places all the time. Purpose-built accommodation was needed and it was decided to form a non-profit-making company to run a hall of residence and to appeal for funds to support the cause of the higher education of women in Cambridge. A hall was built on land in Newnham, then on the outskirts of Cambridge, designed by Basil Champneys. Mary Paley describes how Champneys and Marshall measured out the ground for the college together (Newnham Notes: Talk, 32/15). In 1877, Newnham Hall was launched as a limited company. Both Alfred Marshall and Mary Paley contributed generously to the cause: Mary Paley bought one share of £50 and donated a further £100; Alfred Marshall donated £50 and another £10 to the gymnasium fund (one of four donors).

In the first years of Newnham, the majority of students concentrated on the Higher Local Examinations and only about one in nine took Tripos examinations.[14] Their main aim was to return to, or, in a number of significant cases, to found, schools, and to bring habits of scholarship and discipline into the teaching of girls. Their pupils formed the next generation of women able to take advantage of the opportunities for higher education opening up to them at Cambridge and elsewhere in the country. By the mid-1890s, over 80 per cent of Newnham students entered for Tripos examinations, and the Higher Local Examinations became largely a college entrance requirement. Mary Paley continued to be revered as one of the five 'pioneers' and to command respect for her astonishing achievement in the Tripos.

9.3   CAREER AS A TEACHER

After her degree examination in December 1874, Mary Paley returned to Ufford for a few months. Here she took the remarkable step of giving a series of lectures in the nearby town of Stamford. 'I did it off my own bat. I had a class of 15 and gave a course of 6 lectures with papers once a week' (Newnham Notes, ch.2).[15] It can be assumed that the lectures were only open to women and were patterned on lecture schemes for women which were proving so successful in northern towns and elsewhere in the country (cf. note 35). The lecturers for such schemes were normally university men. This, therefore, was a very bold move for a young, unmarried woman to make on her own. As a result of her enterprise, so Mary Paley believed, she was invited to return to Newnham College from October 1875 as resident lecturer to take over the economics teaching from Marshall. At the Annual Meeting of the Association for Promoting the Higher Education of Women in Cambridge on 30 October 1875 it was announced that:

> Miss Paley obtained so much distinction in the Moral Sciences Examination, that the Committee thought themselves justified in selecting her to deliver lectures on Political Economy for the Association, in place of Mr Marshall who wishes temporarily to withdraw from the work. (Minute Book of the Association)

In May 1876, Mary Paley became engaged to Alfred Marshall and they were married in August 1877. The couple contracted themselves out of the clause whereby the woman vows to obey her husband (M.P. Marshall, 1947, 23). A.J. Clough, in her annual report in June that year, wrote:

> From October 1875 to June 1877, Miss Paley was in residence as Lecturer on Political Economy. She taught a class of nine Students, of whom six obtained a star of distinction in this subject in the Higher Local Examination. ... I cannot conclude this Report without mentioning the very valuable help I have received during the last two years from Miss Paley, who besides her teaching for the Lecture Association, has done much to encourage good feeling and a high standard of conduct and work among the students of Newnham Hall. (The Principal's Report to the Meeting of Shareholders of the Newnham Hall Company, June 1877)

On marriage, Marshall had to resign his college fellowship and find other means of support. Mary Paley Marshall, as she now signed her written work and letters, had inherited some money from her family, but her income, she records, was insufficient to support them. Other plans which would involve their both working, a radical departure from the norm, were considered: 'One plan seriously discussed was that we should become Board-school teachers. Just at that time, however, the Principalship of University College, Bristol was advertised, with a salary of £700 a year, and after much anxious consideration, Alfred decided to apply' (M.P. Marshall, 1947, 22).

The University College in Bristol had opened in the spring of 1876. John Percival, headmaster of Clifton College, the 'middle-class public school' in Bristol, had for some years run schemes promoting the liberal education of both women and the working classes as a way of tackling the social problems thrown up by industrialization and urban living. Percival sponsored lecture courses in Bristol in a number of subjects given by the members of staff of the boys's school. In his pamphlet, *The Connection of the Universities and the Great Towns*, published in 1873, he put forward ideas drawn from Matthew Arnold and John Henry Newman for colleges of liberal culture in major industrial and commercial towns. The towns were to provide the buildings and equipment, the universities of Oxford and Cambridge would endow chairs and supply the teaching personnel. The idea was taken up in Bristol by wealthy members of the Nonconformist and Quaker communities, while university support was provided by Balliol and New College, Oxford. The Master of Balliol, Benjamin Jowett, took a personal interest in the scheme and is credited with insisting that the Bristol institution should offer not only science subjects, the local preference, but also literature, and that women should be admitted to courses on the same terms as men (Carleton, 1984, 1–4).

Although it was originally hoped to attract someone who could combine the work of principal with that of professor of mathematics or classical history and literature, the post was eventually offered to Alfred Marshall, together with a chair in political economy.[16] Marshall's arrival marked an upswing in the number of students attending economics lectures. One student, Marian F. Pease, records particular excitement at the arrival of the young couple:

> in 1877, we heard that Mr Marshall, a Fellow of St John's College, Cambridge, was appointed Principal and some of us knew that his bride ... was Mary Paley who was one of the six first students of Newnham College, that she had been allowed to write the papers for the Moral Sciences Tripos and that she had shown that her brains were equal to those of the men. That she was the [great] granddaughter of 'Paley's Evidences' – which at home we had had read to us on Sunday afternoons, added to the interest. (Pease, 1942, 6)[17]

Marian Pease speaks in glowing terms of the impression made on her by Marshall's public inaugural lecture, where he infected the audience with his enthusiasm and his faith in economic science as furthering the cause of social improvement. Pease continues:

> Mrs Marshall's graceful charm attracted everybody and to us she represented Newnham and the cause of the higher education of women. It is difficult for this

generation [1942] to realise what that cause meant to us. There were then no degree or professional examinations open to women and no college which they could enter on the same terms as men except our own (and possibly one other) – women who wanted to be doctors had to fight their way through incredible difficulties – the High School movement was only just beginning to give women teachers some sort of status and Girton and Newnham only existed on sufferance and got their students examined by the personal kindness of men like Dr. Sidgwick and other Fellows of Cambridge Colleges. ... Mrs Marshall had taken her part [in this struggle] and we felt indeed honoured to have her amongst us. (Pease, 1942, 7–8)

After settling into their new house in Clifton, Mary Marshall 'was pretty busy socially' during this first year of married life. There was also work to be done completing the *Economics of Industry*, which the couple had begun to work on together during their engagement. Making no mention of the absence of pregnancy which could be expected to fill the life of a young, Victorian bride, Mary Marshall records that the couple planned to share some of the College work:[18] 'both Alfred and I were anxious that I should /be allowed to/ help in the work of the College especially as it was the first College to start mixed education' (Newnham Notes, ch.3).

The suggestion was brought before the Education Board in May 1878, that she should superintend the admission of female students and generally advise such students in their choice of subjects: 'The Board desires to express its cordial thanks to Mrs Marshall, and recommends the Council to devise some scheme that will enable the College to profit by her services in the capacity referred to' (University College, Bristol, Minutes Book of the Educational Board, 4 May 1878). Later the same month, she was appointed to take over Marshall's morning lectures, at his request (Council Minutes, 15 May 1878).[19]

During Marshall's first year, 30 women had attended economics lectures, compared with only five the previous year. The numbers of male students were also up, from 14 to 20. However, only one man attended the day classes and it was therefore felt suitable for Mary Marshall to take over the daytime teaching. It should be noted that this arrangement was made a year before Marshall's illness obliged him to cut down on his teaching; thus the decision to give Mary a teaching post was not an emergency arrangement. For the academic year 1878–9, she lectured twice a week and held a class for one hour on Mondays, allowing her husband to reduce his teaching to one class and one lecture a week for two terms.[20] On the whole, Mary Marshall did more teaching, and more advanced teaching, than her husband did during these years. Her lectures followed closely the pattern of the chapters of the *Economics of Industry*, with the addition of lectures on the principles of taxation, English taxes and their effects on the various classes of the community, the economic functions of government, and the methodology of economics and its relation to other branches of social science (University College, Bristol, *Calendar*, 1881–2).

The appointment of a woman as a lecturer (as she was described in the College *Calendar*), was reported with some pride at the Annual General Meeting of Governors of University College, Bristol. The secretary explained that:

> permission had been given to the Principal to delegate to Mrs Marshall the day lectures on political economy which are chiefly attended by women; a permission which the Council felt justified in giving, from the high testimonials of Mrs Marshall, and the great success which attended her teaching at Newnham-hall [*sic*], Cambridge. In pursuance of this arrangement, Mrs Marshall now delivers the day lectures on political economy and the Council have every reason to be satisfied with the results. (Newspaper report inserted in Council Minutes, 21 December 1878)

In the spring of 1879, Alfred Marshall fell ill. The trouble was diagnosed as a kidney stone and he was in considerable pain. He was ordered a complete rest, with no exercise. Fearing he would be an invalid for a long time, he determined to give up his post as principal. However, great pressure was brought to bear, 'for it was thought that to change Principal would be a distinct evil'. One source of this pressure was Benjamin Jowett, a member of the Council, and already a close friend of both the Marshalls. Marshall tendered his resignation, but it was not accepted and he was asked to remain for a further year.[21]

Marshall submitted his resignation again in May 1881, citing his inability to cope energetically with the external and social engagements which the post of principal entailed. He also resigned from his post as professor of economics. Blaming himself for taking on duties 'which I was not strong enough to discharge', Marshall added:

> It is my one consolation with regard to the past, that in all directions in which her influence could reach, my wife has more than made up for my deficiencies, and it is my chief regret with regard to the future that her work must be lost to the College. (Letter, dated 11 July 1881, copied into the Council Minutes, 18 May 1881)

The Council accepted the resignation with regret, recording its high appreciation of the 'great ability, energy and devotion to the interests of the College displayed by [Marshall] and Mrs Marshall during the whole period of their connection with the Institution'. Jowett was still not prepared to lose them and wrote to Marshall the following month suggesting that they could perhaps both return to the college as professors of political economy or that Marshall could be made a fellow of Balliol with minimum residence requirements, once the new statutes came into effect allowing the appointment of married fellows.[22] Both could then continue their work at Bristol (B. Jowett to A. Marshall, 9 August 1881, Marshall Archive 1/40).

After spending the winter in Sicily, Marshall had recovered sufficiently for the couple to travel slowly back through Europe in the spring, sightseeing on the way. Bristol University Council Minutes record the reappointment of Alfred Marshall as professor of political economy on 24 May 1882 and note that Mrs Marshall was to assist him in giving some portion of the day lectures. A year later, the Minutes contain a letter of resignation from Marshall on his acceptance of a lectureship at Oxford. A similar letter of resignation was received from Mrs Marshall. These were accepted with 'deep regret at the loss of their valuable services and to assure them of the warm appreciation of the devotion they have ever shown to the interests of the College which is entertained by the Council' (Council Minutes, 23 May 1883).

Mary Paley Marshall's work was long remembered at Bristol, where she was one of the very first woman university lecturers in the country and a source of particular inspiration to her students. Two years after Marshall's death, she was honoured for her lifelong work as a teacher of economics with the award of the degree of D Litt by the University of Bristol.[23] In presenting her for the degree, Professor Crofts, the Dean of the Faculty of Arts, described her as 'a distinguished scholar in her own right, who has devoted the best of her powers to collaboration with her husband in researches which have brought economics out of the cloud of surmise into the daylight of true science'. In her lectures on economics at Bristol, she had 'set before the students of the University College those high ideals of scholarly work and corporate effort, to which, as a University, they endeavoured to remain true' (reported in the Newnham College Roll *Letter*, January 1928).

At Oxford, Marshall took over the post of lecturer to the Indian Civil Service candidates left vacant by the death of Arnold Toynbee and was made an honorary fellow of Balliol. The Marshalls had their entry into Oxford society smoothed through their friendship with Jowett, and it is likely that he introduced Mary Marshall to the men and women who were active in the women's higher education movement there. An organization, similar in objective to that in Cambridge, had been formed in Oxford to run an ambitious scheme of extramural lectures, preparing women for the Oxford Examination for Women over Eighteen Years. Two halls of residence had been opened in 1879, one based on broad Church of England principles (Lady Margaret Hall) and the other non-denominational (Somerville).

In her first term at Oxford, Mary Marshall does not appear to have been formally involved with this scheme. We do, however, have some indication that she was actively engaged in teaching for the women's education movement, since she is recorded in the membership list of the (old students')

Newnham College Club as 'Teacher by Correspondence'. Correspondence courses were run by the women's education schemes in both Cambridge and Oxford at that time. They were 'intended to promote the self-education of women who are unable to obtain efficient oral teaching and to assist them in preparing for the Higher Local Examinations' (Newnham College Report, 1881).[24]

The first lecturer in political economy under the Oxford Association for the Education of Women (AEW) had been Arnold Toynbee. William Sidgwick took over in 1881–2, but the subject was dropped in the academic year 1882–3. Mary Paley Marshall began her lectures in the Lent [sic] Term, 1884, lectured in both the Summer and Michaelmas Terms and was scheduled to teach again in Lent 1885. Her arrival gave a tremendous boost to the number of students interested in economics. Whereas Sidgwick had been able to attract at most seven women in 1881–2, 34 women gathered to listen to Mary Marshall's weekly lectures on 'Labour, Wages, Poverty &c.', that is, 25 per cent of the total attendance at women's lectures in Oxford at that time (Bodleian Library, papers of the AEW, MS. Top.Oxon.c.818). These numbers reflect not only a particular interest among women in economics and its value in understanding the problems of poverty, but also a certain amount of curiosity about the 'lady lecturer from Newnham', admiration for her as a pioneer in the cause of women's education and, it can be assumed, the convenience of attending a lecture without a chaperone which a female lecturer entailed. Many of her students chose to continue with her course for a second term, and she again attracted just under 25 per cent of the total attendance.[25] She was also available to coach women students who needed special help, a task she shared with Michael Sadler and Robert Ewing.

She made many friends in Oxford and found life there 'simpler and less expensive' than at Cambridge: 'we had made up our minds that Oxford was to be our home in the future' (Newnham Notes, ch.5). Marshall was perhaps less settled: '[The] Oxford climate did not suit him and he never got thoroughly *en rapport* with Oxford life and thought, though he always was grateful for [the] immense kindness shown to us there' (Newnham Notes: Talk, 18/40).[26]

This Oxford interlude was interrupted by the death of Fawcett, the Professor of Political Economy in Cambridge, in November 1884 and the appointment of Alfred Marshall to the chair the following month. Although Mary Marshall was committed to teaching in Oxford for the Lent Term, 1885, there was to be no compromise involving two households for a few months. Before the end of December, 1884, she had given her new Cambridge address to the Newnham College Club.

It might be assumed that, in returning to Cambridge as the wife of a professor, Mary Marshall would assume a high profile as an economics lecturer at

Newnham. This was not the case; in fact, it becomes quite difficult to trace her work as a lecturer in economics from this point. From 1886 until 1890, her name even disappears from the membership list of the Newnham College Club and, when it reappears again in 1890 and for subsequent years, there is no indication given as to occupation. Newnham College Reports describe her as lecturing in moral sciences from 1885 for the college but, although she was a member of the College Council for 1891–4 and again for 1907–9, she appears to have done little or no committee work until after Marshall's retirement.[27] For example, she does not appear to have become a member of the Education Committee until about 1909. One reason for this may be that the number of Newnham students taking economics as a Tripos subject was small.

Winnie Seebohm, however, has left us with a fascinating portrait of Mary Marshall at this time, her appearance and teaching methods. She described her in a letter to her family after attending an introductory lecture:

> She *is* Princess Ida.[28] She wears a flowing dark green cloth robe with dark brown fur round the bottom (not on the very edge) – she has dark brown hair which goes back in a great wave and is very loosely pinned up behind – very deep-set large eyes, a straight nose – a face that one likes to watch. Then she is enthusiastic and simple. She speaks fluently and earnestly with her head thrown back a little and her hands generally clasped or resting on the desk. She looks oftenest at the ceiling but every now and then straight at you. She looks at Political Economy from a philanthropic woman's point of view, and talks to each separately about the books we might read and the other subjects we are working at. (Glendinning, 1969, 71)[29]

In 1885, Mary Marshall still lectured to students who came to Newnham to study for the Higher Local Examinations, but by the mid-1890s the overwhelming majority of Newnham students were studying for a Tripos. Prior to the foundation of a separate Tripos, economics papers were optional in the History Tripos and obligatory in Part 1 and optional in Part II of the Moral Sciences Tripos (for details of reforms involving economics in these Triposes, see Groenewegen, 1990). Neither Tripos was particularly popular among the women students and the number requiring teaching in economics would be small.[30] With the foundation of the Economics Tripos in 1904, Mary's role as teacher assumed a new significance. The number of women opting to take an economics degree was small in the early days, but they now had a three-year course of study in economics in which they required teaching and guidance. From 1904 to 1916, Mary Paley steered 55 women through the new examination, gaining an outstanding success in 1908 when two of her students gained First Class degrees (McWilliams Tullberg, 1993a).

At the beginning of the Michaelmas Term 1908, the first term of Marshall's retirement, the Principal of Newnham announced to the Education Committee that:

> Mrs Marshall had ceased to lecture on Economics for the College as the lectures provided by the University meet our needs but she was very kindly coming for $1^1/2$ hours a week to talk over work with students and would if necessary give papers and other assistance. (Newnham Education Committee Minutes, 20 October 1908)

However, as she now became a member of the Education Committee, the extent of her teaching commitments to the College are recorded in the Committee's minutes over the following eight years. She acted as Director of Studies for all students reading economics, whether as a whole Tripos or a paper in the History Tripos. This meant that she organized their teaching, especially extra teaching or coaching, advised them on their choice of subjects, guided their reading, looked over weekly and term papers, and assessed their progress.[31] In Michaelmas Term 1910, while expressing her willingness to remain as Honorary Director of Studies, she proposed that one of her most successful students, Lynda Grier, should take on part of the work of advising economics students (Newnham Education Committee Minutes, 18 October 1910). Mary Marshall continued in this role for some years, the outbreak of war in 1914 postponing any plans she may have had for complete retirement. Lynda Grier was appointed Assistant Lecturer in Economics by the College in 1913 and Lecturer in 1915, but in that same year was given leave of absence from Newnham to fill the place of D.H. Macgregor, Professor of Economics at Leeds University, who had been called away on war work (Newnham Education Committee Minutes, 21 October 1913 and 19 October 1915). Mary Paley Marshall stepped in again as Director of Studies for economics students for the academic year 1915–16 but was finally able to hand over her task to two more of her most successful students, Eva Spielman and, later, Geraldine Jebb.

After the turn of the century, Newnham students began to have access to a new breed of women teachers who had gone through the Cambridge Tripos mill and who were actively pursuing and publishing their own research work. Mary Marshall was still much liked and respected by her students as a kindly old lady who had done something significant for women's education ten years or more before they were born, but, to these young women of the twentieth century, her teaching lacked the glamour of independent scholarship. Mary Agnes Adamson (Mrs Hamilton, Newnham, 1901–4), who first read classics but in her third year had to switch Tripos, 'out of the plain necessity of speedy equipment to earn a living' described Mary Marshall's teaching as follows:

> For this, Economics appeared more relevant; ... the way in, at this time, was still Part II of the History Tripos – a pretty mixed bag, with Economic Theory as its most important element. The school was dominated by Alfred Marshall; his vast Principles was its Bible. Mrs Marshall taught us; ... she regarded the Principles as

verbally inspired. This I could not feel even after, having ventured some extra-Marshall opinion in an essay for her, she squashed me with the remark – 'Fools rush in where angels fear to tread'. (Hamilton, 1936, 40–41)

Some years later, the same observation was made by Ann Carr (Newnham, 1908–11):

> Every [economics] seminar was devoted wholly to the worship of her husband and the PRINCIPLES. I can't remember any other subject being mentioned. We girls combed the PRINCIPLES through and through to find one dot or comma misplaced and later editions of the great book ought to owe a little to us. There was some naughtiness of spirit mixed with great affection for Mrs Marshall. (Ann Carr to John Maynard Keynes, 29 October 1944, Keynes Collection, King's College, Cambridge, JMK A/44)

In Mary Marshall's defence, it might be argued that the style and content of her teaching lacked vision and originality not simply because of her identification with Marshall's work, but also because she had herself been taught in a Cambridge tradition which still encouraged personalized *coaching*, in the sense of cramming a specific syllabus for the purpose of passing a necessary examination or achieving a high position in a competitive Tripos.[32] Throughout her teaching career, she had spent her energies in helping women gain a foothold on the first rungs of the academic ladder; even later in the century, when students had received the benefits of good schooling, economics was not a subject which they had previously studied and they still needed a good grounding.

Nonetheless, her latter-day students accused her of lack of scholarship. Were they being unreasonable? The early women academics saw teaching as their primary duty. A majority of Newnham students (and this was the college ethos) felt their task was to improve their own educational standard and then quickly return to teaching in one form or another to raise the level of education for the next generation of women. This they did with astounding success. It is true that many men graduates of the same generation also ended up as teachers, although fewer felt they were responding to a call to duty in quite the same way. For those men who chose to remain at the university, there were, mid-century, very few official teaching posts or well-paid fellowships available. They turned instead to full-time coaching, which could provide an adequate income and was a lucrative profession for the most successful. It left little time for research, even if that had been a respectable alternative. Research was felt to be the task of the few professors, and in some quarters was viewed with grave suspicion as an excuse for anarchic rethinking. As Rothblatt explains, reformers who proposed that all university teachers unite German practices of scholarship with English teaching skills 'encountered formidable opposition' (Rothblatt, 1968, 201–2). Many of the men who fought to establish women's colleges in Cambridge, Marshall included, also campaigned for educational reform at the university: 'They were distinguished by their professional interest in scholarship, by their intention to make university teaching a career and by their desire to revive the unique feature of the collegiate university, the close relation between fellows and students' (Rothblatt, 1968, 227). In the final quarter of the century, great strides were made towards this goal, with the expansion of college lectureships and fellowships for which proven research ability became a sine qua non.

The women's colleges, however, continued to emphasize the sound grasp of fundamentals and the ability to teach these to others, coupled with organizational ability, as the skills most needed to advance women's education. There was little time and no money for anything else. For, as research opportunities within the University expanded for men, Cambridge women were excluded from those vital teaching posts, research fellowships, essay prizes and postgraduate degrees which would have enabled them to take up research.[33] There were even practical difficulties in their way; they had, for example, no greater rights at the university library than the general public. Among some members of the women's colleges, there was a growing realization that their academic goals needed to be reconsidered. As Ethel Sargant, a noted botanist who had been a student at Girton, put it in 1901:

> The truth is we do not sufficiently realise that the experimental stage is past. ... Now that college life has left its stamp on a generation, we may fairly seek to criticise the system in order to amend it. The great defect in it is that in the effort to satisfy University tests we have neglected the pursuit of learning for its own sake. (Sargant, quoted in Vicinus, 1985, 132–3)

But it was not until the turn of the century that the women's colleges were able to fund research. The first Research Fellowship was endowed at Newnham in 1898 and at Girton in 1900.[34]

Mary Paley Marshall devoted her teaching career, stretching as it did over 40 years, to grounding women students in the fundamentals of economic theory and analysis. She contributed significantly to the rapid progress made in women's education – which in turn made her own teaching practices obsolete. Yet her own lack of independent scholarship cannot be explained away so simply. It still might be argued that, married as she was to a man with a secure income, with no children, with access to books and a taste for the simple life, she might have achieved more. It is therefore necessary to examine further aspects of her life before her apparent lack of originality can be explained.

9.4 PUBLICATIONS AND PUBLIC ADDRESSES

Mary Paley Marshall's first excursion into authorship remains her most controversial. Shortly after returning to Newnham as lecturer, she was approached
by Professor Stuart, who wanted a simple textbook in economics for the
University Extension Lectures for which he was becoming the driving force.[35]

> Prof. Stuart asked me (fresh from my Tripos and rather cocky) to write a small
> cheap text book for the Extension lectures, which had just started. In a weak
> moment and with a light heart I agreed ... not knowing what a hard job it was.
> However, Mr Marshall came to the rescue and the book gradually became almost
> entirely his. In fact, its Book II contains the germ of his Theory of Distribution.
> But he insisted on my name appearing on the title page. He always disliked the
> little book for it offended against his pet dogma 'That every dogma that is short
> and simple is false', and as he said 'you can't afford to tell the truth for half-a-
> crown'. (Newnham Notes: Talk, 19–12)

The *Economics of Industry* was published in 1879 and reprinted nine
times, with minor revisions in 1881. Marked copies of the 1884 and 1886
reprints indicate that at some point a revised edition was contemplated. In the
early 1890s, Marshall, in his own words, 'had the book suppressed' and he
continued to condemn it for many years. His most successful manoeuvre was
to produce another book in 1892 'made chiefly from scissors and paste out of
my *Principles*', of which he was the sole author. Although the full designa-
tion of the 1892 book is *Elements of the Economics of Industry*, the spine
bears the title *Economics of Industry*, to the confusion of readers and librarians alike. Keynes said of the original *Economics of Industry*:

> It was, in fact, an extremely good book; nothing more serviceable for its purpose
> was produced for many years, if ever. I know that my father [John Neville
> Keynes] always felt that there was something ungenerous in Marshall's distaste
> for this book, which was originally hers, but it was allowed to go out of print
> without a murmur of complaint from her when there was still a strong demand for
> it. (Keynes, 1985b, 239)

A number of reasons have been adduced to explain Marshall's dislike for
the book. Marshall's own explanations were that it proved too difficult to
combine simplicity with scientific accuracy, and that he had said something
in the book on American Trusts about which he later changed his mind.
Others have suggested that he was irritated by having to defend himself in
academic journals during the 1880s against misunderstandings which had
arisen because of the book's brief treatment of certain subjects, that he had
profoundly altered his treatment of normal values in the *Principles* so that the
concept was now a relative one rather than something absolute, as it had been

in the *Economics of Industry*, and that holding as he did a view of women's intellects as inferior and incapable of advanced theoretical work, it was inappropriate that he should himself be co-author of a book with a woman (Keynes, 1985a, 201–2; Whitaker, 1975, 1, 67–83; these objections and further details concerning the *Economics of Industry* can be found in McWilliams Tullberg, 1992).[36]

It seems probable that Mary Marshall's contribution to the book was twofold: first, a large share in the authorship of the early chapters, and second, editorial work throughout the book. Book I deals with the agents of production, the law of diminishing returns, the organization of industry, the division of labour and the tenure of land, and is largely definitional and descriptive. The analytical core of the book is in Book II, covering normal value, demand and supply, rent, wages and profits and the earnings of management, while Book III examines market values, market fluctuations and their causes, and contains the valuable discussions on trade unions and cooperatives. The preface to the 1881 reprint explains that the first chapters of the book were printed at a time when it was proposed to give the work a more elementary character than later proved possible. It does not appear unreasonable that a recently-graduated student in the moral sciences, of which economics was one of four major subjects, well taught by Alfred Marshall and highly regarded by her examiners could, under guidance, produce the material 'of elementary character' given in Book I.[37] Book II, however, contained analysis which only someone who had been thinking, reading and discussing points of economic theory for some years could produce. Similarly, Book III covers topics of which Mary Marshall at that time could have had little direct experience, unlike Marshall, who had promoted the cause of the Agricultural Workers Union in East Anglia, contributed to the socialist press and observed industrial conditions in Britain, Germany and the United States.

When J.N. Keynes heard that Marshall was to help Mary Paley with the little textbook, he wrote in his diary: 'with Marshall's matter and her style, Miss Paley's book will probably be a great success' (J.N. Keynes diary, 15 June 1877, Cambridge University Library, Manuscript Collection).[38] There is a clarity of style and directness in the *Economics of Industry*, sorely missing from the *Principles*, which must in some measure be attributed to Mary Marshall. Left to his own devices, it seems unlikely that Marshall would have or could have produced the *Economics of Industry* alone. The record of the production of the eight editions of the *Principles*, of *Industry and Trade* and *Money, Credit & Commerce*, not to mention the abandoned second volume of the *Principles*, demonstrates his incapacity for producing books on time and of limited length. Extension lecture students, candidates for the Higher Local and Bankers' examinations and those of limited means and leisure no doubt had reason to thank Mary for the little book's existence.[39]

The part which she played in the production of the 'big books' is unclear. In the preface to the first edition of the *Principles*, Marshall wrote: 'My wife has aided and advised me at every stage of the MSS and of the proofs, and it owes a very great deal to her suggestions, her care and her judgement.' He was less generous in his thanks in the next three editions, but from the fifth edition he returned, in content, to the original acknowledgement. However, these tributes could mean that Mary Paley was primarily concerned with secretarial and subeditorial matters, not with drafting or determining structure or content. C.R. Fay, in his memoir, cited a postcard received from Marshall in thanks for some printing errors he and Edwin Cannan had found in the *Principles*; Marshall wrote: 'thanks for the *errata*. I have handed them to Mary. The mistakes are her department' (Fay, 1982, in Wood, 1982, 1, 87). Professor Austin Robinson had the impression that she was used as a sounding-board for Marshall's written work: if she could catch his point, then so could the general reader.[40] There is no record anywhere that he asked her advice as an economist. Jowett certainly thought Mary could influence Marshall in matters of style, begging her to ensure that Marshall did not allow mathematics to assume a dominant role in the *Principles* (B. Jowett to M.P. Marshall, 14 December 1884 and 30 December 1886; and to A. Marshall, 24 July 1890; Marshall Collection, Marshall, 1/43, 1/47 and 1/53). However, it seems unlikely that Marshall needed any encouragement to restrict his use of both geometry and algebra, the latter being kept for a mathematical appendix.

The aid and advice given by his wife was also acknowledged by Marshall in the *Elements of the Economics of Industry* and both editions of *Industry and Trade*. This latter work included material which had been typeset as far back as 1904 but, in view of Marshall's declining health and mental powers, the completion of the book must owe a great deal to Mary's skill in bringing coherence to Marshall's many drafts, notes and previously printed pieces. This is even more the case with *Money, Credit & Commerce*, which was published in 1923, one year before Marshall's death. In the notes which she made for Keynes to use in writing his biographical memoir of Marshall, she explained: 'After [*Industry and Trade*] came out [1919] his health began to fail, though he did not know it. On this account, I did all I could to hasten the appearance of [*Money, Credit & Commerce*], especially as Dr. Bowen told me in 1921 that his working life was over and that he was incapable of constructive work.'[41] Further evidence for her work in producing *Money, Credit & Commerce* can be adduced from the fact that, whereas she is warmly thanked in a draft Preface, there are no acknowledgements made to her in the published version.

The Marshalls' first experience of co-authorship was not a happy one and neither may have been inclined to repeat it (see in particular the correspondence with Foxwell during 1878 and 1879 given in Groenewegen, 1991, 15).

Marshall made his dissatisfaction with the book widely known; how far Mary Marshall resented his takeover of the textbook with which he had originally agreed to help and then his negative attitude towards it remains her secret.[42] We can guess that her feelings were mixed; she was perhaps aware that she could not complete the project herself, but unhappy to detect an ungracious, domineering side of Marshall's character. Professor Becattini has suggested that the timing of this discovery can be connected with the blossoming of her interest in painting, which allowed her to express herself independently of Marshall (see below, p. 179). Marshall reputedly had difficulties in cooperating and delegating. William Ramsay, the man chosen to succeed Marshall as Principal of University College, Bristol in 1881, having worked under him as Professor of Chemistry for a year, reportedly noted Marshall's inability to work with others: 'Marshall, though ably seconded by his wife, herself an economist, was essentially a solitary worker' (Ramsay papers, Travers, in Introduction to Vol.5, pts 1 & 2).

In the 15 years which followed publication of the revised edition of the *Economics of Industry*, Mary Marshall published nothing. She then made two contributions to the *Economic Journal*. In the first of these, under the heading 'Notes and Memoranda' in March 1896, she commented on some of the contributions to the Conference of Women Workers which had taken place in October 1895 in Nottingham under the auspices of the National Council of Women. By 1893, an estimated half a million middle-class women were working 'continuously and semi-professionally' in philanthropy, while another 20 000 supported themselves as 'paid officials' in charitable societies (Prochaska, 1980, 224, quoting Louisa Hubbard's 'Statistics of women's work' published in 1893). To these should be added a large number of women who worked part-time for charity, as did Mary Marshall herself (below, p. 178). Many women regarded social service as their profession, albeit unpaid, and met on a regional or local basis as Unions of Women Workers to pool professional experience and coordinate their activities. In 1895, a central Union body was established, known at the time as the National Council of Women.[43] Some of the topics discussed at the three-day Nottingham meeting were concerned with philanthropic subjects; others related to the women's own position as philanthropists. Mary Marshall expressed doubts that anything of value could result from such a wide-ranging discussion.

She singled out three papers for special attention. Eleanor Mildred Sidgwick, the principal of Newnham College, spoke on the changing efficiency and earnings of women teachers in secondary schools over the previous 30 years. Earnings were still inadequate. A woman needed to save for her retirement which, because of the fashion which gave preference to teachers under 35, could be forced on her at an early age. Despite this, E.M. Sidgwick felt that women who were not in need of a salary should not be discouraged from entering the profession, since 'the dignity of the profession is raised by its being pursued as an art or vocation rather than a trade' (M.P. Marshall, 1896, 107). Mary Marshall makes no comment on this perverse view of incomes policy by someone who had the future of the teaching profession at heart; she presumably agreed that raising the social tone of the profession would increase the demand for girls' education, and would thus be ultimately more efficacious in improving salaries than would restricting the pool of available teachers. Given the prevalent social snobbery and the fact that parents had to be persuaded to give their girls a good secondary education, there may have been some force in the observation.

Ella Pycroft discussed domestic science teaching and the theme, apparently familiar at the time, that continental housewives were better able to produce good food on small incomes than their British counterparts. This she put down to domestic economy lessons for girls in both lower- and middle-class schools on the Continent and their absence in Britain. Mary Marshall makes no comment on this, at least in part, it can be assumed, because Pycroft reflected the views of Alfred Marshall who criticized the English and American housewives who 'make limited means go a less way towards satisfying wants than the French housewife does, not because they do not know how to buy, but because they cannot produce as good finished commodities out of the raw material of inexpensive joints, vegetables etc. as she can' (Marshall, 1961, 119, note 1, unchanged from the second edition of 1891).[44]

The lengthiest section of her review is devoted to a paper by Beatrice Webb who argued for 'Further restrictions on women's labour' so as to raise their efficiency and economic independence. B. Webb argued that trade unionism could not help the majority of women workers before legislation had ensured them a minimum of health and vigour:

> Before wage-earners can exercise the intelligence, the deliberation, and the self-denial that are necessary for Trade Unionism, they must enjoy a certain standard of physical health, a certain surplus of energy, and a reasonable amount of leisure. It is a cruel mockery to preach Trade Unionism, and Trade Unionism alone, to the sempstress sewing day and night in her garret for a bare subsistence; to the laundrywoman standing at the tub eighteen hours at a stretch; or to the woman whose health is undermined with 'Wrist-drop', 'Potter's-rot' or 'Phossy-jaw'. (Beatrice Webb, quoted in Adam, 1945, 12)

Mary Marshall criticized Webb's piece on a number of grounds. She took exception to Webb's typically Fabian response to social ills, that legislation is necessary to improve the wages and conditions of women workers because of the weakness of the individual worker vis-à-vis the employer. In her opinion, there were many examples of industries in which this was not true, though she offered no examples. Further, the view that trade unions and government action are alike in restricting the so-called liberty of the worker, and that, for women in their current situation, legislation must precede unionization struck her as particularly 'bold' (which in Victorian feminine parlance could mean 'outrageous').

She also claimed that 'more moderate advocates' of further restriction of women's labour based their case on the benefits which this would have for the health and happiness of children, whereas Beatrice Webb held that it was important to legislate for adult women from the point of view of the women themselves 'to increase their economic independence and efficiency as workers and citizens no less than as wives and mothers' (M.P. Marshall, 1896, 108). One of Mary Marshall's 'more moderate advocates' was her husband, who was severe in his criticisms of women workers. He insisted that women working outside the home neglected their household duties and failed to invest 'in the personal capital of their children's character and abilities' (Marshall, 1961, 685, unchanged from the first edition. See also 1920, 198, 529 and 564).[45]

This particular piece of writing by Mary Paley Marshall is limp and impersonal. Where views are expressed, they correspond with those of Alfred Marshall. Had she lost the ability to express any opinion of her own through constant deference to her husband? Or did perhaps breeding, good manners and friendship with the three authors concerned prevent her from expressing herself more forcefully? A possible interpretation in this particular case is that she simply found the collection of papers scarcely worth reviewing.

Fortunately, she contributed another review to the *Economic Journal* six years later which was far more substantial. In 1902, Clara Collet published a collection of her papers in a book with the title *Educated Working Women*. It was reviewed the same year by Mary Marshall. Collet, who was a pupil and friend of H.S. Foxwell from London University,[46] had worked with Charles Booth on *Life and Labour of the People of London* in the 1880s, as an assistant commissioner on the Labour Commission of which Alfred Marshall had been a member, and then at the Labour Department of the Board of Trade.

Mary Marshall applauded Collet's view that a woman's intellect differs from that of a man because it is formed by a different set of interests and emotions. Women's successes were to be built on work which complements rather than competes with that of men – this point being a favourite Marshallian hobby-horse.[47] The implication was that the numbers of women employed in industry would fall and those in the service sector rise. However, 'natural characteristics' – by which was meant a woman's marital and child-rearing habits – produced a great many 'economic paradoxes and discords' in relation to women's work and wages. Collet's data, given in 'The prospects of marriage for women', a paper originally published ten years previously, showed that, while almost all women in the poorer classes could expect to marry, this was not the case in the middle and upper classes. Analysis of census returns by district revealed a great disproportion in the number of marriageable women to men in those middle- and upper-class areas studied, even after allowing for the living-in female servants.[48]

Collet described how each successive social group required a higher standard of life if status was to be maintained. But a misplaced belief that their work filled only a temporary interval before marriage led single women to accept earnings below this standard. With regard to the earnings of women in the upper-middle classes in particular, 'chaos reigns supreme'. Collet's analysis of the 'Expenditure of middle-class working women' showed that many high-school teachers did not earn the efficiency wages that permitted the necessary rest and recreation 'in an occupation requiring freshness, vitality, and energy, and ... provision in old age' (M.P. Marshall, 1902, 255). The chief reason for these low salaries was that parents were not prepared to spend much money on their daughters' education, since they expected them to marry after a few years and be supported for the rest of their lives. 'If parents recognised frankly the need for their daughters to be self-supporting, there would be a demand for better teaching, and salaries of high-class teachers would rise' (M.P. Marshall, 1902, 256). Mary Marshall added that teaching is an oversupplied profession and that the less academic girls could find work teaching domestic economy to the lower classes. An increasing number of careers were opening to the well-educated girl and she quoted approvingly Collet's suggestion that men in business should train their daughters as they do their sons; that there was much scope in business for them as designers, chemists, foreign correspondents and as factory managers; and that to become at least capable of economic independence was good for a woman's character: 'A fine character needs self-respect and it is impossible for a woman to have much self-respect if she has to marry for a living' (M.P. Marshall, 1902, 256). The role of daughters was changing, as women 'refuse to become decrepit'. They find they have a longer period of efficient life than previously and no longer need an adult daughter to stay at home and care for them (M.P. Marshall, 1902, 257).

There was much in this review which challenged Marshall's publicly avowed views on the position of middle-class women. The centrepiece of his argument against women at Cambridge was that first, young (middle- and upper-class) women could not be spared full-time away from home because of their duties to their parents, siblings and relations, and second, even if women were so selfish as to disregard these claims, an advanced intellectual training was unnecessary, since it was doubtful if they could benefit from it and they would, in any case, spend their lives performing domestic duties, caring for their husbands' needs and bringing up children, or running a home for a male relative. Such women, it was to be understood, would be economically provided for by a male (McWilliams Tullberg, 1990b, 219 and 226).

The whole question of the number of single women among the upper and middle classes had been a source of controversy between Marshall and E.M. Sidgwick at the time of the great debate on the granting of degree titles to Cambridge women in 1897.[49] In an eight-page fly-sheet opposing the proposal, Marshall claimed that 90 per cent of women students would spend their lives in charge of a home as a wife or sister. They were therefore in need of neither a Cambridge education nor a degree. E.M. Sidgwick replied with the results of her own statistical enquiry, published in Cambridge in 1890, into the marital status of all the girls, whether student or not, in the families from which the women's colleges drew their students. This indicated that the marriage rate in these families was low, under 50 per cent, and that the girls tended to marry late, whether student or not. The Collet paper analysing census returns, which had been published in 1892 in the *Nineteenth Century*, a widely-available journal, also showed that marriage prospects for middle- and upper-class women were poor. Marshall, in private correspondence with E.M. Sidgwick, admitted that there was a large element of conjecture in his estimate. However, he did not believe that his figure of 90 per cent was too high, but, preferring to understate his opinion, he was prepared 'to put my guess at about 85 or even 83 per cent' (A. Marshall to E.M. Sidgwick, 16 February 1896, Newnham College Archive). Six years later, in her *Economic Journal* review, Mary Marshall demonstrated that she was willing to give more credence to Collet's statistical analysis than to Marshall's guesses – clearly, a large body of women needed to provide for themselves throughout or at least for part of their adult lives. She also accepted Collet's point that women needed a high-quality education which would prepare them for a well-paid career, and that 'men in business should train their daughters as they do their sons' since there was much scope in business for highly educated girls. In April 1902, Marshall wrote his *Plea for the Creation of a Curriculum in Economics* in which he proposed a Cambridge education in economics for just such sons; later the same year, his wife suggested indirectly that the same education would do for daughters.

Finally, she paraphrases, without negative comment, the view of Collet and others that economic independence was good for a woman's character and self-respect and that to be obliged to marry for a living was a destructive humiliation. Marshall held the view that men would only encumber themselves with a wife if their chivalrous instincts were called into play. Men would refuse to marry women who demonstrated their independence. In an exchange on women's suffrage with Beatrice Webb, Marshall is reported to have said:

if women attempt to equal men and be independent of their guidance and control, the strong women will soon be ignored and the weak women simply starved: it is not likely that men will go on marrying, if they are to have competitors as wives – Contrast – is the only basis to marriage and if that is destroyed we shall not think it worth our while to shackle ourselves in life with a companion whom we must support and must consider. (7 June 1889, microfiche typescript of diaries of Beatrice Webb, no. 1057)[50]

Marshall repeated his uneasiness over 'the present drift towards new-woman-hood' in a letter to Benjamin Kidd (14 February 1898, Cambridge University Library, Add Ms 8064.M254). Edgeworth, in his 'Reminiscences' confirmed that it was an issue which concerned Marshall profoundly (Pigou, 1925, 72).[51] Peter Groenewegen, in his forthcoming biography of Marshall, argues that Marshall was apprehensive about the future progress of the race should upper- and middle-class women gain their independence, and that his stance on women formed part of his evolutionary scheme for the progress of society. Marshall must certainly be applauded for his perspicacity if he realized that more choice for women might lead to fewer marriages and fewer children per marriage. However, if he saw the problem clearly, he chose to obfuscate. No attempt was made to suggest how matrimonial relationships and social organization might best respond, in an evolutionary fashion, to this new development. He reacted instead with a mixture of threats and ridicule to keep women in the position which he had determined for them in the society of the future. Men, according to Marshall, would reject independent women, and not vice versa; women, he claimed, lacked the intellectual equipment needed to contribute to society beyond the home and its extensions (his 'low opinion' of women's intellects was, for example, noted in 1889 by Henrietta Barnett, who knew the Marshalls well, as being among his 'fads ... concerning the destinies and capacities of our sex')[52]. Whether held sincerely or as a matter of convenience (and he may have succumbed to his own powers of persuasion), Marshall does not appear to have convinced his own wife that men should be providers and women subordinate, half-educated carers.[53]

Mary Paley Marshall's talents as a descriptive writer were first made evident in a five-page article on 'The growth of Newnham College' contributed to the Newnham Club *Letter* for 1884. She vividly recalls the companionship and intellectual excitement of the early days, the dedication of the male lecturers who gave as much time to one or two women students 'as if we had been a large class of men' and the gradual realization that some of the students could attempt the same degree examinations as the men (M.P. Marshall, 1884, 6).[54] In her second and third years 'a wave of Moral Science was at its height; Political Economy was rampant; Mental and Moral Philosophy were almost as bad' (M.P. Marshall, 1884, 6). This charming picture is almost identical with the one she was to produce over 40 years later. She

remained a typically Victorian memoir writer, positive, restrained, impersonal and uncontroversial, or, as she later put it, 'safe'.

Only the death of her close friend and fellow Newnham 'pioneer', Mary
Kennedy (Mrs Wright), in 1939, prompted her to reveal something of her
own aspirations and the partnership she might have wished for herself. Writing for the Newnham Roll *Letter*, she recalled how, as young women, they
had studied political economy together.[55] After her degree examination, Mary
Kennedy lectured on political economy for some years in London and in
1887 married R.T. Wright, fellow and tutor of Christ's College. Mary Kennedy
was talented both in singing and painting, but had been prevented from
training to a professional level by her parents:

> Her husband, Mr R.T. Wright, a warm and constant friend of Newnham, thought
> highly of her artistic talents and encouraged her to study at the Slade and for six
> months in Paris and painting was her favourite pursuit throughout her life. ... But
> though devoted to art she did not neglect her children. When she was attending
> the Paris studios and her two elder girls were about four and two, she would get
> up at six, bathe and dress her children, give them their breakfast and be in the
> studio by eight. (M.P. Marshall, 1940, 52)

Here was a man who had supported his wife's ambition to develop her talents
and a woman who had shown that the pursuit of education or a career by a
middle-class woman did not mean, as Marshall insisted, that she had to
neglect her children.

Towards the end of her life, at the instigation of G.M. Trevelyan, Mary
Paley Marshall wrote her reminiscences and left him a copy with a request to
do as he thought fit about publishing it after her death (G.M. Trevelyan to
John Maynard Keynes, 17 April 1944, Keynes Collection, King's College,
Cambridge, JMK L/MM).[56] Remembered by those who knew her in her old
age as warm and humorous, with a self-effacing calm, it was probably not in
her nature to dwell on those periods or areas of her life which had not been
entirely satisfactory. This may explain the brevity of her book and its emphasis on her early days. It is no more than 50 pages long and covers her
childhood in the Ufford Rectory, the early years of Newnham College,
Marshall's illness, the eight-month convalescence in Europe, especially
Palermo, friends at Oxford, particularly Jowett, visits to Cambridge of economists and others, Marshall's books and holidays at home and abroad. The
years in Cambridge from 1885, when Marshall became professor, are dealt
with in eight and a half pages which say nothing about his university work
and the book ends abruptly with his death in 1924.

There is little in the early notes for the book, beyond a sentence here and
there, which deviates from the printed version. One item of interest is a
chapter outline which indicates that, at an early stage, no chapter on Cam-

bridge was planned.[57] Another is the detailed interest she showed in their combined income and expenditure, which was given a less prominent treatment in the published version (M.P. Marshall, 1947, 25–7). This reveals her pride, not only in her mastery of Marshall's gospel of correct expenditure, which condemned spending on display and ignoble entertainments, but also that she herself had contributed to the family income through her earnings and inheritance. A third feature is the greater emphasis placed on her friendship with Jowett: 'Leaving Oxford to me meant leaving him [Jowett] for he had become our dearest friend' (Newnham Notes, ch.4, 7 – *the sentence is crossed out*).

Although the book was to contain her own memoirs, it is clear that she felt her readers really wanted to know about her husband. She protested that most of what she wanted to say could be found in Pigou's *Memorials* (1925), especially in the piece by Benians: 'However, I will try to fill in a few odds and ends; and anyhow I am on *safe ground* when talking of my own student life in Cambridge from 1871–74 nearly 60 years ago' (Newnham Notes, ch.2, reverse p. 5, emphasis added).[58] These memoirs were to be kept on 'safe grounds' in two meanings of the expression: first, in growing old, she found her clearest memories related to the early years: 'it is the years between 1870 and say 1910 that I can most vividly recall' (Newnham Notes: Talk, 1); second, she admitted that Marshall had been sensitive, perhaps oversensitive: 'He had extraordinarily sensitive fingers, a sign of an extraordinarily sensitive nature' and, in explaining Marshall's resignation as principal at Bristol, 'we felt that a man physically strong and less sensitive to pin-pricks would do the work better and yet be able to carry on his own studies' (Newnham Notes, ch.2, 18; ch.3, 9). Clearly her loyalty had been severely tried by Marshall's behaviour to friends and colleagues following his return to his alma mater in 1885 and during his campaigns to promote the academic study of economics, to keep women out of the university and to keep his colleagues and students conforming to the path of Marshallian economic wisdom.[59] It was no doubt 'safer' to ignore these topics completely.

Mary Marshall spoke in public on a number of occasions, though always to limited audiences. In 1903, she was one of five speakers at a Women's University Settlement Society meeting at Newnham College. The five stood in for Charles Loch of the Charity Organisation Society (COS) who was prevented by illness from speaking; the topics of their talks were not recorded. In 1908, she read papers on 'Social aims' and the following year on 'Land taxation' to the same society; details of these talks have not come to light (Newnham College Roll *Letter*).

Keynes mentions two occasions on which she addressed groups in Cambridge with memories of her husband. These were on the presentation of a copy of the Marshall portrait by Rothenstein to the Marshall Library, and at a gathering in celebration of the Marshall centenary in 1942. The undated notes deposited in Newnham College relate to a meeting that she addressed of the Marshall Society, chaired by Austin Robinson, but they may well have been used on these other occasions.[60] Here she emphasized that the founding of the Economics Tripos was Marshall's great achievement and gave an account of the status of economics in Cambridge at the turn of the century and of the opposition to Marshall's project spearheaded by William Cunningham and John McTaggart. Her choice of 'greatest achievement' is revealing. Was she simply appealing to her audience, members of the Cambridge Faculty of Economics, who had a particular interest in the Economics Tripos? Did she recognize that Marshall's written work, into which he had poured so much effort, had not had the impact he had hoped for on the nation's conduct of its social and economic life? Or did she remember that the new Tripos had re-established her importance as a teacher of economics at Newnham and, through spectacular Tripos successes, provided proof of her teaching skills?

From the material examined here, it can be concluded that Mary Paley Marshall had great facility as a writer, but chose to use her pen uncontroversially, only once during Marshall's lifetime publishing views with which he could not agree. Her reticence is to be regretted; her wit and charm and clarity of expression would have been of great value to groups arguing the case for women's education and suffrage, among many others. She chose instead to assist Marshall in his authorship, while her own creative talents she directed into the non-controversial and non-competitive sphere of watercolours.

9.5 OTHER ACTIVITIES

Describing life at Balliol Croft, Maynard Keynes wrote:

> [Mary Marshall] never, to the best of my recollection, discoursed on an economic topic with a visitor, or even took part in the everlasting economic talks of Balliol Croft. For the serious discussion she would leave the dining-room to the men or the visitor would go upstairs to the study, and the most ignorant Miss could not have pretended less than she to academic attainment. (Keynes, 1985b, 242).[61]

As a student and young lecturer, she certainly did not shy away from discussion, even in mixed company. At Bristol University College she started a women's debating society, as she had done in Newnham, and she was the first president of both societies (North Hall Diary, Newnham; Pease, 1942, 8). At Newnham, the debates related to social behaviour, reflecting the unique position in which the first women students found themselves. In Bristol, the debates were 'so lively that on one occasion at least the debate had to be adjourned' (Pease, 1942, 8). The subject on that occasion was Irish Home Rule, when some of the women students, admirers of Parnell, clashed with the daughters of 'cultivated and attractive' Irish families who opposed them 'with fearful eloquence' (Pease, 1942, 8).[62]

When Benjamin Jowett and Henry Smith attended meetings of the College Council in Bristol, they stayed with the Marshalls and the four of them sat up talking until past midnight (M.P. Marshall, 1944, 36). When they moved to Oxford, the Marshalls attended meetings of Sidney Ball's Society for the Discussion of Social Questions and the newly-founded Charity Organisation Society, public lectures addressed by Henry George, H.M. Hyndman and Ruskin, and listened to the Barnetts describe the work done from the newly-founded Toynbee Hall Settlement in the East End of London. There were house parties at the Master's Lodge, when Jowett delighted in assembling groups of politicians and academics to discuss current issues; there were small dinner parties at the Marshall home. Life at Oxford, in Mary Marshall's words, was 'full of interest and excitement' (M.P. Marshall, 1944, 35). When they returned to Cambridge, if the Keynes story is correct, she shared less in intellectual exchanges with her husband's visitors. This may explain her colourless description of life in Cambridge: 'One year passed much like another' (M.P. Marshall, 1947, 42).

In Michaelmas Term 1886, she was largely responsible for founding a Cambridge Ladies Discussion Society for the purpose of obtaining information on and discussing 'what are commonly called social problems'.[63] The club was open to 'ladies resident in Cambridge' as well as to the students at Girton and Newnham. The Committee invited authorities on subjects suggested for discussion to come to Cambridge and read papers before the society. The first meeting was addressed by Mary Clifford of Bristol on pauper children and a Miss Mason on boarding out, the second by two women who had practical experience in connection with emigration, a popular solution at that time to the problems of poverty and overcrowding (Newnham Club *Letter*, 1886, 14). Topics discussed in 1888 included 'Benefit societies for women', 'Open spaces for the poor', 'The present working of the Elementary Education Act' and 'The changes in the social conditions of the Northern mines in the last generation' (Newnham Club *Letter*, 1888, 10). Papers were read at the meetings by both men and women speakers; for example, in 1891, Miss Calder spoke on technical education, Clement Edwards on new unionism, Elizabeth Garrett Anderson on the medical profession for women and Tom Mann on the economic and social aims of the working classes (Newnham Club *Letter*, 1891).

One of the Society's most important meetings was held in the Lent Term 1887, and was addressed by Mrs Barnett, who read a paper on Toynbee Hall and university settlements, and by two former students from Girton and

Newnham who had started a small settlement in one of the 'poorer districts of London'. The interest roused by these papers was so great that a Women's University Settlement was established shortly afterwards (Gardiner, 1887, 19–20).[64] Henrietta Barnett described the Marshalls as playing a large part in the active organization of the settlement (Barnett, 1918, vol.2, 32). Their original support may have been moral and financial but, at some point, Mary Marshall became the Newnham representative on the executive board of the settlement, remaining there until 1909.

The aim of the settlement movement was to bring back the 'leisured classes' to inner city areas where they would live their middle-class lives among the poorer classes, and by instruction and example help deprived people to realize their 'best-selves' – a goal defined in terms of middle-class values. The reformers recognized the alienation among the poorest classes which had resulted from industrialization and urbanization; social reintegration was to be achieved by the creation of a new sense of community which would follow on the re-establishment of a proper social hierarchy. At the outset, the settlement movement was highly critical of the upper and middle classes for their failure to carry out their duties on behalf of the poor. University graduates were encouraged to spend some months or years in residence at a settlement, pursuing if necessary their own occupations or studies during the day and devoting their free time to making individual friendships with their poor neighbours and running educational and recreational projects on their behalf. The Women's University Settlement concentrated its efforts on training, entertainment and outings for women and children. Many of the Oxford and Cambridge residents had daytime jobs as teachers, school managers or Poor Law guardians.

When Marshall died in 1924, the Settlement Society noted that they had lost a 'true friend in Professor Marshall. He proved his friendship in many ways, by his generosity, by his interest'. Mary Marshall replied: 'From the very first, my husband was much interested in [the settlement], and his interest increased as time went on and whenever I came home from its meetings, he wanted to know what had been done and was glad to make suggestions about the work' (Newnham College Roll *Letter*, 1925, 46).[65]

She was an active member of the COS committees in both Oxford and Cambridge. When questioned before the Royal Commission on the Aged Poor, 1893, Marshall was able to claim a 'good deal of indirect experience of the working' of the Society, not only through careful reading of the Society's journal, but also as 'a supernumerary member of the Committee' through discussions with his wife at mealtimes following her attendance at a committee meeting:

We make it an invariable rule to discuss the questions in detail, if [the committee] have any difficulty, at the next meal after she comes back [from a meeting]. We always do that, and we always take up the question of whether the case is rightly treated, of what it would be best to do; and at the next meeting of the committee, if from the conversation anything arises which she thinks it would be worth while to bring before the committee, it is so brought. (Keynes, 1926, 217)

Marshall again used his vicarious experience of COS work to defend himself against Bernard Bosanquet, the Society's theorist, who had criticized Marshall's old age pension proposals as the work of a writer lacking in experience in charity administration (Marshall, 1892, 372). Marshall was not a supporter of COS hard-liners for whom the definition of 'deserving' was extremely narrowly drawn, although he believed that relief must be discriminatory. Unfortunately, no details exist of Mary Marshall's activities as a committee member, where she would have been called upon to decide on the merits of cases put before them by a case worker.

The Marshalls were both members of the Cambridge Ethical Society, founded in 1888.[66] The Society's programme was the application of reasoned thinking (as opposed to authority and tradition) to the moral aspects of social, political and educational questions and to the dissemination of these ideas among the working classes and young people. Marshall was a member of the organizing committee from the start but attended no further meetings after the first; she became a member of the committee in October 1889 and attended regularly, this being a further example of the familiar family division of labour whereby Mary Marshall attended meetings, undertook committee work and reported back on organizations of whose methods and social goals Marshall approved.

Besides her teaching, Mary Paley Marshall's greatest interest was in painting, mainly in water-colours. While she claims that she was interested in colour from childhood, and was caught up in the pre-Raphaelite movement with regard to dress and furnishings as a student and in the early days of married life, it was during Marshall's convalescence in Palermo that painting first appears to have become an important hobby.[67] It is clear that she expected to spend considerable time painting, since windows were introduced into the otherwise unbroken 'catslide' roof which covers two floors of the north-facing rear of Balliol Croft, the house which the Marshalls had built for them on their return to Cambridge. Here she had her 'studio'. She joined the Cambridge Drawing Society in 1885, became its president during 1912–14 and was still a member in 1939. She presumably gained inspiration and technical advice from her close friend, Mary Kennedy, and both women exhibited their work.

Mary Marshall left a volume of her water-colours, about 100 pieces relating to Sicily and the Tyrol, to C.R. Fay for presentation to the Marshall Library. He asked Professor W.G. Constable to write an appreciation of her work (C.R. Fay to J.M. Keynes, postmarked 20 April 1944, Keynes Collection, King's College, Cambridge, JMK L/MM); when this was done is unclear, but the piece was published by Claude Guillebaud in *The Eagle*, the St John's College magazine, in 1960.[68] There Constable described her as 'an artist of complete integrity, who used no tricks or clichés in trying to express what she saw and felt'. Some of the earliest paintings in the volume were from the winter and spring of Marshall's convalescence, including views of Palermo, Capri, Rome, Venice, Bavaria and the Rhine. They were the work of 'a conscientious beginner who had had some lessons from a Victorian drawing master'. The next painting dates from 1894, by which time, Constable feels, she had 'found herself as a painter':

> Here is a new breadth of handling, a new feeling for tone relations, and consequently a closer adjustment of technique to express a conception. What had happened to bring about that change, I don't know; but probably much quiet practice combined with the study of other watercolour painters. Possibly, too, in mountains Mrs Marshall had found material to which her imagination responded ... or possibly, since Marshall preferred to spend his holidays among mountains, necessity had truly become the mother of invention. (Guillebaud, 1960)

The next group of paintings are records of holidays, mostly spent in the Tyrol. When, in 1906, the mountain venue was exchanged for the Riviera and North Italy, Constable found the paintings less successful, but 'a visit in 1912 to Mentone secured the rewards of hard work. In subjects akin to those found in Sicily and Italy thirty years earlier, amateur timidity [had] been replaced by [a] confident mingling of breadth of treatment and subtlety of observation' (Guillebaud, 1960).

Her work has a secondary feature of particular interest to economists; she often noted on her paintings the stage which Marshall had reached in his writing. Thus the single painting from 1894 is inscribed 'White Elephant idea occurred'. In her notes for the Marshall Society talk, she explained: 'Much time was lost in the next 15 years, and this loss of time was chiefly due to "The White Elephant" as he called it in later years':

> at Stuben ... he devised a Treatise which reminds one of the next scheme which Adam Smith projected. For he also left fragments of a great work to be illustrated by the History of Astronomy, Ancient Logic and Metaphysics. As time went on he became convinced that he was working on too large a scale. One gets glimpses in *Industry and Trade* of the amount of material [Marshall] amassed. He wrote a quantity on the History of Money, of Banking, of Railways, on the details of Scientific Management and of Cartels and Trusts: but gradually he boiled down this mass of material, or filled the Waste Paper Basket, and in its more manageable form it at last appeared as *Industry and Trade*. Still, the time had only been partly wasted, for his intimate knowledge of men and things drew the attention of Business Men. Mr Peace at the University Press told me he had never known such

demand for a big and serious book. He said it might have been a 'Shilling Shocker'. (Newnham Notes: Talk, 30–31)

Constable concludes his assessment of this Victorian amateur who 'grew in mastery while retaining her humility and sensibility' by wondering how she accomplished this in view of 'all her other responsibilities' and asking, rhetorically, if Marshall realized that Balliol Croft sheltered an artist.

9.6   CONCLUSION

If we are to believe her own description of events, Mary Paley Marshall drifted into higher education as a distraction from an ill-considered engagement and without any particular goal in sight. At Newnham, she discovered she had a liking and aptitude for economics and became the first woman to succeed (and succeed well) in a degree examination in the subject. She clearly considered a career in adult education, possibly teaching economics, as her lecture series in Stamford demonstrates. She accepted a lectureship at Newnham, replacing Alfred Marshall, and even agreed to produce an elementary economics textbook. She then found a perfect partner, an economist, a man who had supported a scheme for women's education at Cambridge from its inception, and one who seemed to offer her an exciting, modern partnership:

> The ideal of married life is often said to be that husband and wife should live for each other. If this means that they should live only for each other's gratification it seems to me intensely immoral. Man and wife should live, not for each other but with each other for some end. (Mary Paley Marshall was quoting from Marshall's lectures on Moral and Political Philosophy, given to women Tripos students over the years 1873–4: M.P. Marshall, 1947, 19)[69]

Undoubtedly, her path to academic heights had gone very smoothly. Unlike many women, both before and after her, she did not have to surmount any great obstacles placed by her family or the academic establishment in the path of her pursuit of education. She had the active support and assistance of her father and her Cambridge teachers, and had experienced very little opposition from the Cambridge authorities who, in these early days, were not yet alert to the 'dangers' of allowing women to make use of the university's examination papers.[70] Nonetheless, she had shown a certain independence of spirit and a willingness to challenge social norms. Her initial engagement had not had her father's approval, even less so her rejection of religion and her decision, together with Marshall, to contract herself 'out of the marriage vow of obedience' (M.P. Marshall, 1947, 10, 13, 23). Studying for a Tripos was not what society expected of a young lady, nor was a certain eccentricity of dress, nor a willingness to debate on serious topics in both female and mixed company.

After her marriage in 1877, she appears to have come up against setbacks and opposition for the first time. The task of writing a simple textbook proved more difficult than she had anticipated. It was taken over by her husband, who not only made it his own, but who also criticized it with increasing harshness, especially the first part, which probably included her own main contribution to the work. Then her husband fell ill and she took upon herself the task not only of nursing him but also of assisting him in the work he was contracted to do as Principal of University College, Bristol and the work he wanted to do of publishing his economic ideas. Her willingness to help was clearly exploited both by the college and by Marshall. The college refused to accept Marshall's resignation and failed, probably from lack of funds, to appoint an administrative assistant to relieve him of some of his duties for almost a year; Marshall not only clearly enjoyed being nursed (Newnham Notes: Talk, 33/57), but also felt that the time spent on the *Economics of Industry* had been wasted and that the move to Bristol had been a mistake, a move 'forced' on him by his marriage and therefore, indirectly, by his wife (Marshall, 1933, 222; McWilliams Tullberg, 1991, 247–8).[71]

Quite how their relationship developed at this point is not known. Was she 'converted' by Marshall the preacher – her own description of him – to his modified view of marriage, 'That man and wife should share each other's life; that the aims of one should be important to the other' (Newnham Notes: Notes, 16), the aims of Alfred assuming primary importance? Was there perhaps criticism and argument, ending in a compromise agreement: she could teach and paint, on the understanding that Marshall and his work came first? It is quite possible that, meeting resistance for the first time, Mary Marshall simply drifted into an ancillary role, no longer believing she had anything unique to offer the partnership. The return to Cambridge, which Marshall regarded as his rightful home, completed the process. He was appointed to the chair of Political Economy and determined to establish the country's leading school of economics in Cambridge; she returned to teaching at Newnham, no longer sole resident lecturer and right hand of the Principal, but one of a growing number of women lecturers. She also found herself at times in an uncomfortable position, as the result of Marshall's stubbornness, tactlessness and outspoken views on a number of topics, including the subordinate role to be played by women. Thus the 'cocky' young Newnham student who had passed a Tripos examination 15 years earlier and started on a career as the country's first lady lecturer in economics is scarcely recognizable in the 39-year-old woman described by Beatrice Webb attending the Co-operative Conference in Ipswich in 1889:

That gentle unassuming lady – badly dressed with protruding teeth, weak eyes and quickly changing colour – a former student of Newnham and present lecturer, who sits by [Marshall's] side, selects his food and guards him from obtrusions – is his wife. It is true they are childless: and they live only for his work – he being dyspeptic and somewhat hypochondriacal. (Webb, diary entry 4 June 1889, microfiche no. 1050)

The question arises: was Mary Paley Marshall obliged to sacrifice a career which included independent scholarship because of Alfred Marshall? I think not. After all, research was a luxury that few qualified Cambridge women could hope to indulge in until after the turn of the century. I believe that she felt that her vocation lay in teaching and that she sought her personal development through art, and there is much evidence to suggest that she was both a highly successful teacher of economics and a talented amateur landscape artist. No doubt she would have liked to have much more support and encouragement from her husband. Marshall supported her in her work for the COS and the Women's Settlement, areas of action which he held were particularly suited to a woman's insight and sympathies, but resented her success in getting women students through the Economics Tripos (McWilliams Tullberg, 1993a). When she married in 1877, it was still the very early days of the women's higher education movement and few men or women had thought through the implications of giving women access to university education. Marshall was soon to decide that giving women such an education would lead to their independence and rejection of male control; this, he claimed would endanger the future of the race. She learnt to accommodate this but was no doubt deeply disappointed that this one-time radical now felt so threatened by the expansion of educational and economic opportunities for a large social group.

When Archbishop Benson died in 1896, his widow, Henry Sidgwick's sister, Minnie, wrote: 'There is nothing within, no power, no love, no desire, no initiative: he had it all, and his life entirely dominated mine. Good Lord, give me a personality' (quoted in Moore, 1974, 89). Mary Paley Marshall did not suffer this appalling fate when Alfred Marshall died in 1924; she certainly did not find herself without a personality. She had never surrendered completely to his preaching, never accepted his views on the intellectual capacities of women nor his repudiation of the need for educational opportunities for women at the highest possible level. Through her art, she had also carved out a space in her life which Marshall had not been able to invade and take over. As far as her work for Marshall was concerned, she wrote to John Maynard Keynes in 1922: 'to have been for so many years his companion, and to have helped, however little, such a life as his is an enviable and delightful lot' (M.P. Marshall to J.M. Keynes 27 July 1922, Keynes Collection, King's College, Cambridge, JMK EJ/6.4).[72] Claude

Guillebaud, in an unpublished obituary of his aunt, gave an admirable summary of the situation:

> Until [Marshall's] death in 1924, she lived only for him collaborating with him in his writing and tending him with a self-sacrificing devotion that could hardly be exceeded. She was 74 years of age when he died, but instead of resigning herself to the inactivity of old age, her individuality blossomed forth in what became for her a real St Martin's summer. ... Age never warped the kindly, tolerant and humorous attitude towards life which made her such a delightful companion. (Unpublished obituary, Keynes Collection, King's College, Cambridge, EJ/6.4)

Keynes completed the picture by describing the use to which she put her new freedom – by generously devoting time and money to ensure that students might have access to that prerequisite of good scholarship, a well-stocked library and a knowledgeable librarian: 'Every morning till close on her ninetieth year ... she bicycled the considerable distance from Madingley Road to the Library. ... There, she spent the morning in charge of the Library' (Keynes, 1985b, 249).

Many of the books had been donated by Marshall for the use of students during his lifetime. On his death, his private library was handed over to the university and formed the core of the Marshall Library of Economics. Mary Marshall sat in the library each morning, advising students in their reading, and compiling a remarkable subject index of current economic periodicals (Guillebaud, unpublished obituary, Keynes Collection, King's College, Cambridge, JMK A/44). She ended her days doing what she thought was most important – helping young students make the best use of their educational opportunities – but now without any distinction as to sex.

NOTES

1. I should like to thank the librarians and archivists of the following libraries for their generous help: Cambridge City; Humberside; Stamford; Cambridge University; Newnham College, Cambridge; Bristol University; Lady Margaret Hall, Oxford; Bodleian, Oxford; and University College, London (William Ramsay Papers).

   I am grateful to the fellows of Newnham College and the Faculty of Economics and Politics, Cambridge for permission to publish material from their archives; to the provost and scholars of King's College, Cambridge for permission to quote from material from the J.M. Keynes archive; and to the fellows of Lady Margaret Hall, Oxford for permission to publish material from the Lynda Grier papers.

   Finally, I should like to thank Professors A.W. Coats, P.D. Groenewegen, G.C. Harcourt, A. Kadish, M. Perlman, E.A.G. Robinson and J.K. Whitaker for their most valuable comments and suggestions, and my husband, Hasse, for much practical assistance and encouragement while I have worked on this chapter.

2. The archdeacon's best-known work, his 'Evidences', was still required reading for Cambridge undergraduates at the beginning of the twentieth century (Phillips, 1988, 100: 'Paley's ghost').

3. He was the 27th Wrangler in the Mathematical Tripos. Thomas Paley's biographical details are drawn from the unsigned obituary appended to Mary Paley Marshall's *What I Remember* (1947, 51–4) and reprinted from *The Eagle*, the college magazine of St John's College, Cambridge, December 1899.

4. Mary Paley's maternal grandfather was described in the 1851 census as a 'landed proprietor and magistrate'. The family was at that time living in Barton-on-Humber, just south of Hull.

5. The rectory is still standing, though in private hands, and the garden is certainly large enough to have kept young children happily entertained as Mary Paley Marshall remembered it. The parish of Ufford-cum-Bainton is now amalgamated with that of Barnock in the diocese of Peterborough.

6. Mary may have misinterpreted her father's rigidity. Arthur Gray, then Master of Jesus College, wrote to John Maynard Keynes in 1933 recalling that he had first met Mary Paley in the house of her father's cousin around 1872 (A. Gray to J.M. Keynes, 22 March 1933, Keynes Collection, King's College, Cambridge, B/1). Frederick Apthorp Paley was, like Mary Paley's father, a grandson of Archdeacon Paley, and also a renowned classical scholar, a writer on church architecture and a prominent Catholic. He was a graduate of St John's and had rooms there until 1846 when he was suspected of having encouraged one of his pupils to convert to Catholicism and was ordered to leave. He returned to Cambridge in 1860 on the partial removal of religious disabilities there. Had her father been less tolerant, Mary Paley would certainly have been forbidden to meet him. She also describes her father as dancing with the Principal of Newnham, another activity incompatible with strict evangelicalism (M.P. Marshall, 1947, 11).

7. Use will be made throughout the chapter of manuscript notes made for *What I Remember* and for the talk given by Mary Paley Marshall at a Marshall Society meeting in the 1930s. They were passed to Ruth Cohen as Principal of Newnham College in 1960 by Mary Marshall's nephew, Claude Guillebaud, and have only recently come to light. They will be referred to as Newnham Notes. The notes are written on small, or very small, pieces of paper, sometimes on both sides. They are numbered non-consecutively and in some cases twice. Where the notes are tied together as forming a chapter, the chapter number will be given. Those which appear to relate to the talk will be described as 'Newnham Notes: Talk'. Material given between obliques represents non-trivial corrections made by Mary Paley Marshall to her manuscript (see McWilliams Tullberg, 1993b).

8. Mary Paley grew up with a sister and brother who were close to her in age and then a much younger brother (brothers). Alfred Marshall had an elder brother, two younger sisters and a younger brother.

9. Interesting work on the family's finances will be presented in the forthcoming biography of Marshall by Peter Groenewegen.

10. Given the dozens of such schools advertised in the *Stamford Mercury*, it has proved impossible to identify this one.

11. Thomas Paley's strategy can be contrasted with that of William Marshall, who forbade Marshall's sister Mabel to marry the man of her choice (Coase, 1990, 20). The Cambridge Higher Local Examinations for Women were first held in 1869; five years later they were opened to male candidates. For the whole background to women's higher education in Cambridge, see McWilliams Tullberg, 1975 and forthcoming, App. A.

12. In *What I Remember*, she also mentions taking logic, which her father advised was such a *safe* subject (M.P. Marshall, 1947, 13).

13. For the examination paper which Mary Paley sat and details of Alfred Marshall's essay prize, see McWilliams Tullberg, forthcoming, Apps A & B.

14. Newnham students were not only part of an experiment in female tertiary education but also part of Henry Sidgwick's other experiments in university reform: for example, unlike Girton students, Newnham women were not allowed to enter for the ordinary or pass degree. In 1881, the university gave its formal permission for women students at Girton and Newnham to make use of the Tripos examination papers and to have them marked, but at the same time refused them permission to enter for the pass degree. In the latter half of the century, for every 100 men students at Cambridge, on average 41 took honours

degrees, 34 pass and 25 no degree (Royal Commission on Oxford and Cambridge Universities 1922 x Cmd. 1588).

15. No record of these lectures has been found in the *Stamford Mercury*, but it is unlikely that Mary Paley or her students would have courted publicity.

16. University College, Bristol: Council Minutes 16 March 1877 and 26 July 1877. Five candidates had been called for the final interview. It can be assumed that Marshall was quizzed particularly on his attitude to working-class and female education.

17. Typing errors have been corrected and some punctuation added.

18. It is possible to speculate endlessly as to who could not or would not have children in the Marshall marriage. John Maynard Keynes's comment to Lytton Strachey that he believed Marshall 'became sterile soon after marriage' simply raises more questions than it answers, the most central being what, if anything, was understood about male sterility in the 1870s and 1880s and again in the 1920s (23 October 1924, Keynes Collection, King's College Archives, PP/45). The fact of childlessness is clearly of importance in understanding the Marshall relationship, but it cannot be analysed in the absence of information about its cause. It should, however, be noted, that, except in medically very enlightened circles, childlessness in a consummated marriage was long felt to be the 'fault' of the women. It was also commonly held in the latter half of the nineteenth century that women who studied did this at the expense of their reproductive organs, drawing blood away from them to the brain (McWilliams Tullberg, forthcoming).

19. 'Mrs Marshall is now delivering lectures on Political Economy at the University College, Bristol with great success' (Newnham Hall Company, Report, 1878). She was reappointed as day-lecturer on 21 May 1879, 26 May 1880, 18 May 1881 (University College, Bristol: Council Minutes).

20. The following year, she added to her timetable a class for advanced students, for which papers were to be written. She also set papers occasionally for the beginners. Marshall held one lecture and one class a week and also held occasional classes for advanced students (*Calendar*, 1879–80). He dropped these the following year, but advanced classes continued to be held by Mary Marshall during the day. For the academic year 1881–2, she planned to include a twice-weekly advanced lecture course in her teaching schedule. She would set written papers at both the elementary and advanced levels and give special teaching to members of both groups in the work required for Group D of the Cambridge Higher Local Examination, now open to both men and women (*Calendars*, 1880–81 and 1881–2).

21. It was agreed that arrangements be made to relieve him of some part of his duties (Council Minutes, 19 November 1879). To this end, the duties and salaries of the secretary and clerk were reconsidered but it was not until October 1880, after sifting through 146 applicants, that the post of registrar and secretary was filled.

22. Mary Paley Marshall is therefore one of an élite group of women in Britain who have been offered chairs in economics in the past 110 years!

23. The College at Bristol was granted its University Charter in 1909 and awarded Alfred Marshall an honorary doctorate in 1911. Ironically, Marshall had not supported the move to university status. In the typescript of his autobiography, Morris W. Travers quotes correspondence with Marshall who felt this involved the risk of hasty action and raised doubts about standards. In effect, Marshall abandoned both his early educational ideals, of making university education available in the provinces and for women.

24. The Cambridge scheme had been available since 1871 and in the early years attracted two to three hundred students a year. Mary Paley Marshall is known to have worked for the scheme in its early years (see M.P. Marshall to H.S. Foxwell, April 1878, in J.K. Whitaker's edition of the Marshall correspondence, forthcoming). In 1883, there were 144 students, of whom half took the examinations, some with outstanding results. The numbers dropped after 1885 as the result of improved education given in girls's schools, the increase in university extension lectures and classes, and competition from other correspondence classes with lower fees. The scheme was disbanded in 1894. The Oxford scheme was started in January 1883 and political economy became available in the academic year 1883–4. However, it attracted only one student.

25. Her attendance record for the Michaelmas Term 1884 sank to 12 per cent. It may have been the case that she was repeating the course given the previous year.

26. Marshall confirmed this in his final lecture in 1908: 'Oxford has made movements, Cambridge has made men. Cambridge tends to make people with a higher standard of truth for the sake of truth than can be got by any other system of education' (Newnham Notes: Talk, 29; see also McWilliams Tullberg, 1993a).

27. In 1893, Mary Paley Marshall became one of the first 30 Associates of Newnham College. These were chosen from among former students and members of staff as persons deemed most fit to advance education, learning and research. The Associates were an important body of academic women which could influence the Council, acting as a counterweight to the many men who, as teachers, officers and long-term advisors, were in a strong position to determine College policy.

28. The heroine of Tennyson's poem, *The Princess*, 1847, who founded a university. The story of Princess Ida had been revived in 1884 in the operatic satire by Gilbert and Sullivan, *Princess Ida*.

29. Seebohm, an asthmatic, overprotected by her family, was persuaded to leave Newnham after only one term and died shortly afterwards.

30. It is not easy to estimate the numbers of students studying economics because of the individual nature of the study programmes. A list of students probably dating from 1886 suggests that Mary Marshall had about 20 first- and second-year students attending classes in economics at some level, of whom 12 later took Triposes. In 1896, the number of Newnham students in all three years (1894–6) reading history was 29 and the number reading moral sciences, ten.

31. In a long letter to the Education Committee on 12 October 1909, and in cadences familiar from the writing of Marshall, Mary Marshall describes how the first-year economics students are 'apt to waste a good deal of time; and, unless they are very able, they never make firm foundations. ... When once they are well grounded they are able to cope with the subject themselves, and I think that as a rule they are more likely to become strong and self-reliant students if they do not have much individual help in their later years.' Proposing that Lynda Grier should give one hour of extra teaching to the first years, she adds: 'I, as directing the Economics students, should make all arrangements as to classes to be attended (including Miss Grier's), and for any extra coaching that might be required. I should be in Newnham for an hour each week to advise students generally and especially those in their second and third years and I should also wish to test the work of all who were doing Economics, my term papers given at intervals so as to be able to report efficiently on their progress.'

32. After describing how teaching had passed out of the hands of the colleges into those of private coaches by the mid-nineteenth century, Rothblatt continues: 'The reputation of a coach was measured by his ability to cram an undergraduate, to drill him intensively for a high place in the examination list' (Rothblatt, 1968, 199). Since the arrangement was a private one which could be terminated, it also required the coach to gain the confidence of the individual pupil and the teaching could be of very high quality. But there was little room for *scholarship*. The practice of private coaching had lost ground by the 1890s and disappeared in 1907, when ranking of Mathematical Tripos candidates was abolished (Rothblatt, 1968, 197–208 and 230–35).

33. A popular comment on this situation was that Cambridge University's loss was London University's gain!

34. 'The 1890s saw a shift away from graciousness and bad food towards professionalization and bad food' (Vicinus, 1985, 132). Vicinus, 1985, 132–5 and 147ff, is particularly useful on the role of women university teachers.

35. This scheme grew out of the work of the North of England Council for Promoting the Higher Education of Women founded in 1867. Stuart lectured for the Council from the start, his subject being the history of physical science and astronomy. The scheme spread throughout the country and, in 1872, Cambridge gave its official recognition to the scheme for 'University extension'.

36. Claims for the overriding importance of the change in definition of normal value from an

absolute to a relative concept between the *Economics of Industry* and the *Principles* as the explanation for Marshall's behaviour have been pressed by a number of Marshall scholars in recent discussion. I am still tempted to apportion this point less explanatory weight, since it was not mentioned by Keynes, Mary Marshall or other contemporary commentators who knew the emphasis Marshall placed on different parts of his work, nor by Marshall himself who could have been expected to want to draw attention to such an important shift in his thinking.

37. In a letter to a Japanese translator in 1910, Marshall wrote: 'Those who suggested that an educational work on economics should be written by a young student [who had obtained only a very elementary knowledge of it and did – *this phrase heavily crossed through*] were not economists and did not know that the task of combining simplicity with thoroughness is more difficult in this than in almost any other subject' (Alfred Marshall to Kumakichi Kawabe, 2 May 1910, Marshall Archive, Marshall 1/63).

38. This date is interesting; Mary Paley Marshall says that she and Marshall began working together on the book nine months earlier (M.P. Marshall, 1947, 22).

39. Further details of the production of the *Economics of Industry* and discussion of Marshall's attitude towards the book can be found in Groenewegen (1991).

40. Private conversation, September 1990.

41. She seems to have understood this decline in mental faculty before it was confirmed by Marshall's doctor; she began making notes on 'Recollections of Alfred' as early as January 1920 (Newnham Notes: Talk, 52). Mary Marshall's part in the production of *Money, Credit & Commerce* is discussed in detail in Groenewegen's forthcoming biography of Alfred Marshall.

42. On one occasion, when talking privately to Professor Selig Perlman in 1939, possibly following references to the Webbs, Mary Paley Marshall admitted her disappointment over Marshall's unwillingness to recognize her intellectual contribution to their partnership. (Private information from Professor Mark Perlman.)

43. B. Webb described the Union as follows: 'This National Union of Women Workers sprang out of a sort of federation of philanthropic societies to befriend young girls. Louise Creighton [wife of Bishop Creighton], with great energy and considerable capacity has organized it into a somewhat incoherent federation of all societies of women dealing with industrial, philanthropic and educational matters. Its chief function is to hold an annual conference to which all women who work are invited to listen to papers on any conceivable topic and discuss … . The conference consisted of about six hundred, mostly middle-aged, well-to-do, but a good many hardworking professional philanthropists, guardians of the poor etc.' Originally on the Executive Committee, Webb resigned in protest at the religious and non-political tone of the organization which was 'dominated by bishops' wives and deaconesses'. See entries for 18 October 1895, 5 October 1896 and 29 October 1897 in MacKenzie and MacKenzie, 1983, vol.2).

44. Marshall concludes: 'The greatest faults in domestic economy, among the sober portions of the Anglo-Saxon working-classes at all events, are faults of production rather than of consumption.' It seems unlikely that Marshall had had much first-hand experience on which to base his claim. And if there was any truth in the comparison, perhaps the clue lay in the ready access to wine and fresh herbs, denied to most working-class English wives, with which the Continental housewife could add flavour to the most boring stew!

45. The experience of field-workers in developing countries today is that educating women and giving them a skill with which to earn a living is, besides vaccination, one of the best methods of reducing child mortality. In most cases, women use their new knowledge and incomes to improve the quality of life of their families. Like a great many of their contemporaries, the Marshalls continued to preach middle-class values at the poorest classes, while closing their eyes to economic realities.

46. See the letter to Collet quoted in Coats, 1972, in Wood (1982, , vol. 4, 239–40), in which Foxwell pours out his anger and disappointment at being passed over for the Cambridge chair after Marshall's retirement.

47. Marshall, however, believed that women's intellects were inferior. For Marshall's views on female competition, see McWilliams Tullberg, 1990b, 220.

48. Collet's description of early marriage among working-class women is given a Marshallian embellishment by Mary Marshall in her review: the 'expectation and desire of marriage often lead to a great waste of faculty before marriage, to choice of work which, whilst requiring little training, offers freedom from restraint, to wasteful expenditure on dress and amusements and to a disinclination to save or to take part in Trade Unions and Benefit societies' (M.P. Marshall, 1902, 254; cf Marshall, 1961, 88, fn.1; M.P. Marshall, 1947, 19–20). Collet's proposals for part-time schooling and the teaching of domestic science for working-class girls were commended.

49. The first women took Cambridge degree examinations in 1872. In 1881, women were granted formal permission to take Tripos examinations. In 1887 and 1897, their requests to be granted the titles of their degrees were refused. In 1923, they were granted degree titles and given other university privileges, and in 1947 they were permitted to graduate, although their numbers were limited to 10 per cent of male students.

50. B. Webb was tempted to point out that celibacy could be 'begun by either party to the matrimonial contract'. She claims to have caught sight of 'the poor little wife's agonised look (for Female Suffrage is a red rag to the Prof's somewhat feminine nerves and shrewish temper)', so she laughed off the matter. At this time (1889), B. Webb opposed female suffrage.

51. See also Pigou, 1925, 468, on Marshall's fear for family life 'under the influence of aggressive womanhood'.

52. Letter from Henrietta Barnett to Beatrice Webb, 20 June 1889, Diary of B. Webb, microfiche 1139. See also McWilliams Tullberg, 1975, 124–5, and 1993a.

53. This is not the place for analysis of the roots of Marshall's attitude to the changing role of women – and without fuller information about his childhood and marriage, this could be only speculation. See Groenewegen, 1995; McWilliams Tullberg, 1991, 248, note 16. On the relationship between women's education and social and racial progress, see Dyhouse, 1976.

54. Marshall's role in the early women's education movement at Cambridge is not mentioned in this piece. Elsewhere, Mary Kennedy wrote that it was Alfred Marshall who had persuaded the women to attempt a Tripos, another sensitive point avoided by Mary Marshall (Phillips, 1988, 3).

55. She also recalls an incident which confirms that Marshall was regularly teaching 'curves' to his students in the early 1870s: 'There was the incident of the blackboard, which seemed to Mary and me to have got too old and greasy for all the complicated economic curves. So we put our money together and bought a large handsome one. However, it refused to let the curves be rubbed out and was ignominiously set aside for the old one. What an impression those curves must have made on her; for only a few days before she died she wrote me a long letter on some fallacy in the subject which they illustrated and which I had quite forgotten' (M.P. Marshall, 1940).

56. Going through his aunt's papers, Claude Guillebaud found some notes which had been used in the preparation of the reminiscences (C.W. Guillebaud to John Maynard Keynes, 28 March 1944, Keynes Collection, 8, King's College, Cambridge, JMK L/MM). It seems likely that these are the notes now in the Newnham College Archives and described in this chapter as 'Newnham Notes' – see above, note 7 (C.W. Guillebaud to Ruth Cohen, 3 June 1960, Newnham College Archive).

57. The chapter heads were:
    1. Life in a country rectory in the 50's and 60's
    2. The beginnings of Newnham
    3. Income & expenditure
    4. From our roof in Palermo
    5. Oxford in the 80's
    6. Jowett and others
    7. Sarah
    8. Travels in England
    9. The Dolomites and our last visit in 1920 – The Lightening Strike
    10. Sea Vale (Newnham Notes, ch.5, reverse of p.2).

58. This same expression, 'safe ground' is used again in the notes for the talk (Newnham Notes: Talk reverse p.1).

59. See, for example, Mary Marshall's letter to John Maynard Keynes, about meeting Foxwell, a close friend and colleague of Marshall's who had been edged out of the economics teaching at Cambridge after the turn of the century and finally passed over, with the support of Marshall, in favour of Pigou when Marshall's successor was appointed in 1908. 'I was so glad of an opportunity to make friends with Foxwell whom I had never seen since the terrible breach in 1908. We talked about the old days when he had coached me and Mary Kennedy' (M.P. Marshall to John Maynard Keynes, 16 June 1935, Keynes Collection, King's College, Cambridge, JMK L/MM). On the Foxwell dispute, see Coats, 1972, and Coase, 1972. On Marshall's campaigns to promote economics at Cambridge, see Groenewegen, 1990; on women, see McWilliams Tullberg, 1975, 1990a, 1990b and 1991; on conformity, see, for example, Maloney, 1985, 223–4).

60. Professor Robinson tells me that a typist was 'smuggled into the meeting' to make a record of her talk and it was this typescript she kept by her side and added to at intervals. There may have been more than one typescript (cf. p. 174 above), but the important point, confirmed by Professor Robinson, is that her talk to the Marshall Society was a repetition of the material later published in *What I Remember*.

61. Keynes would only be able to comment on the situation from personal experience after 1900 or even later – though he would probably be familiar with the situation in the Marshall household through his parents.

62. Parnell was the leader of a group of Irish members of Parliament demanding Irish independence and, at that time, disrupting the work of Parliament. By 'cultivated and attractive Irish families' is meant middle- or upper-class Protestants opposed to Irish Home Rule. Professor Becattini has suggested that his wife's apparent engagement in political debate may have embarrassed Marshall; he was trying, with little success, to interest the Anglican Tories, who dominated the city and its institutions, in the pressing economic needs of the new University College.

63. Her role in the founding of this society is mentioned in Gardner, 1921, 73, although it is mistakenly called the Society for Discussing Social Questions, the name of a club originally founded by some young male fellows and graduates in 1883 (Kadish, 1989, 106–7). Kadish notes that some joint meetings were held by the two societies (Kadish, 1989, 172).

64. The Oxford women's colleges joined the scheme later in the term.

65. Mary Marshall reports in her book *What I Remember* that women selected by the settlement were given a holiday in the Marshall home in Cambridge, while the Marshalls were abroad during the summer. The women were looked after by the Marshalls' servant, Sarah, who had been with them since their Bristol days.

66. The information given in this paragraph is drawn from Peter Groenewegen's research on the Marshalls' association with the Cambridge Ethical Society for his forthcoming biography of Alfred Marshall.

67. 'Perhaps one recollects earliest the things that one cares for most; certainly I have always had a love for colour' (M.P. Marshall, 1947, 1). Remembering the Marshalls's house in Bristol, G.H. Leonard describes 'the books and the pictures, and a new charm and beauty of its own within, which ... I should like to call "aesthetic"' involving 'a new sense of joy and loveliness in colour and form' (letter dated 7 October 1924 addressed to editor of the *Times and Mirror*). Elsewhere Mary Marshall, describing their honeymoon, wrote of the fortnight spent in Cornwall that 'I preferred the Lizard because of the beautiful colouring; Alfred preferred the [*sic*] Land's End and its fine forms. I always /loved/ preferred Colour and [Alfred] the Form throughout our lives' (Newnham Notes, ch.3, reverse of p.5).

68. W.G. Constable, 1887–1976, read law and then Part II of the Economics Tripos in 1910, where he took a First and got to know Marshall, who by then had retired. After being injured in World War I, he turned to art. He trained at the Slade and then worked in various art collections and as an arts writer and critic. In this latter capacity he was often called on to give the annual criticism of the Cambridge Drawing Society. After two years as Slade Professor of Fine Arts at Cambridge, he became Curator of the Boston Museum of Fine Arts in 1938, remaining in the United States for the rest of his life.

69. Biagini has argued that, from the outset, Marshall meant no more than that women should receive a measure of training which would enable them to offer intelligent assistance to men in some areas of their serious business of running the country (Biagini, 1991, 333). I believe that Marshall well understood and supported the aims of the women's education lobby of which he was a very active member in its early days. The Newnham faction wanted to give economic independence to middle-class women. Marshall went further and suggested that they should aim for academic excellence per se (see McWilliams Tullberg, forthcoming).

70. Evidence of this can be adduced from the absence of real opposition to women at Cambridge in the early days of the movement. Opposition manifested itself first when women began to return spectacular successes in the competitive Tripos examinations and to compete for university resources.

71. It is true that Marshall had to give up his fellowship on marriage; he could, however, have stayed at Cambridge, earning a modest living by coaching the small number of moral sciences students while waiting for a college lectureship and reform of the celibacy requirements. He was not 'forced' to go to Bristol; it was probably an attractive alternative at the time, because it incorporated two of his favourite projects – tertiary education for women and for the lower classes – and because of the generous salary.

72. Ann Carr, who read economics at Newnham during 1908–11 and later became a journalist, looked back at the relationship she had observed 30 years earlier: 'What kind of man was he to swallow such idolatry from his wife, to swallow so much and yet be jealous of her having any independent reputation as an economist?' (A. Carr to J.M. Keynes 29 October, 1944, Keynes Collection, King's College, Cambridge, JMK A/44).

REFERENCES

Adam, H.P. (1945), *Women in Council-Jubilee Book of the National Council of Women*, London: National Council of Women.

Barnett, H.O. (1918), *Canon Barnett, His Life, Work and Friends*, 2 vols, London: John Murray.

Biagini, E.F. (1991), 'Marshall's 1873 "Lectures to Women"', *Quaderni di Storia dell'Economia Politica*, **9**, (2–3), 333–51.

Biagini, E.F., R. McWilliams Tullberg and T. Raffaelli (eds) (forthcoming), *Alfred Marshall's Lectures to Women*, London: Croom Helm.

Carleton, D. (1984), *A University for Bristol: an Informal History in Text and Pictures*, Bristol: University of Bristol Press.

Coase, R.H. (1972), 'The appointment of Pigou as Marshall's successor: a comment', *Journal of Law and Economics*, **15**, (2); reprinted in Wood (1982), vol. 4, no. 113.

Coase R.H. (1984), 'Alfred Marshall's father and mother', *History of Political Economy*, **16**, (4), 519–27.

Coase R.H. (1990), 'Alfred Marshall's family and ancestry', in McWilliams Tullberg (1990a), 9–27.

Coats, A.W. (1972), 'The appointment of Pigou as Marshall's successor: a comment', *Journal of Law and Economics*, **15**, (2); reprinted in Wood (1982), vol. 4, no. 114.

Dyhouse, C. (1976), 'Social Darwinistic ideas and the development of women's education in England, 1880–1920', *History of Education*, **5**, (1), 41–58.

Fay, C.R. (1982), 'Reminiscences of a Deputy Librarian', in Wood (1982), vol. 1, no. 6.

Gardiner, M.I. (1887), 'Women's University Association for work in the poorer districts of London', Newnham College Club *Letter*.

Glendinning, Victoria (1969), *A Suppressed Cry: Life and Death of a Quaker Daughter*, London: Routledge & Kegan Paul.

Groenewegen, P.D. (1990), 'Teaching economics at Cambridge', *Scottish Journal of Political Economy*, **37**, (1), February.

Groenewegen, P.D. (1993), 'A weird and wonderful partnership: Mary Paley and Alfred Marshall 1877–1924', *History of Economic Ideas*, **I**, (1), 71–109.

Groenewegen, P.D. (1995), *A Soaring Eagle: Alfred Marshall 1842–1924*, Aldershot: Edward Elgar.

Guillebaud, C.W. (1960), 'Art and Economics in Cambridge', reprinted from *The Eagle*, **59**, (255), April 1960.

Hamilton, Mary Agnes (1936), *Remembering My Good Friends*, London: Jonathan Cape.

Kadish, A. (1989), *Historians, Economists and Economic History*, London: Routledge & Kegan Paul.

Keynes, J.M. (1926), *Official Papers of Alfred Marshall*, Royal Commission on the Aged Poor, Memorandum and Evidence of Alfred Marshall, 199–262, London: Macmillan.

Keynes, J.M. (1985a), 'Alfred Marshall', in *Essays in Biography*, D. Moggridge (ed.), *Collected Writings of John Maynard Keynes*, London: Macmillan for the Royal Economic Society, vol. 12, ch. 14; originally published in the *Economic Journal*, September 1924.

Keynes, J.M. (1985b), 'Mary Paley Marshall', in *Essays in Biography*, D. Moggridge (ed.), *Collected Writings of John Maynard Keynes*, London: Macmillan for the Royal Economic Society, vol. 12, ch. 15; originally published in the *Economic Journal*, June–September 1944.

MacKenzie, N. and J. McKenzie (ed.) (1983), *The Diary of Beatrice Webb, vol. 2, 1892–1905, All the Good Things in Life*, London: Virago, in association with the London School of Economics and Political Science.

Maloney, J. (1985), *Marshall, Orthodoxy and the Professionalisation of Economics*, Cambridge: Cambridge University Press.

Marshall, A. (1933), 'Alfred Marshall: the mathematician as seen by himself', *Econometrica*, **1**, April, 221–2; first published 1907.

Marshall, A. (1892), 'The Poor Law in Relation to State-Aided Pensions', and 'Poor Law Reform', *Economic Journal*, **2**, 186–91; 371–9.

Marshall, A. (1961), *Principles of Economics*, ed. C.W. Guillebaud, London: Macmillan for the Royal Economic Society, 9th (variorum) edn in two volumes; vol. 1, text, vol. 2, notes; first published 1920.

Marshell, A. and M.P. Marshall (1879), *Economics of Industry*, London: Macmillan; reprinted, with introduction by D.P. O'Brien, Bristol: Thoemmes Press, 1994.

Marshall, M.P. (1884), 'The growth of Newnham', Newnham College Club *Letter*.

Marshall, M.P. (1896), 'Conference of Women Workers', *Economic Journal*, **6**, March, Notes and Memoranda, 107–9 (review of *The Official Report of the Conference of Women Workers*, 1895).

Marshall, M.P. (1902), '*Educated Working Women* by Clara E. Collet', *Economic Journal*, **12**, 252–7.

Marshall, M.P. (1940), 'Obituary of Mary Wright (Kennedy), 1871–75', Newnham College Roll *Letter*, January.

Marshall, M.P. (1947), *What I Remember*, Cambridge: at the University Press.

McWilliams Tullberg, R. (1975), *Women at Cambridge – a Men's University, though of a Mixed Kind*, London: Gollancz.

McWilliams Tullberg, R. (ed.) (1990a), *Alfred Marshall in Retrospect*, Aldershot: Edward Elgar.

McWilliams Tullberg, R. (1990b), 'Alfred Marshall and the "Women Question" at Cambridge', *Economie Appliquée*, **43**, (1), 209–30.

McWilliams Tullberg, R. (1991), 'Alfred Marshall and the male priesthood of economics', *Quaderni di Storia dell'Economia Politica*, **9**, (2–3), 235–68.

McWilliams Tullberg, R. (1992), 'Alfred Marshall's attitude to the *Economics of Industry*', *Journal of the History of Economic Thought*, **14**, Fall, 257–70.

McWilliams Tullberg, R. (1993a), 'Marshall's final lecture, 21 May 1908', *History of Political Economy*, **25**, (4), 605–16.

McWilliams Tullberg, R. (1993b), 'Marshall Papers in the Newnham College Archive', *Marshall Studies Bulletin*, **3**, 36–47.

McWilliams Tullberg, R. (forthcoming), 'The Women's education movement at Cambridge', in Biagini *et al.* (1995).

Moore, K. (1974), *Victorian Wives*, London: Allison & Busby.

Moorman, M. (1980), *George Macaulay Trevelyan: a Memoir*, London: Hamish Hamilton.

Official Report of the Conference of Women Workers (1895), Office of the National Union of Women Workers, 25 Mecklenburg Square, London WC.

Pease, M.F. (1942), 'Some Reminiscences of University College Bristol', unpublished manuscript.

Phillips, A. (ed.) (1988), *A Newnham Anthology*, Cambridge: for Newnham College at the University Press.

Pigou, A.C. (ed.) (1925), *Memorials of Alfred Marshall*, London: Macmillan.

Prochaska F.K. (1980), *Women and Philanthropy in 19th Century England*, Oxford: Clarendon Press.

Rothblatt, S. (1968), *The Revolution of the Dons*, London: Faber & Faber.

Vicinus, M. (1985), *Independent Women: Work and Community for Single Women 1850–1920*, London: Virago.

Webb, B. (1873–1943), microfiche typescript of diary, Cambridge: Chadwyck & Healey Ltd.

Wood, J.C. (ed.) (1982), *Alfred Marshall: Critical Assessments*, four vols, London: Croom Helm.

10. Women's wage rates and total earnings: two early 'scientific' studies

James P. Henderson

10.1 INTRODUCTION

The British Association for the Advancement of Science (BAAS), the premier scientific organization in Great Britain, recognized the scientific possibilities of economics early when it established Section F at its third meeting in 1833. This was called the 'Statistical Section' until 1856, when its name was changed to 'The Section of Economic Science and Statistics'. Though there is some indication of the dwindling importance of Section F to economists beginning in 1890, when the British Economic Association and the *Economic Journal* were launched, the British Association gave economists a formal tie with the scientific community that these newer institutions lacked. Moreover, the British Association was an important source of funds to finance research projects. During the first two decades of the twentieth century, the British Association financed two studies on the role of women in industry. The first project, initiated in 1900 and completed in 1903, considered 'The Economic Effect of Legislation regulating Women's Labour'. At the outbreak of World War I, the scientific community turned to the economists to identify, investigate, analyse and recommend solutions to the pressing economic problems confronting the nation. A significant share of both the research money appropriated and grants paid by the British Association between 1915 and 1920 went to Section F projects, including 'Women in Industry' (1915–1920).[1] Here attention will focus on the issues surrounding women's wages and earnings that were uncovered in these two research projects. Given that focus, a review of the variety of wage payment practices in Britain is necessary.

In 1892, David Schloss distinguished the 'two branches' of the 'Labour Problem': the first 'relates to the amount, the other to the method, of industrial remuneration' (Schloss, 1892, 1). He identified 11 methods of paying workers, these being divided into two main categories: wages paid to individuals and wages paid to groups of workers – collective wages. Generally, the wages received by workers were alleged to correspond in some manner to the amount of work performed. This correspondence 'is but loosely maintained' in the case of time wages, it being assumed that the time occupied measures the amount of work performed by the individual worker (Schloss, 1892, 3). Time wages guarantee workers a minimum income. Task wages and piece wages more exactly proportion the work done and the pay received, but give the workers no guaranteed minimum income. Task wages are a combination of piece wages and time wages: the worker was expected to accomplish a given task within an allotted period of time. Failure to do so resulted in a deduction from the worker's task wage; exceeding the performance standard, however, was not rewarded with a premium (Schloss, 1892, 19). While task wages relied on a negative incentive, 'progressive wages' provided a positive incentive. Workers were guaranteed a minimum wage, supplemented by a premium paid to those who exceeded the output standard within the allotted time (Schloss, 1892, 48).

Wages were also paid on a collective or group basis. The best known form of this was subcontracting. Here the workers were hired by and worked directly for the work leader ('foreman') rather than for the person who let the contract. The work leader had an incentive to execute the work as efficiently as possible, since the leader pocketed the difference between the revenue received for the project and the wages paid to the employees (Schloss, 1892, 105–6). Subcontracting was the payment method found in sweated industries. On the other hand, in contract work the labourers were directed by the work leader, while remaining the employees of the person who let the contract. As defined by Schloss, in contract work the employer apportioned a lump sum of money 'between the group by, first, deducting the time-wages of the subordinate members, and then paying to the principal member or members, out of balance thus left, a piece-work remuneration, the amount of which varies directly with the rate of speed in working maintained by the group'.

Schloss found four additional methods of collective or group wages. In the first three the employer apportions a lump sum among the members of the group. This takes the form of a 'collective task-wage', a 'collective piece-wage' or a 'collective progressive wage'. Finally in 'cooperative work' the lump sum paid to the group was 'apportioned amongst the members of the group in such proportions as they, at their own discretion, shall determine' (Schloss, 1892, 12). Cooperation took two forms: profit sharing, where 'the power of the employer remained paramount', the workers having no control of the business, but receiving their wages and sharing in the firm's profits, and 'industrial partnership', where

(1) each of the group of workers is to be associated by their own free choice, (2) ... these associates shall work under a leader elected and removable by them-

selves, and (3) ... the collective remuneration of the labour performed by the
group shall be divided among its members ... in such a manner as shall be
arranged upon principles recognised as equitable by the associates themselves.
(Schloss, 1892, 150, 141–2)

Any number of these methods of industrial remuneration were unpopular
with the workers. Through their trade unions, they sought to modify or eliminate several of them. By 1918, G.D.H. Cole saw a need to revise Schloss's
work. He identified 'two bases of payment within the wage-system – payment
for time worked and payment for output' produced (Cole, 1918, 1).[2] Within
Cole's categories wages were paid to workers either individually or collec-
tively. The categories, though distinct in theory, have a common basis:

A time-work system is never wholly without relation to output; for the employer
inevitably expects a certain amount of work from the worker whom he employs,
and if this work is not forthcoming, he finds his remedy in discharging the worker.
Payment by output, again, is never wholly without relation to a time standard; for
piece-prices are invariably determined to a great extent by the income which
constitutes the normal standard of life for the workmen concerned. (Cole, 1918, 1)

Cole identified a new system, 'Scientific Management', which combined
the task wage and the progressive wage (Cole, 1918, 3). After a standard of
output had been defined, those workers who produced less were penalized
with a deduction, while those who exceeded the standard were paid a premium. Piece wage systems had become more sophisticated and the trade
unions were quite successful in their efforts to guarantee minimum incomes
(usually tied to the standard time wage) for those workers paid by the piece.
Where jobs were numerous and complicated, the trade unions had established
'the principle of collective bargaining in relation to piece-work prices' (Cole,
1918, 4). Where the trade unions were strong, a standard price list, 'a long
list, usually printed and sometimes of quite extraordinary complexity, setting
forth in full the piece-work prices to be paid for every job regularly executed
in the industry' was adopted (Cole, 1918, 4–5). These price lists might apply
industry-wide or might vary between districts or particular firms. Where
price lists were not employed, 'mutuality' – 'the fixing of a piece-price for an
individual job by mutual agreement between the employer' and those who
perform the job – was often practised (Cole, 1918, 5). As before, bonuses
were superimposed on piece wage or time wage systems. A new premium
bonus scheme, the 'Halsey system', had been developed in which the time
necessary to complete a job was specified and the worker was paid a bonus
for completing the task in less than the allotted time:

if the standard time allowance for a job is ten hours, and the worker does the job
in six hours, payment will be made for six hours, and in addition for a proportion,

very often a half, of the four hours saved in the job. This payment is made at the standard hourly rate. (Cole, 1918, 6)

Finally, Cole mentioned the variety of profit-sharing systems.

For women compensated under 'payment for output' systems, equal pay for equal results could be obtained if they could secure the same piece rates and bonus terms as those offered to men. Yet this was an uncommon practice in most industries in Great Britain, where both jobs and the pay rates usually differed between women and men. And even if women could secure identical rates or bonuses, their weekly incomes would still not be equal to the men's if they were less productive, if they were forced to work at processes that were less productive, or if there were restrictions on the number of hours they could work. The Factory Acts set limits both on the number of hours and the time (at night) that women could work. This denied women access both to overtime rates and to the premiums paid for working during undesirable periods. Women working on a 'payment for time' basis were usually paid at lower rates than men, regardless of the comparability of the work. Even when their hourly wage rates were equal, the Factory Acts' limitations on the hours and time worked resulted in lower weekly and monthly earnings.

10.2 INVESTIGATIONS OF THE ECONOMIC EFFECTS OF THE FACTORY ACTS

At the meeting of the BAAS in 1900, a grant was awarded to a committee formed to study 'The Economic Effect of Legislation regulating Women's Labour' (*Report of the BAAS – 1900*, xci).[3] The report, in the *Economic Journal*, of this meeting of the British Association mentioned the appointment of the committee and its membership. The *Economic Journal* also noted that Mrs MacDonald presented a paper, 'Labour Legislation for Women' which 'attracted attention' (*Economic Journal*, December 1900, 600).[4] No other papers presented at that meeting evoked comment in the journal.

In 1901, the committee was granted an additional sum and issued the first of three reports (*Report of the BAAS – 1901*, c).[5] Though no actual findings were enumerated, the committee established its 'Scheme of Investigation' identifying these 'points' which the 'Commissioners should observe':

I.   The effects of the legislation *generally*.
(1)   Has it necessitated or induced any alteration of custom, or merely enforced what was customary before, in the case of the *women* themselves, in the industry in question, or in others related thereto?
(2)   Has it necessitated any alteration in the case of *other workers* (men, young persons, or children) in the industry in question, or in others related thereto?

II.   The effects of the legislation *specially* on the position of women, whether (a) prejudicially: –
(1)   Has it lowered the wages of women relatively, either temporarily or permanently?
(2)   Has it caused any displacement of women?
(3)   Has it initiated any important changes in the use of machinery or the division of labour?
Or (b) beneficially: –
(1)   Has it increased the efficiency of all women themselves as industrial agents; and is this efficiency due to all, or only to some, of the legal restrictions?
(2)   Has it increased their economic efficiency as members of society (*e.g.*, with relation to home life, the health of the children, the morality of the race), and are these effects due to all, or only to some, of the legal restrictions?
(N.B.– The legislation may affect the demand for women's labour (1) directly, in the industry in question by adding to difficulties of management, or by diminishing the output of the women themselves, or others engaged in the work; (2) indirectly, by effects on other industries related to the industry in question; or it may increase the supply of women and their substitution for men by rendering the work healthier or easier.) (*Report of the BAAS – 1901*, 400)

In 1902, the British Association added £25 to the committee's 'balance on hand' (*Report of the BAAS – 1902*, xc).[6] The committee's second report summarized a number of findings as well as returns from several foreign inquiries.[7] The 'Third and Final Report of the Committee' was published in the 1903 *Report ... of the British Association.*[8] This final report was based on further accounts from the committee's investigators, 'general statistics of Women's Employment from Miss Collet', and 'reports [issued since 1834] of the Chief Inspector of Factories' (*Report of the BAAS – 1903*, 316).[9]

The Committee's Final Report in 1903 generally follows the structure of the 'Scheme of Investigation' established in its 1901 Report.[10] Of most interest are the findings in 'Section V – effect on women's rates of wages and total earnings'. The committee took care to make three important distinctions: first, discriminating 'between changes of rates per hour or per piece and changes in total weekly earnings'; second, separating the immediate changes which were brought on by the Acts from 'the change that may be observed after sufficient time had elapsed to allow a return to equilibrium'; and, finally, where 'greater regularity week by week' followed the Acts, the committee considered 'how monthly and annual earnings changed'. Fundamentally, the committee concluded 'that neither theory nor evidence enable us to decide whether earnings increase or decrease after restriction[s]' were imposed on working conditions by the Factory Acts (*Report of the BAAS – 1903*, 337). The committee's findings were divided into theoretical and statistical results.

It is clear that the economists on the committee had a strong hand in writing the theoretical conclusions. They isolated factors which 'would tend to produce a fall' from those 'circumstances [which] would tend to produce a rise' in women's incomes – carefully distinguishing between wage rates and earnings. Three conditions 'tend to produce a fall' in income:

[1] the substitution of other labour or machinery (in rates and earnings); [2] the diminution of the product in proportion to the time cut off (in earnings, probably); [3] the spreading the same output more regularly among the same workers (in earnings, but only if overtime had been paid at a higher rate). (*Report of the BAAS – 1903*, 337)

Five factors were found to cause income to rise:

[1] the attempt to produce the same output in a shorter time by workers of the same class, causing a demand for more workers (in rates, earnings might fall or rise); [2] the diminution of the product, increasing the demand for it relative to the supply (in rates); [3] the greater efficiency of the worker caused by the regulation of hours (fall in piece-rates, rise in time-rates, and in both cases rise in earnings); [4] the more rapid output per hour caused by the attempt to make the same earnings in the shorter time; [and 5] the greater demand for women workers caused by the introduction of machinery. (*Report of the BAAS – 1903*, 337)

The fifth factor raised an issue that will recur in the later studies on women economic conditions during World War I. There the investigating committees and the employers tended to focus on the added costs of introducing machinery, while ignoring the benefits that accrued to employers as a result of introducing new technologies and machines.

A comparison of the countervailing factors influencing women's income led the committee members to conclude that 'it cannot be said *a priori* whether either rates or earnings will rise or fall' as a result of the Factory Acts (*Report of the BAAS – 1903*, 337).[11]

The committee concluded from its examination of the statistical evidence that:

no permanent fall in wages can be connected with restrictive legislation, while in many cases a rise is recorded at a time, if any, when the legislation might have caused a fall. These figures are important in that they show that restrictive legislation is not inconsistent with rising wages, but of course they do not show whether it furthered or hindered that rise. (*Report of the BAAS – 1903*, 337)

On the basis of both the theoretical and statistical evidence, the Committee could produce no significant proof

of any loss of wages or earnings traceable to the Acts; nor did it have any definite evidence of any gain, which (if it accrued), would be due to influences which take time to produce effect, and whose action would be indistinguishable from that of other causes. (*Report of the BAAS – 1903*, 339)

The Committee closed its report announcing that its members were 'unanimous in expressing the following opinions' (*Report of the BAAS – 1903*, 340). In all, 21 'opinions' were developed. While the 'opinions' numbered 12, 13 and 14 speak directly to women's earnings, most of the others concern conditions that could also alter their incomes. Opinions 1–6 and 17 and 18 might influence total earnings by changing the number of hours worked. Conclusions 7–10 would affect total incomes by changing the opportunities for the bonuses and premiums that could be earned by working at undesirable times. Number 11 speaks to the demand for women workers. Items 15 and 16 might affect earnings by changing the skills required to perform certain types of work. Opinion 19 dealt with elderly women workers and their employment, and hence earning, opportunities.

1.   The Factory Acts have reduced weekly hours of work in some cases and regularised them in many, and have abolished night work for women.

2.   The maximum allowed is in general greater than the number of hours worked by men in trades regulated by agreement between employers and Trade Unions.

3.   In some cases legislation has enforced the custom of the better managed firms, in others it has made compulsory hours that would not have been obtained otherwise.

4.   In nearly all cases employers admit that the *normal* hours allowed are sufficient, and welcome the restriction; frequently the hours actually worked are less than those allowed.

5.   Employees, so far as their opinions have been gathered, are unanimous in approving the restriction to the maximum allowed.

6.   But for the compulsory restriction the hours would often be lengthened against the will of the majority of all concerned.

7.   The Acts have had considerable effect in spreading work more uniformly through the week, month, or year, where there is occasional pressure.

8.   In the great majority of cases there is approval of or acquiescence in the restriction of *overtime*; but in some few cases greater elasticity in arranging hours of work and the removal of the prohibition of overtime is urgently desired by employers.

9.   It appears that in a small minority of cases the partial removal of the prohibition of overtime authorised by the Acts tends to economy and greater ease of production without overworking the employees, particularly where occasional times of pressure follow periods of slackness and in the other cases contemplated by the Acts. There is great danger of any relaxation being abused, but when trial has shown that overtime cannot be altogether abolished (as *e.g.* where there is actual employment of more expensive labour to carry on work which women are prevented by law from doing) the authorities should give careful consideration to the circumstances of the case. The Committee have not enough evidence to recommend relaxation in any particular case.

10. There are very few cases where women's labour has actually been displaced by restriction.

11. The information as to the general demand for women's labour does not show any appreciable change that can be traced to the Acts, but the statistics are of such a nature that a change might easily escape observation.

12.   Women have lost some opportunities of overtime, but it is very doubtful whether either the total number of hours worked or the total earnings made have been diminished in any important cases.

13.   There is no conclusive evidence that the course of either rates of wages or earnings has or has not been affected appreciably in consequence of the Acts.

14.   As regards rates of wages and the allocation of work between men and women the Acts are at the utmost among the less important of the determining factors.

15.   The Acts have in some industries exerted a small but steady pressure in favour of the more efficient and of the larger factories or workshops.

16.   In a few cases legislation has hastened the introduction of machinery and of new arrangements of work which have promoted efficiency of production, even where hardship or inconvenience has been caused.

17.   There is some evidence that the regularisation of hours has promoted the efficiency of women as productive agents.

18.   In some important industries as a whole, and in some processes in others, the limitation of women's time has caused a limitation of men's work, but the hours even thus limited are still more than those which obtain in the majority of organised men's trades.

19.   There appears to be a falling off in the relative number of elderly women returned as occupied. It is expedient that in considering legislative measures care should be taken not to diminish any desirable opportunities for their employment, but so far no want of employment has been traced directly to the Acts.

20.   The Acts may have caused some inconvenience and perhaps hardship in special cases, in the main of a temporary character; the better adaptability of the more recent Acts tends to reduce these to unimportance.

21.   The benefits which the Acts have conferred are in the long run great and out of all proportion to any inconveniences or injury they have caused. (*Report of the BAAS – 1903*, 340–42)[12]

One wonders how these conclusions might have been influenced by the changes in the membership of the committees and investigators. The original nine-member committee in charge of the investigation included only one female member, Mrs J.R. (Margaret E.) MacDonald. The first report indicated that the committee had grown to 12 members and Miss A.M. Anderson, Miss C.E. Collet and Mrs. H.J. Tennant now joined MacDonald. Both Anderson and Tennant left the committee in the third year and Miss Helen Blackburn was added. The final committee membership included the return of both Anderson and Tennant. Women members were added after the first year and some explanation of this is offered in the committee's reports, where it is remarked that the committee 'sought the assistance of Mrs. H.J. Tennant, late H.M. Principle Lady Inspector of Factories, Miss A.M. Anderson, her successor in office [and] Miss C.E. Collet, of the Board of Trade'. These three women had expertise developed in their careers that the committee found essential for its investigations.

Moreover, the number of women listed as investigators engaged in data gathering and report writing was indicative of the committee's confidence in their performance of these duties. Some women were put in charge of report-ing on geographic areas: Birmingham was investigated by Miss B.L. Hutchins, while the report on Canning Town and the Isle of Dogs was done by Miss Hadley; both Miss A. Harrison and Mrs F.H. Spencer investigated Liverpool, and Miss Irwin covered Glasgow and the South of Scotland. Other women investigated industries: Miss Thornewell did the Potteries and Miss B.L. Hutchins added paper-making near London and several South London indus-tries; a committee organized by the Women's Industrial Council of London studied printing and bookbinding, another committee of the Women's Indus-trial Council of London explored tailoring in London, Mrs Bosanquet exam-ined London industries and West London Laundries, and finally, Miss A.M. Anderson scrutinized laundries (*Report of the BAAS – 1903*, 316). It appears that the male-dominated original committee put aside whatever initial preju-dices they may have harboured about the ability of women to engage in such scientific work as they recognized the expertise offered by several women who held important government positions and as they witnessed the quality of the research produced by women covering geographic areas or industry studies. It is most probable that the women in charge of the industry studies produced more credible reports since the industries they investigated were dominated by female employees, who may well have feared the consequences of answering candidly any inquiries posed by male interrogators.

10.3   THE INVESTIGATIONS PROMPTED BY WORLD WAR I

In the summer of 1915, the discussions in Section F 'aroused considerable interest, and there was a widespread demand that they should be' shared with the public. The outbreak of World War I persuaded the officers of Section F to concentrate attention on three groups of 'problems which were of immedi-ate and pressing importance … the prevalence of industrial unrest, the man-ner in which labour absorbed by the war was replaced, and the state of credit, currency, and finance as affected by the war' (*British Labour, Replacement and Conciliation, 1914–21*, v). It soon became clear that the second issue, the 'replacement of the labour of men by that of women during the war', was of pressing importance. Five different reports of these investigations were issued between 1915 and 1921. These reports on women's role in industry examined the scope and success of the replacement, the relationship between women workers and the male dominated trade unions, and issues surrounding women's wages.

    The first report issued by the committees established by Section F was the 1915 book, *Credit, Industry and the War*. A 'Conference Committee on

Outlets for Labour after the War' was established, with W.R. Scott serving as chairman and A.W. Kirkaldy acting as secretary.[13] The Conference Committee determined to investigate five terms of reference:

> 1. The replacement of men by women in industries during the war. 2. The permanent effects of this after the war. 3. The character of re-employment with respect to changes of tastes and physique amongst those who have served with the Forces and are disbanded. 4. The means by which consequent unemployment may be counteracted or minimised. 5. The possibility of employing disbanded men on the land. (Kirkaldy, 1915, 68)

The last three 'terms of reference' were 'more suitably dealt with by papers and discussion', so the Conference Committee turned its attention to the first two issues (Kirkaldy, 1915, 69). A Committee was created to investigate the 'Replacement of Men by Women in Industry' (*Report of the BAAS – 1915*, lvi).

The following year, 1916, the Research Committee on the Replacement of Men by Women in Industry during the War continued its inquiry, supported by another grant (*Report of the BAAS – 1916*, lvi). Its report appears in a book titled: *Labour, Finance and the War*.[14] In 1917, the Research Committee, with a supplemental grant, continued its inquiry and reported its findings in a book titled *Industry and Finance, War Expenditures and Reconstruction* (*Report of the BAAS – 1917*, xxiii).[15]

The reports of the British Association show that in 1918 the Committee was awarded another grant to continue its work (*Report of the BAAS – 1918*, xi). In the 'Preface' to the 1920 *Industry and Finance (Supplementary Volume)* the editor, Adam Kirkaldy, announced that 'the Committees appointed just after the beginning of the war are not responsible for these supplementary reports' (Kirkaldy, 1920, v).[16] By this time a number of other groups, public and private, were monitoring economic events. Kirkaldy thanked 'Employers, Welfare Supervisors, and Trade Union officials … Government departments and officials [in particular] the Industrial War Inquiries Branch of the Board of Trade … [and] Mr. R.E. Barnett, B.Sc., of the Central Technical School, Leeds' for the valuable assistance they offered the investigators (Kirkaldy, 1920, v–vi).

The final report on the investigations into the replacement of men by women was 'co-ordinated and revised by Miss L. Grier and Miss A. Ashley', then published in 1921 in a last book edited by Adam W. Kirkaldy, *British Labour, Replacement and Conciliation, 1914–1921*. In 1919, the report of the British Association noted that an additional grant had been made to the Committee (*Report of the BAAS – 1919*, lxiii). As before, attention here is focused on the findings relating to women's wages.

In its first report in 1915, *Credit, Industry and the War*, the committee appraised women's wages and estimated that 'women receive 50 per cent. to

75 per cent. of the wages paid to men in similar occupations'. In their evaluation of the 'chief factors' which account for this disparity they noted that employers claim to pay the individual worker 'what in the employer's opinion he or she is "worth"' (Kirkaldy, 1915, 87). However,

> Men's Trade Unions and many of the women's organisations ... object to the payment to women of lower rates than those paid to men for similar work. In some cases the policy of the men on this point is opposed to that of the women in the same industry – the men asking for equal rates for men and women, and the women objecting on the ground that this would lead to their effectual exclusion from the trade. (Kirkaldy, 1915, 87)

The male-dominated labour unions frequently demanded equal pay for men and women for equal work, but this was intended to keep women out of the jobs they controlled. This tactic relied on the widely held belief that men were more productive than women workers. If that premise was accepted by employers, they would reject women applicants if they we required to pay them the same wages as they paid the 'more productive' male workers. Women's organizations soon realized the consequence of this labour union tactic and began demanding equal employment opportunities, rather than equal pay.

The committee divided the justifications for paying women lower wages than men into two groups. The first group 'resolve themselves' into four specific complaints which reflect the alleged 'limitations to the industrial employability of women':

> 1. Women can perform only the lighter processes.
> 2. The output of women is less than that of men.
> 3. Women are less skilled and experienced than men and are rarely willing to devote much time to training even if employers thought (as they rarely do) that the short duration of their industrial life justified a long training.
> 4. Some conditions, such as night work, are more objectionable in the case of women than of men. (Kirkaldy, 1915, 88)

The second 'limitation' was proved wrong in numerous cases as the war progressed. The third 'limitation' – women's lack of skills and experience – was as much the result of opportunities denied them by both employers and labour unions as it was due to the women being 'rarely willing to devote much time to training'. The final 'limitation' was a consequence of the Factory Acts. Thus the alleged 'limitations to the industrial employability of women' were largely a social construct, rather than a biological fact.

The committee observed that men's wages, particularly during the earlier phases of their careers, were 'reckoned in two dimensions – the size of the wage and the prospects of promotion and higher pay after a period of training or experience' (Kirkaldy, 1915, 88). Since women's industrial careers were shorter and 'in the majority of cases she has fewer prospects and is employed for her intrinsic output', the committee concluded that 'it would seem only equitable that, other things being equal, a woman's wage in the earlier stages, instead of being lower than that of a youth doing the same work, should be on a higher scale' (Kirkaldy, 1915, 88).

In addition, the committee reviewed the various arguments put forward to establish that the work done by women was not 'equal work' to that of men. First, the committee asserted that the work done by women 'is very rarely similar as regards either processes or conditions' to that of male workers:

> With the introduction of women the work has often to be subdivided, and the men generally have at least the arduousness of their work increased with oft-times the addition of overtime and night work and a larger amount of work entailing a greater strain. Where workshops have been recently built for women workers they have been equipped with machinery of a very different type from what would have been installed had the management been able to procure skilled men. (Kirkaldy, 1915, 89)

The last argument indicates that the shortage of skilled labour created an incentive to innovate and invest in equipment which increased worker productivity, regardless of the worker's gender, while ignoring the benefits, both financial and productive, that resulted. The committee also claimed that, while women could be trained to operate certain, relatively simple machines, 'a long training is necessary in operating other tools' and machines. It was believed that there was not enough time to provide such training, given the wartime emergency. Finally, even where men and women operated identical machines their work was unequal, 'as only in rare instances can the women "tune" or "set" their machines' (Kirkaldy, 1915, 89). Millicent Fawcett's analysis of this complaint blamed the problem on the male-dominated labour unions. Not only had the trade unions excluded women from the higher paying skilled jobs, they were allegedly responsible for women not having the training necessary to perform all aspects of the jobs they did hold. Thus, to the old complaint that women could not 'tune' or 'set' their own machines but required male workers to perform that crucial task, Fawcett answered:

> These facts are indisputable, but in connection with them another fact must be remembered – namely that stringent Trade Union rules prevented women from being taught to 'set' and 'tune' their machines. They did not do it, because they were not allowed to learn it. (Fawcett, 1917, 198)

The committee concluded that 'the apparent simplicity of the "equal pay for equal work" test is in practice found to be extremely complicated and difficult to apply' (Kirkaldy, 1915, 89).

The second group of justifications for paying women lower wages were labelled 'social custom', and included these claims:

> the needs of women are smaller than those of men. It is argued that a man's wages have normally to be used for the support of a household, while a large proportion of working women have only themselves to support. Some employers also state that, as women ask for less wages than men, they are paid less in consequence. Others follow social custom in regarding women workers as of a lower status than men. (Kirkaldy, 1915, 89)

These arguments were fabricated by employers, yet the committee concluded that 'the difference between the wages of men and women is often more than can be justified by any difference in efficiency, and that this has the result of making it profitable for a firm to introduce the largest possible amount of female labour' (Kirkaldy, 1915, 89). While the male-dominated trade unions might agree 'on the basis of "to everyone according to his needs"', they also assumed that 'the low demands of women workers are partly the result of lack of organisation and of industrial ambition among them' (Kirkaldy, 1915, 90). The unions vehemently opposed women underbidding men's wages, those who did so were labelled 'blacklegs'. Yet the male unions discouraged, and even forbade, women from joining their ranks, so that women were forced to establish their own trade unions.

The committee noted that low-paid labour is not necessarily cheap labour. They found evidence showing that, when women workers were substituted for men, the employers' labour costs frequently rose. 'Often two women have had to be employed instead of one man, and three women instead of two men is a fairly common occurrence.' On the other hand, when such a substitution is accompanied by 'a greater subdivision of processes', the cost of production is 'frequently found' to be reduced (Kirkaldy, 1915, 90). It is no surprise to find that both the division and specialization of labour coupled with increased investment in new technology would reduce costs, yet this admission was unusual. More frequently the committee reported employers' complaints about the cost of introducing such technology, while the employers and/or the committee ignored the financial benefits and productivity gains that also resulted. The committee concluded that 'skilled workmen are thus in some cases undercut in the labour market as effectively as though women offered to do equal work for a smaller wage' (Kirkaldy, 1915, 90). But new technologies, and the consequent deskilling of workers that accompany their introduction, is an issue unrelated to the gender of the workers involved and the statement merely makes women the scapegoats for this process.

Finally, the 'Fair Wages Clause' included in all government contracts proved an ineffective safeguard for women's wages. The clause was 'framed apparently on the assumption that, in the trades to which it applies, standard recognised rates of pay can be ascertained'. Widespread evasion arose when employers changed production processes and then introduced women. Employers also were able to evade the clause by classifying the newly hired women as 'learners' and then paying them on a reduced 'learners' scale of wages (Kirkaldy, 1915, 90–91).

In the committee's 1916 report, *Labour, Finance and the War*, it was noted that the government decided to adopt minimum wage rates for women who replaced men in occupations that had been exclusively male before the war. The Central Labour Supply Committee issued 'Circular L2' in October 1915. This was later approved by the prime minister and the minister of munitions, at the insistence of the trade unions. The minister of munitions was given the power 'to fix minimum wages for women doing munition work in establishments of a certain class'. The committee also noted that 'practically the whole of the easily available reserve of female labour had been drained' resulting in scarcities of labour in the 'women's fields' (Kirkaldy, 1916, 61–2). Thus, during the early years of the war, experienced women workers shifted from existing jobs in 'women's fields' into industries previously dominated by male workers. It seems that few forces operated to attract additional women into the labour force.

In 1916, the committee identified four 'forces ... in operation tending to raise the rate of wages of women in general industry'. The first force was the new minimum wage rates 'established by three Orders under the Munitions of War (Amendment) Act, 1916'. In judging whether such wage rates should be considered high or low, the committee discerned that 'such wages were a minimum and, from the scarcity of women in other industries, they seem to compare favourably with the general level of wages' (Kirkaldy, 1916, 90). The second force that raised wages came from the trade unions which settled wage agreements with those employers who replaced men with women. The third force, 'the operation of economic laws', raised women's wage rates because of the scarcities of labour created in those industries not subject to 'Trade Union influence, or Trade Board regulations' or minimum wage requirements. These scarcities were created in those industries by women leaving them for the obvious attractions of those industries subject to such income-raising forces. Here the committee discovered a new phenomenon. In any number of firms, women employees were divided into two separate groups within the same shop – one group doing work subject to minimum wage conditions, the other exempt from minimum wages, even though a similar amount of skill was involved in their jobs. As a result

> two sets of wages were in operation. A double standard of wages as between men and women has long been a well recognised fact of industry; but a double standard, as between one set of women and another, in contact with each other, and on

work involving similar powers, is a new phenomenon. It is clear that, women being forthcoming at the lower rate, as soon as the legal enforcement of the minimum is withdrawn, there may be a considerable fall in the wages of the women affected, which will probably spread to other industries. (Kirkaldy, 1916, 91)

The final force at work raising women's monetary wages was rising prices. After reviewing the price level increases, the committee concluded that, while nominal wages had gone up, 'it is doubtful how far real wages have risen'. One thing was apparent, though: 'there is a greater correspondence between men's and women's wages for the same work than there was before the war' (Kirkaldy, 1916, 92–3). Only in some cases was this due to trade union influence. Wage rates were not the sole determinant of earnings and the committee considered that 'high earnings are sometimes due to an expenditure of energy which is of the greatest value to the nation at the present time' (Kirkaldy, 1916, 93). However, the committee did not expect that such bursts of energy were likely to continue for very long, or under more normal, peacetime circumstances.

While the trade unions had several reasons for opposing the introduction of women into men's jobs, their major concern was the wage issue. Both the employers and the unions sought a solution which would fix the wages of women so 'as to enable them to be employed and yet to avoid their undercutting men'. Examining the most popular solution, equal pay for equal work, the committee noted that 'there are many processes in which the introduction of women necessitates extra supervision and technical changes in process which reduce the women's value to the employer' (Kirkaldy, 1916, 94). Here, once again, the committee ignored the financial benefits and productivity gains which accompany such 'technical changes in process'. The committee judged that 'the policy of equal pay for equal work is not unanimously held, even by the strongest supporters of women's rights; and it is very doubtful whether the mass of women workers could ever be prevailed upon to stand out [i.e. strike] for this equality' (Kirkaldy, 1916, 94). We have already seen why women opposed, and the men's unions promoted, 'the policy of equal pay for equal work'.

Later in the report, the Committee estimated which of these forces were likely to continue exercising a strong influence on wages after the war, and narrowed its list to these three: the minimum wage restrictions imposed on certain war industries, the trade union demands, and rising consumer prices. The fourth force, which the committee identified in 1915, 'the operation of economic laws' which raised wages in response to labour scarcities, it believed was likely to disappear after the war. The 1916 committee expected continued pressures from the unions, though they were unwilling to estimate the success of those demands. The influence of inflation was 'also an incalculable factor'. The minimum wage requirements were designed to end 'twelve months after peace is declared, and we have reason to believe that the immediate result will be a drop in the wages of the women still remaining in that work and, consequently, in other industries also'. Believing that 'it is almost inconceivable that the women, having earned wages comparable to those of men, will be willing to return to the lower paid trades at the old rates', the committee agreed that such an event 'may prove to be the force which will unite the women together as workers' (Kirkaldy, 1916, 98).

In 1917, in its report *Industry and Finance, War Expenditures and Reconstruction*, attention was drawn to a number of new 'orders [which] have been issued [by the government] determining the remuneration of women engaged in work on munitions of war'. These orders had appeared since the release of the Committee's previous report in 1916. While the employers' reaction was described as being 'seldom in favourable terms', nonetheless there seemed to be 'no uniformity of practice as to the women's rate, and the matter is ... still the subject of unsettled dispute' (Kirkaldy, 1917, 76). The employers were allowed to pay their women employees at a reduced rate, up to 10 per cent lower, if they could prove the 'expense of setting up, or skilled supervision' added to their costs of employing female help. This penalized women for not having skills or not performing tasks, when the required training had been denied them. The committee's investigations of women's wages in some industries revealed that 'female operators can make good pay'. Moreover, it was clear that not only was 'the increase in the skill of the worker' a factor in these high earnings: three other factors were also at work – 'improvements in the machines themselves, in the tuning-up of these machines, and in the management of the factory'. Yet there remained considerable variation in the women's earnings, greater variation than could be accounted for by the differences in workers' skills, which caused 'some amount of dissatisfaction' (Kirkaldy, 1917, 76). The committee recommended that there be a 'levelling-up' of women's earnings by either a 'payment on a time rate, with a production bonus system' or 'by taking the present total cost of the [commodity] as produced, and readjusting the payment for separate operations on it, so as to result in the possibility of almost equivalent payment to the women operators' (Kirkaldy, 1917, 77–8). While the committee had not made detailed inquiries into industries not covered by the various governmental orders, the question of women's wages kept coming up. Here

it was found to be a common stipulation in the trade agreements between Trade Unions and Employers' Associations, that women introduced shall be paid the same wages as men for equivalent work – a stipulation which, while accepted in the exigencies of the present time, is said, likewise, to be one of the surest safeguards of the position of the men after the war. (Kirkaldy, 1917, 78)

In 1921, the 'results of conferences and investigations by committees of Section F of the British Association' were published in a book: *British Labour, Replacement and Conciliation, 1914–1921.* In the chapter on wages, the committee attributed the increase in women's wages to 'three main causes'. The first was 'the keen competition for labour' which developed shortly after the outbreak of the war. 'Secondly, the rise in the cost of living' was an important factor in driving wages upward. The third cause was that, 'where women were doing men's work, the men insisted on good payment for the women so as to safeguard their own interests, while the women naturally demanded the same rate of pay as the men whom they replaced' (Kirkaldy, 1921, 93). The similarities and differences between these 'three main causes' of increased women's wages and the findings in 1915 and 1916 will become clear as we examine them in more detail.

With the disruptions and rapid conversion of production during the early months of the war, the employment of women actually fell. This was attributed to the rapid decline in the demand for goods produced by industries which normally employed women which was not offset by increased demand for their services elsewhere. Thus, during the early months of the war, 'schemes were introduced to find work for them. Such schemes soon became unnecessary'. Yet this increase in the demand for women workers had little impact on women's wages during the early stages of the war. It was 'during the last 18 months of war, [that] competition resulted in raising women's wages in all occupations'. Even during this period, the results were uneven. Women's wages rose

> more markedly in those [industries] they were entering than in those they were leaving. Occupations normally employing many women were forced to put up their payment if they were to retain even a smaller number than before, to meet the competition of those trades which wanted women in greatly increased numbers, but war forces were not at work long enough for this competition to bring about any equality in the rates offered in different occupations. Variations were great. (Kirkaldy, 1921, 93)

The committee noted that 'the cost of living rose fairly steadily throughout' the war. Reviewing the data provided by the *Labour Gazette*, the committee reported that

> the retail price of all the items 'ordinarily entering into the working class family budget' rose by about 50 per cent. above the pre-war level by August, 1916; 110 per cent. above it by August, 1918; and by the end of July, 1920, it was 155 per cent. above the level of July, 1914. (Kirkaldy, 1921, 94)

At first it was not widely recognized that this rapid price inflation was wiping out the buying power of the wage increases brought on by the war. 'But once it was seen that the rise in prices was continuous, there arose in one industry after another the demand that wages should follow that rise.' The committee realized that, during the early years of the war, 'the rise in wages was nominal not real'. Most importantly, 'once public attention had been called to the question of what money wages were worth, the public conscience was awakened to the point of insisting that minimum rates should be fixed which would give a real wage above the pre-war standard' (Kirkaldy, 1921, 94). In the committee's words: 'The principle of a minimum living wage has bitten deeply into the public mind' (Kirkaldy, 1921, 95). The result was a 'great extension of the number and activities of the Trade Boards' which, after the Trade Boards Act of 1918, were able to establish minimum wage levels 'in any trade in which, on account of defective organization, wages are "unduly low"' (Kirkaldy, 1921, 94, 95). The committee's investigations of women's wages led them to two conclusions: '(1) That it was some time before the increased cost of living was used or found as a plea for raising [wage] rates. … (2) That when the Trade Boards really got to work, increases were given which more than out-ran the increased cost of living' (Kirkaldy, 1921, 95, 96). Moreover, the committee found 'that the rise in the Trade Boards [wage] rates was even more rapid when the war had ended than it was before'. The committee concluded from its examination of the first two causes of the rise in women's wages that:

> The competition for women's labour and the rise in the cost of living have been general causes, affecting all industries, though in different degrees. Roughly speaking, it may be said that the first affected the highest, the second the lowest, [wage] rates paid to women. (Kirkaldy, 1921, 96)

The third cause of the increase in women's wages was attributed to the factors surrounding women's replacement of male workers. The committee concluded that it was 'impossible to give any accurate idea of the level to which women's wages have risen in cases in which they have not replaced men' (Kirkaldy, 1921, 96–7). Though they found 'a great mass of evidence relating to the wages paid to women' who performed men's work, nonetheless 'the issue is seldom clear'. Here countervailing pressures were at work:

> On the one side the trade unions were insistent that employers should not be tempted to employ women in men's places when the men returned by finding women's labour cheaper than that of men. On the other, employers protested that they could not pay the same wages to women who were unskilled as to men who were skilled. This difficulty could be overcome by allowing the women to begin at a lower rate than men and approach the men's rate when they became experienced. (Kirkaldy, 1921, 97)

Training women workers to do the men's work turned out not to be a solution since such training frequently took 'too long for the exigencies of the war'; or, when the work involved moving heavy objects, it was deemed 'impossible for women to be fully efficient substitutes' (Kirkaldy, 1921, 97). In these cases, the three solutions most frequently applied were to divide the men's tasks into simpler subdivisions and employ several women to replace one skilled man, or place several women under the direct control of a skilled worker so that he could concentrate his efforts on those aspects of the task that required special skills while the women did the repetitious aspects, or devise machinery to perform the skilled or lifting aspects of the task.[17]

Where women workers directly replaced men, 'with no alteration of process, and one woman completely filled the place of one man, almost any variation of payment might be found'. Women frequently required higher wages, 'since they took the place of lads who accepted a learner's wage, while the women would only work for a living wage'. Sometimes they worked for wages equal to those received by the men they replaced, but more often they received 'lower (at times considerably lower)' wages than the men's rate had been (Kirkaldy, 1921, 99). In this last case, the lower wages were rationalized because 'the mass of substitution occurred during the war either on processes in which it was necessary to employ more than one woman in the place of one man, or on processes in which some form of dilution was introduced, especially the latter' (Kirkaldy, 1921, 100).

After reviewing the various governmental 'Orders' which prescribed the wages that must be paid to women workers, the committee identified several principles which seemed to govern these rules. 'Throughout there runs the principle that the men's rates shall not be adversely affected by those paid to women. ... Throughout an attempt is made to apply this principle by securing to women rates paid to men for the same job' (Kirkaldy, 1921, 102). Yet problems remained. When the government announced special bonuses, 'war wages' or 'war advances', for workers in the war industries, the men's bonus invariably exceeded the women's bonuses. 'Pressure was continually brought to bear on the Government to put up the war advances to women to meet those given to men. Both men's and women's trade unions demanded it, and ... the Government acceded to the demands to some extent in the last months of the war' (Kirkaldy, 1921, 103).

Employers continued to argue that, when required to pay women at 'precisely the same level' as the men, their total production costs rose, 'since the overhead charges for a given output' were greater for women than for men (Kirkaldy, 1921, 102). Again, the employers and the committee ignored the positive gains, both financially and productively, that result from 'the overhead charges for a given output', when that overhead cost is the result of investment in new technology and machinery. Finally, it became impossible to compare men's and women's work, and thus men's and women's wages, where production processes were modified and dilution ensued.

Where wages were negotiated between the trade unions and employers associations, "'equal pay for equivalent output" frequently figured in these agreements, sometimes accompanied by a minimum rate below which women's wages must not fall' (Kirkaldy, 1921, 104). On occasion this led to curious results. In the worsted industry, for example, the custom prevailed of paying women lower wage rates than men, even though 'men and women were doing precisely the same work' and this policy 'was preserved during the war'. 'But when women did exactly the same work on a night turn, they received the same rates as the men, because they were then doing work from which they were normally precluded by the Factory Acts.' The committee described this policy as 'anomalous'; it epitomized 'the working of an old custom side by side with a new principle'. The investigators concluded that the fact that men and women received the same pay rate at night but different rates for the same tasks on the day shift 'was significant'. The committee also noted that the insistence on equal pay for equivalent output probably reflected an assumption that women could not produce as much output as their male counterparts. Thus 'the idea of safeguarding the men's rates was being considered' when equal pay for equivalent output was required. However, when such a rule was accompanied by 'further provisions of a minimum rate for women', it was 'an attempt to safeguard the women's standard of life and part of the movement for the establishment of a general minimum' wage (Kirkaldy, 1921, 105).

In conclusion, the committee summed up its findings on women's wages during the war in these words:

It may be said that during the war there was a great increase in women's wages; that the increase was far greater in the last than in the first years of the war; and that towards the end the rise in wages showed, in the case of women, a tendency to outstrip the rise in the cost of living, though it should at the same time be stated that the cases of phenomenally high wages were relatively few. It would seem likely that the level of women's real wages has been raised, and that the minimum subsistence standard for women is higher than it was before the war. But the cases of really high wages paid to women occurred where women were replacing men, or doing work for which these was a great war demand. Few women have retained posts in which high rates are paid; the work for which they received them has in most instances ceased or been taken over by men. For the most part, men have, in various industries, resumed their monopoly of the best paid work; fortunately the women whom they have displaced, or who have lost their work owing to the cessation of the war, have if they took up other work, generally been able to secure wages which, even at the present high cost of living, represent more real wealth than they were accustomed to earn in old days. Whether the change is permanent is matter for present speculation and future proof. (Kirkaldy, 1921, 106)

As was the case with the committee that investigated 'The Economic Effect of Legislation regulating Women's Labour', the committee that ana-lysed 'The Replacement of Men by Women in Industry' during World War I was dominated by males. The original committee of 15 included no women. Yet for the first investigations, which were undertaken in the Birmingham district, the 23 'investigators' included 16 women: Miss E.B. Ashford, Miss D. Austin, Miss M.E. Bulkley, Miss M. Cross, Miss B. Drake, Miss E. Dunlop, Miss A.C. Franklin, Mrs F.W. Hubback, Miss B.L. Hutchins, Miss B. Keen, Miss Moses, Mrs Pember Reeves, Miss M. Stettauer, Miss L. Wyatt Papworth, Miss N. Young and Miss D. Zimmern. The Report continues: 'The Central Care Committee of the Birmingham Education Committee ... [made] it possible for Miss Anne Ashley to undertake the direction of the investiga-tion. Miss Lee of the Birmingham Women's Settlement was appointed inves-tigator' (Kirkaldy, 1915, 69). Unlike the earlier investigations, women were not added to the main committee, the only exception being Ashley, who served on the 1916 Research Committee (Kirkaldy, 1916, 58). Other women listed as 'investigators' at various times included Miss Mellor and Miss Enfield, while 'Miss Grier, of Leeds University', and her assistants, Miss Madeley in Birmingham, Miss Barrowman in Glasgow, Miss Purdon in Leeds and Miss A. Lawrence in London supervised the investigations by Miss Elliot into engineering and Miss Laycock into tayloring (Kirkaldy, 1920, v). Finally, the final report on these investigations was 'co-ordinated and revised by Miss L. Grier and Miss A. Ashley', then published in the last book in the series edited by Adam W. Kirkaldy, *British Labour, Replacement and Con-ciliation, 1914–1921*. The effect of the general absence of women on the major committees is difficult to judge, though their importance in gathering the data in the investigation phase is clear.

10.4 CONCLUSION

These two early 'scientific' studies of women's wage rates and total earnings frequently reveal, not so much objective science, as an uncovering of socially constructed views and attitudes. For example, Edgeworth served on the com-mittee investigating 'The Economic Effect of Legislation regulating Women's Labour'. The year after that committee published its final report, he pub-lished his first independent contribution to the analysis of women's earnings in a 'Preface' to *Women in the Printing Trades: A Sociological Study*, edited by J. Ramsay MacDonald. There he perceived an interesting paradox, which concerned 'the relation between the use of machinery and the competition of women against men' for jobs. Edgeworth concluded that: 'In some cases the cheapness of women's work averts the introduction of machinery. ... On the other hand ... the employment of machinery makes it possible for the less skilled and lower-paid women to do work formerly done by men' (Edgeworth, 1904, xi). If cheap labour really did 'avert the introduction of machinery' it was because that labour was cheap, not because women did it. Moreover, where 'the employment of machinery' allows the introduction of 'less skilled and lower-paid' workers 'to do work formerly done by' more skilled and higher-paid workers, it has nothing to do with the gender of either group of workers involved.

That these two early 'scientific' studies of women's wage rates and total earnings amounted to something less than objective science is probably to be expected since the data gathered and analysed concerned economic practices. These pay and employment practices reflected attitudes towards women workers at that time and hence these studies expose socially constructed views and attitudes. It is revealing that these committees, whose research was sponsored and financed by the British Association for the Advancement of Science, the premier scientific organization in Great Britain, seemed willing to accept these biases toward women workers almost without question. Were they unaware of these biases, or did they accept them as objective facts?

NOTES

1. From 1900 to 1920, the British Association for the Advancement of Science provided Section F with research funds for the following ten projects: (*years, project title, project chair, funding (A = appropriated and P = paid)*).
   1. 1900–1903: 'Legislation Regulating Women's Labour', E.W. Brabrook; A = £70, P = £70.
   2. 1903–6: 'British and Foreign Statistics of International Trade', (aka 'International Trade Statistics'). E. Cannan; A = £80, P = £29 4s 8d.
   3. 1906–9: 'Gold Coinage in Circulation in the United Kingdom', R.H. Inglis Palgrave; A = £28, P = £12 7s 1d.
   4. 1908–10: 'Amount and Distribution of Income below the Income-Tax Exemption Limit', E. Cannan; A = £35, P = £15.
   5. 1914–16: 'Fatigue from an Economic Standpoint', J.H. Muirhead; A = £110, P = £60.
   6. 1915: 'Enquiry into Outlets of Labour After the War', W.R. Scott; funded by a £100 grant from the Caird Fund.
   7. 1915–16: 'Industrial Unrest', A.W. Kirkaldy; A = £40, P = £20.
   8. 1915–20: 'Women in Industry', W.R. Scott; A = £160, P = £170 0s 11d.
   9. 1915–20: 'Effects of War on Credit &c.', W.R. Scott; in 1915, A = £205, P = £255.
   10. 1919–20: 'Railway Travel', E. Brabrook; A = £5, P = £10.
   For more information on the history of Section F, see J.P. Henderson, 'The Place of Economics in the Hierarchy of Sciences: Section F from Whewell to Edgeworth', in P. Mirowski (ed.) (1994), *Natural Images in Economic Thought: Markets Read in Tooth and Claw*, Cambridge: Cambridge University Press, 484–535.
2. In her article, 'Equal Pay for Equal Work', the labour leader Gertrude M. Tuckwell identified three common methods employed to determine workers' pay: 'wages are computed either on a time basis, a piece-work basis, or on a species of output bonus, known as

the premium bonus system'. The worker's income under both the premium bonus system and piece-work income 'was secured on systems of payment by results' (Tuckwell, 1919, 66).

3. The committee was chaired by E.W. Brabrook, while A.L. Bowley served as secretary. The members included 'Professor [F.Y.] Edgeworth, Professor [William]) Smart, Professor [A.W.] Flux, Mr. S.J. Chapman, Mr. L.L. Price, and Mrs. J.R. [Margaret E.] MacDonald' (*Report of the BAAS – 1900*).

4. In her paper, MacDonald identified two categories of differences between 'men and women engaged in industry': 'physical differences' and 'differences in economic position'. The second category included the claim that, for all women, even those who do not marry, 'marriage is an event which revolutionises the economic condition and industrial outlook of the great majority of women. As a result, women have a lower standard of pay and work than men.' Married women need only 'pocket money'; while unmarried women either need enough money 'only to keep themselves' or, where they do have dependants, 'they are usually overburdened with household cares and [are] unable to stand out for better conditions'. Another difference in the economic condition of women MacDonald attributed to their lack of organization in trade unions. She noted too that women 'are less ready to complain than men'. The comparatively lower standard of women's pay and work 'has an injurious effect upon men's labour', which can be alleviated through state intervention. 'By setting a legal standard [wage] the State compensates to some extent for the lack of organisation and of a high standard amongst the women'(*Report of the BAAS – 1900*, 850). Reviewing the historical impact of previous labour legislation on women workers in the regulated industries, MacDonald found four consequences: '(1) Sanitary conditions have improved relatively. (2) Wages have risen relatively. (3) The number of women employed have increased relatively. (4) Organisation amongst the workers is more general' (*Report of the BAAS – 1900*, 851). MacDonald concluded with a call for extending legal regulation, insisting that these four points be considered:

    '(1) Classes of workers at present unregulated, or very partially regulated, *e.g.* home-workers, shop-assistants, laundry workers, clerks, &c.
    (2) Matters of legislation – *e.g.* hours of work, sanitation, dangerous processes, wages.
    (3) Administration, central *v.* local authorities, women inspectors.
    (4) Codification of present law, accompanied by differentiation to meet special requirements of special trades'. (*Report of the BAAS – 1900*, 851).

5. The first report continues to list Brabrook as chairman and Bowley as secretary. In addition, the list of members now included: Miss A.M. Anderson, Mr C. Booth, Professor S.J. Chapman, Miss C.E. Collet, Professor F.Y. Edgeworth, Professor A.W. Flux, Mrs J.R. MacDonald, Mr L.L. Price, Professor W. Smart and Mrs H.J. Tennant. The new members were added because the Committee 'sought the assistance of Mrs. H.J. Tennant, late H.M. Principle Lady Inspector of Factories, Miss A.M. Anderson, her successor in office, Miss C.E. Collet, of the Board of Trade, and Mr. C. Booth', the well known investigator of the London poor.

6. While Miss A.M. Anderson and Mrs H.J. Tennant were no longer listed as members of the committee, they, along with Miss Helen Blackburn and Professor George Adam Smith, were recognized for their contributions to the study (*Report of the BAAS – 1902*, 286).

7. These reports were on: the West Riding of Yorkshire (investigated by A.L. Bowley), Birmingham (by Miss B.L. Hutchins), Leicester and Northampton (analysed by Mr R. Halstead), on Canning Town and the Isle of Dogs (studied by Miss Hadley) and the cotton industry of Lancashire (researched by Professor S.J. Chapman). Furthermore, the inquiries to foreign countries yielded reports on Switzerland (both federal legislation and cantonal legislation), Holland, the Grand Duchy of Luxembourg, Hungary, Finland, Russia, Sweden, Norway and Denmark (*Report of the BAAS – 1902*, 286).

8. Miss A.M. Anderson, Miss Blackburn (her death is noted and she was remembered as 'a regular and valued attendant at [the] meetings'), Dr G. Adam Smith and Mrs H.J. Tennant are now listed as members of the committee, along with the original company. Thanks were offered to Miss Heather-Bigg and Mrs Bosanquet for their assistance, while 'Miss

Collet wishes it to be understood that she is unable from her official position [with the Board of Trade] to express any opinions on the subject under investigation'. Finally, 'Dr. C. Booth, Professor W. Smart, and Dr. G. Adam Smith have been unable to attend the meetings of the Committee at which this report was prepared and their conclusions on the matters in question have not been communicated to the Committee'.(*Report of the BAAS – 1903*, 315).

9. In addition to the information received in time for the 1902 meeting of the BAAS, this final report included results from Nottingham (investigated by a special local committee) and Sheffield (by G.I. Lloyd). While Mr G.H. Wood researched Kidderminster, Coventry, Derby, and Tinplate Manufacture, Miss Thornewell did the Potteries, Miss B.L. Hutchins added Paper-making near London and several South London industries, and both Miss A. Harrison and Mrs. F.H. Spencer investigated Liverpool. A committee organized by the Women's Industrial Council of London studied Printing and Bookbinding and Miss Irwin covered Glasgow and the South of Scotland. Another committee of the Women's Industrial Council of London explored Tailoring in London, Mrs Bosanquet examined London Industries and West London Laundries and, finally, Miss A.M. Anderson scrutinized laundries (*Report of the BAAS – 1903*, 316). The Committee of the Women's Industrial Council of London which studied Printing and Bookbinding provided the BAAS Committee with notes prepared for their book, *Women in the Printing Trades*, which was edited by J.R. MacDonald and included an important 'Preface' written by F.Y. Edgeworth.

10. Section I of the Final Report treats the economic effect of legislation regulating women's labour on the hours worked by women. This is broken down into two subsections. The first examined 'the total weekly number' of hours that women work. The second addressed 'the distribution of work through the day, week, or year'. Section II of the committee's findings considered the 'influence of restriction of women's hours on the hours worked by other persons' (*Report of the BAAS – 1903*, 322). Section III appraised the 'effects on factories and workshops of different sizes, and on the prevalence of outwork'. Section IV analysed the 'effect on the employment of women, and on the rearrangement of methods of production' (*Report of the BAAS – 1903*, 324). Two additional sections, the 'effect on the efficiency of women as industrial agents' and the 'effect on the efficiency of industrial processes in general', produced no conclusive results.

11. The statistical evidence supporting the findings on wages and earnings were summarized in 'Mr. Wood's paper in the *Journal of the Royal Statistical Society* (June 1902) and in the Appendix to *A History of Factory Legislation*' by Miss B.L. Hutchins and A. Harrison (*Report of the BAAS – 1903*, 338).

12. There followed a brief dissent filed by Miss Heather-Bigg. She disagreed with the final conclusion (21) finding it 'true enough if made of factory legislation generally'. However, since the 'opinions' expressed by the committee applied only to those Acts 'which determine the hours and conditions of women's work, it underestimates the drawbacks and exaggerates the advantages of such regulations'. Conclusion 20 seemed to her invalid since the 'many modifications' in the Acts in recent years 'proves that the hardships have been recognised as substantial and of a kind likely to recur'. Finally, the nineteenth conclusion she found full of too much 'cheerful optimism' in its 'hopes that some of the falling off in the employment of women over 45 may be due to diminished need on their part to work outside their homes'. (*Report of the BAAS – 1903*, 342).

13. The members of this Conference Committee included Archdeacon Cunningham, C.W. Bowerman MP, W.J. Davis, J.St.G. Heath, J.A. Seddon, E.D. Simon, Sir H. Rider Haggard, Sir C.P. Lucas, Sir C.W. Macara, Sir Sydney Olivier, Sir E. im Thurn, Professor E.C.K. Gonner and Egbert Jackson. A subcommittee, chaired by Professor L.T. Hobhouse with Mr J.St.G. Heath acting as honorary secretary, was established to investigate the first two issues outside the Birmingham district (*British Labour, Replacement and Conciliation, 1914–21*, 68). The members of this subcommittee and the investigators (identified by an asterisk) included Professor L.T. Hobhouse, *Miss E.B. Ashford, *Miss D. Austin, *Miss M.E. Bulkley, *Miss M. Cross, *Miss B. Drake, *Miss E. Dunlop, *Miss A.C. Franklin, *Mr. F.H Hamnett, Mr. J.St.G. Heath, *Mr. E.F. Hitchcock, *Mrs. F.W. Hubback, Miss B.L. Hutchins, *Miss B. Keen, *Professor A.W. Kirkaldy, Mr. J.J. Mallon, *Miss Moses, Mrs Pember

Reeves, *Mr. A. Robinson, *Miss M. Stettauer, Miss L. Wyatt Papworth, *Miss N. Young, and Miss D. Zimmern. Within the Birmingham district, another investigating subcommittee was organized by Professor A.W. Kirkaldy. The report continues: 'The Central Care Committee of the Birmingham Education Committee, whose Chairman, Councillor Lord, was keenly interested, made it possible for Miss Anne Ashley to undertake the direction of the investigation. Miss Lee of the Birmingham Women's Settlement was appointed investigator' (*British Labour, Replacement and Conciliation, 1914–21*, 69).

14. The Research Committee, chaired by W.R. Scott, with James Cunnison serving as Secretary, included as well the following members: 'Archdeacon Cunningham, D.D., F.B.A.; Professors Chapman, Gonner, Hobhouse, and Kirkaldy; Messrs. W.J. Davis, J.P., J.St.G. Heath, Egbert Jackson, and Miss Ashley'. The new investigation was 'carried out by local Committees working in London, Birmingham, Glasgow, and Newcastle-on-Tyne' (Kirkaldy, 1916, 58). The report continues:

    Professor Scott organised the inquiry in Glasgow, and it was carried out by Miss Mellor, with the help of an extremely able body of investigators, among whom the Committee are especially grateful for help given by Messrs. J.E. and H.E.R. Highton. In Newcastle-on-Tyne, Professor Hallsworth enlisted the local Economics Society and its able Secretary (Mr. Halliday); and Miss Ashley, Miss Enfield, and Mr. Cunnison continued the work commenced last year in Birmingham and London.

    The reports of these local committees were collated, and the general report written by the Secretary [Cunnison] and approved by the Chairman [Scott]. (Kirkaldy, 1916, 59)

15. The Research Committee, again chaired by W.R. Scott, had a new secretary, Professor J.C. Kydd, and included these members: 'Ven. Archdeacon Cunningham, Professor E.C.K. Gonner, Professor Hallsworth, Mr. J.E. Highton, and Professor A.W. Kirkaldy'. The new information was 'obtained by the help of investigators in Glasgow, Newcastle, Leeds, Manchester, and Belfast'. The Committee made 'special mention' of the following investigators:

    Miss Grier, of Leeds University, and of Miss Mercier and Mr. R.S. Dower, who assisted her; of Miss Powell, of Queen's University, Belfast; of Mr. J.A. Halliday and Miss Stevenson, of Newcastle; and of Miss Barrowman, Miss McLean, Miss Simmons, and Messrs. J. E. and H.E.R. Highton, of Glasgow (Kirkaldy, 1917, 24).

    Later reports of the British Association reveal that the Committee's 1917 grant was £10 11d, rather than the £10 originally awarded.

16. Instead, 'Miss Grier, of Leeds University', and her assistants, Miss Madeley in Birmingham, Miss Barrowman in Glasgow, Miss Purdon in Leeds and Miss A. Lawrence in London supervised the investigations by Miss Elliot into engineering and Miss Laycock into tayloring (Kirkaldy, 1920, v).

17. These solutions were dealt with in some detail in other parts of the various reports of these Section F committees.

REFERENCES

BAAS (1900), *Report of the Seventieth Meeting of the British Association for the Advancement of Science Held at Bradford in September 1900*, London: John Murray.

BAAS (1901), *Report of the Seventy-first Meeting of the British Association for the Advancement of Science Held at Glasgow in September 1901*, London: John Murray.

BAAS (1903), *Report of the Seventy-second Meeting of the British Association for the Advancement of Science Held at Belfast in September 1902*, London: John Murray.

BAAS (1904), *Report of the Seventy-third Meeting of the British Association for the Advancement of Science Held at Southport in September 1903*, London: John Murray.

BAAS (1916), *Report of the Eighty-fifth Meeting of the British Association for the Advancement of Science, Manchester: 1915*, London: John Murray.

BAAS (1917), *Report of the Eighty-sixth Meeting of the British Association for the Advancement of Science, Newcastle-on-Tyne: 1916*, London: John Murray.

BAAS (1918), *Report of the British Association for the Advancement of Science, 1917*, London: John Murray.

BAAS (1919), *Report of the British Association for the Advancement of Science, 1918*, London: John Murray.

BAAS (1920a), *Report of the Eighty-seventh Meeting of the British Association for the Advancement of Science, Bournemouth: 1919*, London: John Murray.

BAAS (1920b), *British Association for the Advancement of Science, Report of the Eighty-eighth Meeting, Cardiff – 1920*, London: John Murray.

BAAS (1922), *British Association for the Advancement of Science, Report of the Eighty-ninth Meeting, Edinburgh – 1921*, London: John Murray.

Cole, G.D.H. (1918), *The Payment of Wages. A Study in Payment by Results Under the Wage-System*, London: George Allen & Unwin, Ltd.

Edgeworth, F.Y. (1904), 'Preface', in J. Ramsay MacDonald (ed.), *Women in the Printing Trades*, London: P.S. King & Son, v–xii.

Fawcett, Millicent (1917), 'The Position of Women in Economic Life', in W.H. Dawson, (ed.), *After-War Problems*, New York: The Macmillan Company, 191–215.

Kirkaldy, Adam W. (ed.) (1915), *Credit, Industry and the War*, London: Sir Isaac Pitman & Sons, Ltd.

Kirkaldy, Adam W. (ed.) (n.d.) [1916], *Labour, Finance and the War*, London: Sir Isaac Pitman & Sons, Ltd.

Kirkaldy, Adam W. (ed.) (n.d.) [1917], *Industry and Finance, War Expenditures and Reconstruction*, London: Sir Isaac Pitman & Sons, Ltd.

Kirkaldy, Adam W. (ed.) (1920), *Industry and Finance (Supplementary Volume)*, London: Sir Isaac Pitman & Sons, Ltd.

Kirkaldy, Adam W. (ed.) (1921), *British Labour, Replacement and Conciliation, 1914–1921*, coordinated and revised by Miss L. Grier and Miss A. Ashley, London: Sir Isaac Pitman & Sons, Ltd.

Schloss, David F. (1892), *Methods of Industrial Remuneration*, London: Williams and Norgate.

Tuckwell, Gertrude (1919), 'Equal Pay for Equal Work', *The Fortnightly Review*, 1 January, n.s., **iii**, (DCXXV), 63–76.

Name index

Abbott, Edith, 3, 4, 5, 7, 9, 11–12, 14–15,
    17, 43, 44, 45, 47, 48, 50, 55, 63
Abbott, Grace, 45, 50, 63
Abramovitz, Moses, 14
Adamson, Mary Agnes, 162
Addams, Jane, 43, 45, 49, 52, 126
American Association of University
    Women, 66
American Economic Association, 1, 3,
    4, 5, 9, 12, 14, 17, 28, 32–3, 56n,
    126, 146n
American Economic Review, 3, 6, 7–8,
    17, 25, 27–8, 63, 65
American Fabian, 53, 57n, 127
American Historical Association, 32
American Journal of Sociology, 145
American Monthly Magazine, 72, 75
American Women's Suffrage Associa-
    tion, 52, 54–5
Amott, Teresa, 12, 133
Anderson, Miss Adelaide M., 201–2,
    216n, 217n
Anderson, Elizabeth Garrett, 42–4, 54,
    56n, 119, 177
Andrews, John, 3
Anstey, Vera, 47
Anthony, Susan B., 52, 126
Antler, Joyce, 40
Architectural Record, 147n
Arnold, Matthew, 156
Arrow, Kenneth, 12
Ashley, Anne, 203, 214, 218n
Association for Promoting the Higher
    Education of Women in Cam-
    bridge, 155
Association of Collegiate Alumnae, 5
Atack, Jeremy, 15
Atkinson, Mabel, 44, 53
Australian Economic Association, 5
Australian Economist, The, 5

Bachelier, Louis, 18

Backhouse, Roger, 12–13
Badham, Edith, 5
Balch, Emily Greene, 4, 5, 6, 45, 48, 49,
    50–51, 56n
Ball, Sidney, 177
Balliol College, Oxford, 156, 158–9
Banks, Olive, 41
Baran, Paul, 14
Barber, William, 8–9
Barnard College, 27, 48
Barnett, Henrietta O., 173, 177–8, 189n
Barnett, Mr. R. E., 203
Bates, Helen Page, 8–9
Baumol, William J., ix, 16–17, 25
Beard, Charles Austin, 19
Beard, Mary Ritter, 12
Becattini, Giacomo, 168, 190n
Becker, Gary, 47
Bedford College, 46, 56n, 104, 116, 118
Bellamy, Edward, 127, 146n
Belloc, Madame Bessie Rayner Parkes
    see Parkes, Bessie Raynor
Benians, E. A., 175
Benson, Minnie Sidgwick, 183
Bentham, Jeremy, 41, 76, 100n
Berg, Maxine, 10, 12, 16, 44, 47, 53
Bergmann, Barbara, 133
Bernard, Jessie, 47–8
Besant, Annie, 51
Bhagwati, Jagdish, 14
Biagini, Eugenio F., 191
Birkbeck Schools, 105, 115, 120n
Birks, Thomas R., 153
Birmingham Women's Settlement, 214,
    218n
Black, Clementina, 11, 12, 17, 44, 50–
    51, 53, 55
Blackburn, Helen, 201, 216n
Blackwell, Elizabeth, 119
Bladen, Vincent, 99n
Blakey, Gladys, 17
Blakey, Roy Gillespie, 17